# Multinational Financial Accounting

# MULTINATIONAL FINANCIAL ACCOUNTING

Ahmed R. Belkaoui

# Q

QUORUM BOOKS

New York • Westport, Connecticut • London

The author and publisher thank the following for permission to use material from:

Financial Accounting Foundation, copyright by Financial Accounting Standards Board, 401 Merritt 7, P.O. Box 5116, Norwalk, Connecticut, 06856-5116, U.S.A. Reprinted with permission. Copies of the complete document are available from the FASB.

*Journal of Accountancy*, November 1989, reprinted with permission from the Journal of Accountancy, Copyright © 1989 by American Institute of Certified Public Accountants, Inc.

"Glossary of Selected Financial Instruments" in "The Challenge of Hedge Accounting," reprinted with permission from the Journal of Accountancy, Copyright © 1989 by American Institute of Certified Public Accountants, Inc.

"Financial Engineering in Corporate Finance: An Overview" by John D. Finnerty, Vol. 17, *Financial Management*, by permission of the Financial Management Association.

**Library of Congress Cataloging-in-Publication Data**

Belkaoui, Ahmed.
  Multinational financial accounting / Ahmed Belkaoui.
    p. cm.
  Includes bibliographical references and index.
  ISBN 0-89930-614-4 (alk. paper)
    1. International business enterprises—Accounting.  I. Title.
HF5686.I56B443    1991
657'.96—dc20        91-8400

British Library Cataloguing in Publication Data is available.

Library of Congress Catalog Card Number: 91-8400
ISBN: 0-89930-614-4

First published in 1991

Quorum Books, One Madison Avenue, New York, NY 10010
An imprint of Greenwood Publishing Group, Inc.

Printed in the United States of America

The paper used in this book complies with the Permanent Paper Standard issued by the National Information Standards Organization (Z39.48-1984).

10 9 8 7 6 5 4 3 2 1

To Hedi J. and Janice M. Belkaoui
On ne sait jamais. . . .

# CONTENTS

# EXHIBITS

# PREFACE

In the last few years, the world has seen the emergence and the workings of a global economy in which national frontiers are losing their importance and partnerships are forming between companies of different nationalities. As a result, investors as well as annual reports are becoming more global, giving the need for a multinational financial accounting. Multinational financial accounting is not to be confused with comparative accounting principles aimed at understanding the accounting principles and practices of individual countries. Instead, it is the branch of accounting that is needed to accommodate the specific international accounting requirements of multinational corporations that are not met by their national accounting systems. These needs are defined by specific features of the international environment and by specific results of foreign operations and are treated in this book.

The book should be of interest to a variety of groups, including researchers in international financial accounting, accounting practitioners interested in international financial accounting issues, and graduate and undergraduate students in international-accounting courses.

Many people helped in the development of this book. Eric Valentine is a true professional and he has my deepest gratitude. Considerable assistance was received from the University of Illinois at Chicago students, especially Elizabeth Kamilis, Kalli Karabatsos, and Sheila Decena.

# Multinational
# Financial
# Accounting

# 1

# THE NEW ENVIRONMENT FOR MULTINATIONAL FINANCIAL ACCOUNTING

## INTRODUCTION

The international business environment is best characterized by the emergence of a global economy and by the global linkages that tie the global economy together. This chapter describes the challenges posed by this globalization of economic activities and their nature, then explores the nature and context of multinational financial accounting.

## GLOBAL ECONOMY

A multinational corporate world in which national borders are losing their importance is emerging. Partnerships are forming between companies of different nationalities that are willing to forget their rivalries in order to share in the profit opportunities of a world market, to share the material costs and risks associated with the development of products ranging from semiconductors to aircraft, to reduce the impact of fluctuating currencies around the world, and of protectionism and such government-imposed obstacles as tariffs, import limits, and regulations. The best example of such global strategy is the decision of General Dynamics Corporation, an American aerospace giant, to collaborate with Japanese companies on the development of the advanced FSX jet fighters. Other examples include the partnership of Whirlpool Corporation and the appliance division of Dutch giant N. V. Philips, and the partnership of Komatsu, Ltd., the largest Japanese construction company, with Dresser Industries, Inc. of Dallas. The strategy amounts to the desire to be present in the three major markets—Japan, the United States, and Europe—a strategy labeled "triad power," consisting of allocating manufacturing, marketing, financial, and administration operations among the three markets.[1]

Another good example of the global economy is illustrated by how U.S. corporate giants try to achieve stronger trade ties in the Soviet Union. In dealing with Aeroflot, the world's largest airline, FMC Corporation, producer of machinery and agricultural products, and Marriott Corporation used different strategies. FMC Corporation opted for countertrading whereby it provides facilities and/or expertise, in this case processing equipment to make apple juice, in exchange for access to the end product, in this case the selling of the apple juice by FMC. This is not to be confused with barter trading, which involves the straight swapping of one product for another. In this countertrade, the profit on sales of apple juice is shared between Aeroflot and FMC Corporation. On the other hand, Marriott preferred the joint-venture strategy with Aeroflot and created a new company, Aeromar, owned 45% by Marriott and 51% by Aeroflot, that operates the Aeroflot food service.

A third example of the globalization movement is the more than 300 joint relationships formed by approximately 25 major car and truck manufacturers, making the world auto industry one great partnership.[2] The question of who has made a vehicle becomes very difficult to answer. As an example, Pontiac LeMans was engineered by Opel (General Motors' West German subsidiary) and is built by Daewoo in South Korea. In addition to these joint ventures, the companies are buying interests in each other.

The fact that natural boundaries are ignored in this global economy is not without its benefits to U.S. corporations and others. It creates manufacturing, financing, and marketing opportunities that exceed local possibilities by providing a global market and a world economy within which to function.

There are, however, several related issues. One issue arising from the global economy is the potential loss of sovereignty as governments lose much of their power to control monetary and economic policies, especially if the policies enacted are made in a national context rather than a global one. What may have sounded a few years ago like fictional scenarios are now part of everyday reality. For example, Japanese and other foreign investors are holding billions of dollars of U.S. government bonds, allowing the U.S. government to fund the continuous federal budget deficit. If these Japanese investors, anxious about a domestic or international development, decide to stop buying these bonds, the Federal Reserve Board will find itself in the position of increasing interest rates to make the same bonds more attractive. The rise in interest rates may slow the economy as Americans reduce their buying of big-ticket items because of higher borrowing costs and as firms reduce their production, investments, and payrolls. What may follow is a recessionary trend in the economy, followed by a reduction in the value of the stocks of American companies, and, if the trend is not reversed, a market collapse may ensue. This scenario may well explain the stock market plunge on October 19, 1987. To avert these issues, policies need to be made in a global context, taking into account major developments in the global economy. Some of these developments are discussed below.

Currency markets are now playing a vital role in the global economy as $50 trillion worth of various currencies are traded each year, compared to a mere $2 trillion of trade in goods. The activity of the currency markets has been made possible by the use of sophisticated data-processing capacity and high-capability communications and by the use of a powerful information technology to move payments cheaply around the globe. Major currency-trading centers include Chicago, New York, London, and Tokyo. Secondary centers include Paris, Frankfurt, Hong Kong, Singapore, and Sydney.

The power and role of the trading in currency markets is a major factor that limits the ability of governments to control their economies. Cooperation among governments, rather than the enactment of policies in a national context, can alleviate some of the impact of currency-market trading. Economic summits among leaders of the seven major industrial nations, as well as cooperation and consultation among central bankers on policies affecting currency exchange rates and interest rates, constitute a first step toward a global strategy and a trend toward making international economic policy a central function of government. Another example of the need for a global strategy was illustrated after the October 19, 1987, stock market crash, when Japanese and American stock-exchange officials, as well as the U.S. Securities and Exchange Commission chairman and the Japanese Securities Bureau director, agreed to set up an around-the-clock telephone link to exchange information on future and spot markets. The idea was to reduce the chances that a "black Monday" in one market would pull other markets down.

Stocks and commodity markets are also edging toward international integration in the form of a global market. According to Balassa, "viewed as a state-of-affairs [integration] can be represented by the absence of various forms of discrimination between national economies."[3] Applied to the markets for real or financial assets, the definition leads to the *law of one price* or the *law of one price change*. While the evidence is mixed on both laws, there are also some obstacles to the globalization of the stocks and commodities markets because countries have persisted in keeping different rules concerning regulation of stocks, voting rights, corporate control, antitrust legislation, and accounting policies, to name only a few. A major obstacle to the globalization of commodities markets, besides outright protectionist policies, is the rising popularity of *managed trade* or *mercantilism,* which is the use of government policies to maximize a nation's exports and minimize imports.[4] Another obstacle to commodity market globalization is the presence in Japan of business networks, known as *keiretsu*, that give the Japanese distinct advantages in the global economy. These networks are used as a structure through which giant Japanese companies share the same financial institutions, insurance companies, and trading companies, and adopt the same industrial strategy. To get an idea of their importance, note that the main Japanese corporate groups, Mitsubishi, Dai-ichi, Kangyo, Sumitomo, Mitsui, Fuyo, and Sanwa, in 1989 comprised 93% of Japanese trade, and subsidiary firms employing up to 5% of Japan's workforce accounted for up to 15% of annual sales.[5]

As more harmonization takes place among nations, the globalization of stocks and commodities will increase. The first evidence of increased globalization we can point to relates to the increasing number of stock markets, reaching four dozen in 1989, almost two per time zone; these markets are not comparable given the small operation of some of them. A good example of one smaller stock market is the 90 minutes of stock trading a day in the Jordanian market. The three most important markets, known as the *golden triangle,* include the New York Stock Exchange (NYSE), the London Stock Exchange (LSE), and the Tokyo Stock Exchange (TSE). These markets open at different times, allowing the great trading houses — Merrill Lynch and Salomon Bros. in the United States, Normura Securities International, Inc. in Japan, and Barclays Bank, PLC in the United Kingdom — to trade stocks, bonds, and currencies around the clock and around the world. This global trading, in U.S. stocks, for example, may start with the trading at Tokyo and other Asian markets until closure, followed by the trading up to one o'clock London time at the London and European markets, at which point the New York market takes over, as do the other South American and North American markets. Profit opportunities abound. For example, on the Istanbul stock exchange, the average return on most stocks in 1989 was 511%, with one stock's value soaring from $373 to more than $3000 in 1985. To get a piece of the action, a U.S. investor could choose from one of two options: buy shares in the Turkey Fund, a closed-end fund trading on the New York Stock Exchange, or wait for the Turkish stocks to be available in the United States through American deposit receipts.[6]

Increased globalization of stocks and commodities is also seen in the increase of direct foreign investment; foreign ownership of national businesses are on the increase despite the emotional backlash it seems to create in all countries affected. In 1987, for example, Europeans spent $37.1 billion acquiring U.S. companies, while U.S. companies spent $2.4 billion in Europe. It is far from being the American challenge (*le défi american*), but rather the European challenge. Such typically American companies as J. Walter Thompson, Brooks Brothers, Firestone, Doubleday, A&P, General Electric, Hilton International, and Marshall Fields are foreign owned. In 1987 alone, the amount of money investors all over the world put into stocks outside their own countries amounted to $1.2 trillion, double the 1986 amount.

Further evidence of increased globalization relates to the increase in commodity trades and, especially, the creation of big trading blocks. The world seems to be edging toward at least five major trading blocks: (1) a North American block, centered in the United States and best illustrated by the free-trade treaty between the United States and Canada; (2) the European block, centered on members of the Common Market; (3) an Asian market, centered in Japan; (4) a communist trading block, centered in the Soviet Union; and (5) an Arab trading block, centered on members of the Arab League. Of these blocks, the most remarkable is the 1992 creation of a European internal market to trade among the 12 members of the European Common Market and its 320 million people in the same manner as free trade among the 50 states of the United States and its 230 million people.

Additional evidence of increased stock and commodity globalization is seen in trading among units of multinational corporations (MNCs), which encompasses up to 50% of the world's trade.[7]

## CHALLENGES IN THE GLOBAL ECONOMY

Various new challenges characterize the global economy, which will take an extraordinary new dimension if a unified Germany again dominates Europe. It is a certainty that the slogan *Wir sind wieder wer* (we are somebody again) will become a reality—giving rise to the new superpower Germany with (based on 1988 data) (1) exports of $354.1 billion compared to $321.6 billion for the United States, $264.9 billion for Japan, and $110.6 billion for the Soviet Union; (2) a surplus balance of trade of $73.9 billion compared to $77.5 billion for Japan, $3.3 billion for the Soviet Union, and a deficit of $138 billion for the United States; and (3) a per-capita gross national product (GNP) of $13,987 compared to $19,770 for the United States, $14,340 for Japan, and $8,850 for the Soviet Union.[8] The question still remains as to whether the reunification, a boost to the German economy, will lead to another *Wirtschaftsurmder* (economic miracle). The German power will undoubtedly be exercised in the council of Europe and affect the vision of the European Common Market.

The new global economy is best characterized by the emergence of new economic powers competing with the established North American and European powers. Their success cannot be explained by classical theories of competitive advantage that focus on the availability of natural resources or other cost factors. The new paradigm is that it is competition itself that motivates the success of nations.

Such is the thesis of Porter, who maintains that the ability of a nation to upgrade its existing advantages to the next level of technology and productivity is the key to international success.[9] Four factors, called the "diamond" of national competitive advantages, are presented as the key to the success of these new technology partners:

1. Factor conditions (a nation's ability to turn factor endowment into a specialized advantage)
2. Demand conditions (the existence of demanding, sophisticated customers)
3. Related and supporting industries that provide supplier clusters to firms
4. Company, strategy, structure, and rivalry (conditions governing how firms in a nation are created and nurtured during times of intense competition)

The impact of these four factors is best summarized as follows:

The fundamental lesson is that the quiet life is an enemy of competitive advantage. Industries thrive when they are forced to overcome high labor costs or a lack of natural resources, when their customers won't accept inferior or outmoded products, when their local competitors are many and murderous, and when government offers no protection from fair competition, although it sets technical and regulatory standards.[10]

In addition, Porter blames the drift in American industry on the following reasons:

In many ways, what the U.S. needs most is a philosophical shift. Defensiveness and loss of confidence have crept into American industry and government. A mind-set had developed that U.S. industry is helped by devaluation, feeble antitrust enforcement, tax regulation, cooperation among leading competitors, policies that create a monopoly in particular technologies, and "temporary" protection. As appealing as these policies may seem in the short run, they will only make further loss of competitive advantage more likely.[11]

The third world, however, is not benefiting to the right extent from the global economy; it is still relegated to the role of provider of basic products. There is a heavy dependence of these countries on the major powers of the world and the fact that third-world countries have little control over world prices of their resources.

The worst potential threat to the global economy, the global banking system, and global security markets is not military warfare, the potential for a President Quayle in the United States, nor Red Army tanks storming through Europe. Instead, a 1990 U.S. Governmental Accounting Office report views it as the threat of sabotage to the computer systems that transfer trillions of dollars daily among banks and security exchanges around the globe. One computer hacker cracking the codes for the banking system or for securities markets could create havoc by introducing a computer virus in the system, which could bring the 53 trillion shares of trading a day to a noisy and fatal halt. It is hoped that these computers are adequately protected.

The impact of greater market internationalization brings several new topics for discussion, namely:

- The appetite for foreign equities will increase, despite terrifying market plunges, because these securities help provide diversification that reduces portfolio risk.

- On any single day, except for times of worldwide panic, most stock exchanges act independently of one another. In general, they respond to specific economic, cultural, and regulatory environments in their own countries—with differences among countries keeping the various equity markets from marching in lock step; for instance, a rise in prices in London does not automatically spell a concomitant rise that day in Tokyo.

- Over time, globalization will reduce the power governments have over their nations' economies. The increased ease with which money can flow across borders means policymakers can no longer assume that their nation's capital is captive. Because of this, some say financial markets will play a larger role in overriding, or even setting economic policy.

- When a worldwide market panic sets in, globalization can take a bad situation in one market and create an international crisis. This took place during the stock market plunge of October 1987 when "hot money" circled the globe from investors seeking to liquidate their positions at any price. Investors have less of a safety net than they once had because there is now no single lender of last resort. In the past, jittery American markets could be calmed by assurances of ample liquidity from the Federal Reserve. While such assurances are still powerful, globalization lessens their impact. This is because central banks all have different national interests and cannot be expected to act as a united front during a crisis.[12]

While the world's prosperity depends on a fluid and unfettered financial system, the lack of control has created a shadow economy of money laundering, serving customers from cocaine cartels to tax-dodging companies, and, in 1989, leading the Internal Revenue Service (IRS) to claim that the tax cheats skim as much as $50 billion a year from legitimate cash-generating businesses to be laundered to avoid detection. Various laundering schemes are used, including the following:

In Willemstad, the Caribbean capital of the Netherlands Antilles, a banker ushers an American visitor through a hotel casino and into a dining room overlooking the harbor. During refreshments, the prospective customer says he expects a six-figure cash windfall soon and would like to bring the money "quietly" into the United States. At first the banker responds cautiously, "This money isn't, ah, tainted, is it?" When the American assures him it is not, the officer of the Curaçao branch of the French-owned Credit Lyonnais Nederland smiles and orders another tonic water. In that case, says the banker, he can arrange a so-called Dutch sandwich.

Under this multilayered plan, the Paris bank would set up a corporation for the customer in Rotterdam, where he would deposit his cash in the bank's local branch. The American would control the newly created Dutch corporation through an Antilles trust company, but his identity as the owner would be protected by the island group's impenetrable secrecy laws. The Caribbean branch would then "lend" the American his own money held in Rotterdam.

If the American were questioned by the Internal Revenue Service or other authorities about the source of his wealth, he could point to his loan from a respected international bank. "Many of your largest corporations, many of your movie stars, do much the same thing here," says the banker. "We wouldn't want to handle criminal money, of course. But if it's just a matter of taxes, that is of no concern to us."[13]

Clear obstacles to an efficiently working global economy are the emerging racism, prejudice, and subjugation of ethnic minorities in the world. Some examples of an intolerant world include the following:

- *Kokusaika*, meaning internationalization, is currently talked about in Japan; the truth is, the country is a hotbed of the most flagrant racial and cultural discrimination against all types of foreigners and against their own *burakumin* (Japanese racial outcasts who are descendants of families employed as tanners, butchers, executioners, and crematorium workers in preindustrial Japan). It is not *kokusaika* that is practiced, but *sakoku* (closed country) that predominates when it comes to racial and cultural tolerance.

- Various ultraright movements are finding a sympathetic clientele in Western Europe. The most despicable is the "leparism" movement in France, aimed at a systematic harassment of the 4.5 million hard-working North Africans.

- A growing, new "underclass" is forming, both in the United States and Great Britain, deepening class divisions.

Another practice in the global economy is to make a deal and not to worry about money. Basically, creativity is the name of the game, combining both money and barter to pay for exchanges. For example, in 1989, to clinch a multibillion-dollar sale of F-16s to Turkey, General Dynamics Corp. agreed to purchase scores of Turkish products, invest in Hilton hotels, and set up a joint venture to co-produce the F-16 and build housing, a school, and a mosque for 4000 local workers. Exotic countertasks are the norm rather the exception. In 1990, Pepsico entered into a $3 billion deal with the Soviet Union to barter Pepsi-Cola for 10 ships and shipments of Stolichnaya vodka. The trend does create some worries. In a 1989 survey of 50 top U.S. defense firms, it was found that $19.9 billion in offset commitments were made against sales worth $34.8 billion, which equaled 57% of total revenues.

## MULTINATIONAL FINANCIAL ACCOUNTING

Multinational financial accounting has been the subject of various definitions with varying breadths of scope. A useful clarification of these definitions was provided by both Qureshi[14] and Weirich, Avery, and Anderson[15] in their identification of three major concepts pertaining to multinational financial accounting: universal, or world accounting, comparative, or international accounting, and parent–foreign subsidiary accounting or accounting for subsidiaries.

The concept of *universal* or *world accounting* is by far the largest in scope. It directs international accounting to the formulation and study of a universally accepted set of accounting principles. It aims for a complete standardization of accounting principles internationally. According to Weirich, Avery, and Anderson, in the framework of the world-accounting concept,

international accounting is considered to be a universal system that could be adopted in all countries. A worldwide set of generally accepted accounting principles (GAAP), such as the set maintained in the United States, would be established. Practices and principles would be developed which were applicable to all countries. This concept would be the ultimate goal of an international accounting system.[16]

While very commendable, this goal is unlikely to be reached in the near future, and may safely be characterized as highly idealistic by some, and even utopian by others. As is demonstrated in the rest of this book, pessimistic attitudes are based on the many obstacles to a complete standardization of accounting principles. Chapter 2 examines in detail some of the factors determining accounting differences internationally.

The concept of *comparative* or *international accounting* directs accounting principles to a study and understanding of national differences in accounting. It involves "(a) an awareness of the international diversity in corporate accounting and reporting practices, (b) understanding of the accounting principles and practices of individual countries, and (c) ability to assess the impact of diverse accounting practices on financial reporting."[17] There is a general consensus in accounting literature that the term *international accounting* refers to comparative accounting principles. According to Weirich, Avery, and Anderson,

international accounting involves a descriptive and informative approach. Under this concept, international accounting includes all varieties of principles, methods and standards of accounting of *all* countries. This concept includes a set of generally accepted accounting principles established for each country, thereby requiring the accountant to be multiple principle conscious when studying international accounting. . . . No universal or perfect set of principles would be expected to be established. A collection of all principles, methods and standards of all countries would be considered as the international accounting system. These variations result because of differing geographic, social, economic, political and legal influences.[18]

The concept of *parent–foreign subsidiary accounting* or *accounting for foreign subsidiaries* is by far the oldest and narrowest in scope. It reduces international accounting to the process of consolidating the accounts of the parent company and its subsidiaries, and translating foreign currency into local currency. Weirich, Avery, and Anderson state that

The third major concept that may be applied to "international accounting" refers to the accounting practices of a parent company and a foreign subsidiary. A reference to a particular country or domicile is needed under the concept for effective internal financial reporting. The accountant is concerned mainly with the translation and adjustment of the subsidiary's financial statement. Different accounting problems arise and different accounting principles are to be followed depending upon which country is used as a reference for translation and adjustment purposes.[19]

## DIMENSIONS OF MULTINATIONAL
## FINANCIAL ACCOUNTING

### Annual Reports Go International

There are clear indications that annual reports of large corporations all over the world are becoming internationally oriented. Early manifestations of this orientation were the translation of annual reports into one or more foreign languages and the separate disclosure of the extent of international business engaged in by the reporting corporation.[20] The current need is to meet the information needs of unique, multiple audiences-of-interest. To accomplish this, three identifiable schools of thought have been developed or advocated: primary and secondary financial statements, single-domicile reporting, and international reporting standards.[21]

*Primary and Secondary Financial Statements*

In 1975, the Accountants International Study Group (AISG) made a recommendation that primary and secondary sets of statements be prepared by an enterprise with financial-reporting audiences-of-interest in more than one country. Essentially, primary financial statements are those prepared to meet the information needs of audiences-of-interest in other countries. Secondary financial statements have one or more of the following characteristics:

• The reporting standards of a foreign country have been followed.

• The statement has been translated into a language that is not the language of the company's country of domicile.

• The auditor's report has been expressed in a form not commonly used in the company's country of domicile.[22]

## Single-Domicile Reporting

Proponents of single-domicile reporting argue that financial statements can reflect only one point of view, that of the company's country of domicile. Mueller gives the following explanation:

The notion of a single domicile for financial statements means that each set of financial statements necessarily has a nationality, reflects style and customs at a particular point of time and has an individual viewpoint or character. Financial statements are anchored in a single set of underlying account data prepared within a framework of quite specific accounting standards, methods and procedures. Restatement of financial statements to a different set of accounting principles produces different relationships between individual account balances and financial ratios. The meaning and implications of these new relationships may convey an entirely different financial substance to statement readers in other countries.[23]

## International Reporting Standards

The advocates of international reporting standards argue that international reporting standards should be set and followed by all countries in the preparation of financial statements. This proposal assumes a complete and international "standardization" of accounting techniques and policies. Needless to say, this alternative would be difficult to reach given the complexity of the international political, economic, and social climate.

## International Auditing

One may logically ask why there is a need for international-auditing techniques rather than depending on the auditing techniques of each country. Several arguments in favor of international auditing are advanced: First, the growth of broad-based, international capital markets depends increasingly on generally accepted auditing standards to assure consistent and complete financial reporting. Second, the accountant must be in a position to look after the needs of his or her client wherever in the world the client chooses to establish operations. This requires that the auditor both undertake to practice in a foreign country and, for the sake of conformity, rely on accepted international auditing standards. Third, given that the standards that exist in various countries in the areas of independence (audit procedures relating to inventory, accounts receivable, and reporting standards) differ from one country to another, a case for international auditing can be made for the sake of understandable communication.

At present, there is a wide diversity of audit requirements. Examine, for example, the following audit requirements for members of the European Economic Community (EEC):

1. In the United Kingdom, each limited company must have an annual audit performed by an independent public accountant.

2. In Belgium, there are virtually no audit requirements.

3. The Netherlands have requirements similar to the United Kingdom, with an exception for small, privately owned companies.

4. In France, a statutory audit requirement exists for all companies.

5. In Germany, only banks, large corporations, and insurance companies are required to have internal audits.[24]

There is obviously a need for some uniform international auditing standards. The most serious difficulty in establishing international auditing standards is the acceptance of such standards by standard-setting bodies. Efforts to harmonize audit requirements and procedures are being made by the International Federation of Accountants (IFAC). Among the seven standing committees created by the IFAC to enable it to carry out its mission of harmonizing the accounting profession, there is an International Auditing Practices Committee, whose charge is to develop guidelines on generally accepted auditing and reporting practices and to promote their voluntary acceptance. The words, *guidelines* and *voluntary*, are significant. In fact, it was clearly specified that these guidelines should be adopted by the member bodies of the IFAC insofar as they do not conflict with local regulations.[25] To date, these guidelines include (1) Objective and Scope of the Audit of Financial Statements, (2) Audit Engagement Letters, (3) Basic Principles Governing an Audit, (4) Planning, (5) Using the Work of Another Auditor, and (6) Controlling the Quality of Audit Work.[26]

These guidelines are a first step toward harmonizing international standards. Notice that the attempts are toward standardization but not rigid standardization:

Rigid standardization across national lines is simply out of the question. We know this instinctively from the sharp differences of opinion on accounting and auditing matters that divide members of the profession within their own nations. Can those divisions do anything but widen as debate becomes international? For this reason, the approval structure for issuance of guidelines allows for the possibility of some dissent among members of the International Auditing Practices Committee. Three quarters of the members must agree to the publication of a guideline, meaning that as many as one quarter can disagree and [still] be overruled.[27]

Besides the harmonization of international auditing standards, other issues remain of importance to international auditing. These issues include government roles in setting auditing standards, the need for statutory or voluntary audits, problems of quality control, and questions concerning review, ethical conduct of management, and internal audits in foreign operating environments.

### International Reporting Problems

Most accounting issues could be termed *international*, which may explain why international accounting is often referred to as a subarea of accounting. There are, however, some issues relevant to international business that create special accounting problems and that constitute the accepted domain of international accounting. These issues, in fact, make international accounting an essential functional area in international business; they have been subdivided into several areas, namely, the following:

A. Private-sector accounting
   1. Comparative analysis
      a. National accounting, reporting, and auditing practice (principles, procedures, standards, and disclosure)
      b. National accounting theory (including historical dimensions)
   2. Policy at the international level (standardization)
   3. Accounting for multinational operations
      a. Financial accounting (translation, consolidation, segmental reporting, inflation accounting, disclosure, auditing)
      b. Managerial accounting (risk and exposure measurements, foreign investment analysis, information systems, transfer pricing, control and performance evaluation, operational auditing, behavioral dimensions)
   4. Taxation (of international operations in different countries)
B. Public-sector accounting
   1. Comparative analysis of national systems (GNP measurement, balance of payments, balance of trade, employment statistics, and so on)
   2. Accounting for governmental agencies and public not-for-profit organizations (overlaps with private-sector accounting because certain industries are nationalized in some countries)[28]

This book limits itself to the financial-accounting issues classified as private-sector, multinational financial accounting.

### Accounting Standards for Multinational Corporations

Investors and creditors increasingly are faced with the problem of making decisions based on financial statements that have been prepared using accounting principles that vary from country to country. Various groups have begun to suggest international standards for reporting the results of multi-national operations and also guidelines for the behavior of these operations. Examples of these groups include the Center for Transnational Corporations, the U.S. Council of the International Chamber of Commerce, the Organization for Economic Cooperation and Development, the EEC, the International Accounting Standards Committee, and the International Federation of Accountants. Questions of immediate interest to users, multinationals, and potential standards setters include: Should there be standards for MNCs? What should be required by the standards? Who should set the standards?[29]

The first question, concerning whether or not there should be standards for MNCs, is usually answered in the affirmative. There are now identifiable international constituencies that demand specific information from MNCs. In fact, the existence of an international investor group with members from different countries has created various unique audiences-of-interest reporting groups. The following reasons are given for the uniqueness of these reporting groups.

- People living and working in different cultures have different characteristics, attitudes, lifestyles, and general behavior patterns. These differences make for differing standards of comparison and, possibly, lead to different decision processes.

- Investment institutions differ from country to country, thus causing differing information needs and usage.

- Accounting principles, as financial-statement users understand them, are different from country to country.[30]

The second question, that of standard requirements, is more difficult to answer, given the lack of knowledge of the decision requirements of the user groups involved. While a minimal list of items of disclosure may easily be determined, more cooperation from the accounting profession and a substantial research effort, as well as a political effort, is needed to develop general accounting standards for MNCs and to resolve various issues, including

1. Defining user information needs
2. The role of general-purpose reports versus special-purpose reports
3. Segmental information, particularly on a geographical basis, or multianalysis by activity and by country
4. Transfer pricing and its impact
5. Employment conditions and prospects
6. Foreign-currency transactions and the translation of foreign-currency financial statements

7. Accounting for groups and the consolidation of financial statements

8. Accounting for inflation

9. Accounting for taxation[31]

Examples of managerial accounting issues include:

1. Foreign-exchange risk management

2. Consolidation of enterprise accounts

3. Investment planning

4. External financial sourcing

5. International taxation

6. Transfer pricing

7. Performance evaluation

8. Information-control systems[32]

The question of who should set the standards is the most difficult and sensitive. One alternative is to let the MNCs set the standards. This assumes an existing, enlightened self-interest by the management of multinational interest groups that establishes claims to disclosure about its worldwide or local activities by the MNC. This point was also made as follows:

Our suggestion to the multinational is to become involved in the setting of standards and guidelines and then use these harmonized reporting and guideline suggestions to more fully communicate your accomplishments to others. While we understand that such standardization of reporting will not solve all multinational/host country disputes or cause a totally rational discussion between labor and business, we do believe a more standardized reporting which addresses the information needs of each may improve the dialogue.[33]

If this first alternative is rejected, consideration must be given to two alternative agencies — the political or the professional. While the professional route is preferable, developments in international accounting seem to show that the political approach has merit. Consider the following statement:

Matters of accountancy appear to have become too important to be left to accountancy bodies. If the levels of accountability are to be defined at the national level in the first instance and ultimately some form of supernational harmonization is to be achieved, then it is difficult to see any alternative to political agencies. At this stage, it also seems likely that such agencies will concentrate on the philosophy of information disclosure — why information is needed and in what form it is required—leaving detailed aspects to be worked out in cooperation with professional accountancy organizations.[34]

## HARMONIZATION OF ACCOUNTING STANDARDS

### The Nature of Harmonization

For a long time, harmonization has been erroneously associated with complete standardization. It is, in effect, different from standardization. Wilson presents this useful distinction:

The term harmonization as opposed to standardization implies a reconciliation of different points of view. This is a more practical and conciliatory approach than standardization, particularly when standardization means that the procedures of one country should be adopted by all others. Harmonization becomes a matter of better communication, of information in a form that can be interpreted and understood internationally.[35]

This definition of harmonization is more realistic, and has a greater likelihood of being accepted, than the concept of standardization. Every host country has its set of rules, philosophies, and objectives at the national level aimed at protecting or controlling national resources. This nationalism gives rise to particular rules and measures that ultimately affect a country's accounting system. Harmonization consists, first, of recognizing these national idiosyncracies and attempting to reconcile them with the objectives of other countries. The second step is to correct or eliminate some of these barriers in order to achieve an acceptable degree of harmonization.

### Merits of Harmonization

There are various advantages to harmonization. There are several favorable arguments that are frequently cited. First, for many countries, there are no adequate codified standards of accounting and auditing. Internationally accepted standards not only would eliminate the set-up costs for those countries, but would allow them to be part of the mainstream of accepted international accounting standards immediately. Some of this work is already being accomplished by the major accounting firms in their international practice. For example, Macrae states that "each of these firms of course has only been able to set and enforce the standards for its own organization, but combined, they determine the standards followed in a substantial portion of international audit engagements."[36]

Second, the growing internationalization of the world's economies and the increasing interdependency of nations in terms of international trade and investment flow act as a major argument for some form of internationally accepted standards of accounting and auditing. Such internationalization also facilitates international transactions, pricing, and resource allocation decisions, and may render the international financial markets more efficient.

A third argument for harmonization is the need for companies to raise outside capital because the insufficiency of retained earnings to finance projects and the availability of foreign loans has increased the need for accounting harmonization. In effect, suppliers of capital, here and abroad, tend to rely on financial reports to make the best investment and loan decisions and tend to show preference for comparable reporting.

**Limits to Harmonization**

Current trends seem to indicate that there is little chance of ever achieving international harmonization. The arguments that follow are usually advanced to justify this pessimistic attitude. First, tax collections in all countries are one of the greatest sources of demand for accounting services. Because tax-collection systems vary internationally, it is expected that these systems will lead to a diversity in the accounting principles and systems used internationally. In support of this point, Seidler states that "since tax collection systems vary widely between countries, and since governments show little sign of desiring to harmonize tax systems (except in the collection of maximum amounts from multinational corporations), there is little reason to expect that this barrier to international accounting harmonization will disappear."[37]

A second argument against harmonization is that accounting policies sometimes are fashioned to achieve either political or economic goals compatible with the political or economic system espoused by a given country. Since there is little hope of having a single political or economic system internationally, it is expected that the differences in political and economic systems will continue to act as barriers to international accounting harmonization.

Third, some of the obstacles to international harmonization are created by accountants themselves through strict national licensing requirements. An extreme example occurred in 1976, when the French accounting profession required foreign accountants practicing in France to sit for an oral examination. As a result of the French experience, the EEC became involved with the qualifications of auditors. The first published version of the Eight Directive draft created several restraints on the ability of foreign accountants to practice in EEC member countries. Consider the following paragraphs from the first version of the draft of the Eight Directive:

The partners, members, persons responsible for management, administration, direction or supervision of such professional companies or associations who do not personally fulfill the Directive (i.e., non–EEC qualified accountants) shall exercise no influence over the statutory audits carried out under the auspices of such approved professional companies or associations.

   The law shall, in particular, ensure:

— that the above-mentioned persons may not participate in the appointment or removal of auditors and that they may not issue to the latter any instructions regarding the carrying out of audits; . . .

— that the confidentiality of audit reports produced by the auditors and all documents relating thereto are protected and that these are withheld from the knowledge of the above-mentioned persons.

## TOWARD AN INTERNATIONAL CONCEPTUAL FRAMEWORK

### Nature of an International Conceptual Framework

The credibility of international financial reporting has eroded and is subject to various criticisms. An international conceptual framework may be needed to correct the situation and provide a more rigorous way of setting standards; this framework might also help financial statement users to increase their understanding of and confidence in financial reporting. An international conceptual framework can be defined as follows:

A conceptual framework is a *constitution*, a coherent system of interrelated objectives and fundamentals that can lead to consistent standards and that prescribes the nature, function, and limits of financial accounting and financial statements. The objectives identify the goals and the purposes of accounting. The fundamentals are the underlying concepts of accounting, concepts that guide the selection of events to be accounted for, the measurement of those events, and the means of summarizing and communicating them to interested parties. Concepts of that type are fundamental in the sense that other concepts flow from them and repeated reference to them will be necessary in establishing, interpreting, and applying accounting and reporting standards.[38]

A conceptual framework, therefore, is intended to act as a constitution for the international standards-setting process. It would act as a guide in resolving disputes in this process by delineating what benefits would result from any conceptual framework; four specific benefits have been identified. A conceptual framework, when completed, will (1) guide the standards-setting body in establishing accounting standards, (2) provide a frame of reference for resolving accounting questions in the absence of specific promulgated standards, (3) determine the bounds for judgments in preparing financial statements, and (4) enhance comparability by decreasing the number of alternative accounting methods.[39]

Currently, there is no international conceptual-framework project. Instead, there are separate efforts to create a national conceptual framework in the United States, Canada, Great Britain, and Australia. Depending on one's perceptions of the likelihood of an international consensus on such theoretical projects, whether these separate efforts will lead ultimately to a final harmonization in the form of an international conceptual framework is either a long-term goal or merely wishful thinking. These separate efforts are examined below as a first step to an international conceptual framework.

## U.S. Efforts

Efforts in the United States to formulate a conceptual framework began with the publication by the American Institute of Certified Public Accountants (AICPA) of APB Statement No. 4, *Basic Concepts and Accounting Principles Underlying Financial Statements of Business Enterprises.* Although it was basically descriptive, which diminished its chances of providing the first accounting conceptual framework, the statement did influence most subsequent attempts to formulate the objectives of financial statements and to develop a basic conceptual framework for the field of accounting.[40]

In response to the criticisms of corporate financial reporting and the realization that a conceptual framework for accounting is needed, in April 1971 the board of directors of the AICPA announced the formation of two study groups. The study group on the establishment of accounting principles, known as the "Wheat Committee," was charged with the task of improving the standards-setting process. Its report resulted in the formation of the Financial Accounting Standards Board (FASB). A second study group, known as the "Trueblood Committee," was charged with the development of the objectives of financial statements. It published the *Report of the Study Group on the Objectives of Financial Statements,* which presented 12 objectives of accounting.[41] Following the publication of this report, the FASB began its work on the conceptual framework. It first identified nine important issues:

*Issue 1:* Which view of earnings should be adopted?

*Issues 2 through 7:* What are the definitions of assets, liabilities, earnings, revenues, expenses, and gains and losses?

*Issue 8:* Which capital-maintenance or cost-recovery concepts should be adopted for a conceptual framework for financial accounting and reporting?

*Issue 9:* Which measurement method should be adopted?[42]

Exhibit 1.1 illustrates the overall scope of the conceptual framework in the United States; four levels attributed to the framework and related documents, issued to date by the FASB, are indicated at each level.

At the first level given by Exhibit 1.1, the objectives identify the goals and purposes of accounting. Two FASB statements are related to this topic. The Statement of Financial Accounting Concept No. 1 (SFAC 1), *Objectives of Financial Reporting by Business Enterprises,* presents the goals and purposes of accounting for business enterprises.[43] SFAC 4, *Objectives of Financial Reporting by Nonbusiness Organizations,* presents the goals and purposes of accounting for nonbusiness organizations.[44]

In the second level of Exhibit 1.1, fundamentals identify and define the qualitative characteristics of accounting information. Related FASB statements are SFAC 3, *Elements of Financial Statements of Business Enterprises*[45] and Statement of Financial Accounting Standard No. 33 (SFAS 33), *Financial Reporting and Changing Prices.*[46]

The operational guidelines from the third level of Exhibit 1.1 are those that the accountant uses in establishing and applying accounting standards; they include the recognition criteria, the use of financial statements versus financial reporting, and type of measurement. SFAS 33 relates to these operational guidelines.

**Exhibit 1.1**
**U.S. Conceptual Framework for Financial Accounting and Reporting**

| | | |
|---|---|---|
| Objectives | Goals and Purposes of Accounting | SFAC No. 1 SFAC No. 43 |
| Fundamentals | Qualitative Characteristics of Accounting Information | SFAC No. 3 SFAS No. 33 |
| Operational | Recognition Criteria Financial Statements vs. Financial Reporting Measurement Type | SFAS No. 33 |
| Display Mechanisms | Reporting Earnings Reporting Fund Flow and Liquidity Reporting Financial Position | |

At the fourth level of the exhibit, the display mechanisms that accounting uses to convey accounting information include reporting earnings, fund flow and liquidity, and financial position.


## Canadian Efforts

The Canadian Institute of Chartered Accountants (CICA) published a research study in June 1980 written by Edward Stamp, *Corporate Reporting: Its Future Evolution,* hereafter referred to as the Stamp Report.[47] The main motivations behind this effort were that the FASB conceptual framework was not suitable for Canada, given the environmental, historical, political, and legal differences between the United States and Canada, and, also, that a Canadian solution to the problem of improving the quality of corporate financial accounting standards would be provided.

The approach advocated in the Stamp Report is an evolutionary one. It identifies problems and conceptual issues. The possible components of a Canadian conceptual framework were provided as solutions to the problems, which defined the objectives of corporate financial reporting, the users of corporate reports, the nature of the user needs, and the criteria for assessment of the quality of standards and of corporate accountability. Unlike the FASB's conceptual framework, which was deemed too normative (if not axiomatic) and too narrow in its scope (its primary concern is with investors), the Canadian conceptual framework, according to the Stamp Report, would be based on an evolutionary (rather than revolutionary) approach and would be less narrow in its scope (its primary concern would be with the reasonable needs of legitimate users of published financial reports). Furthermore, a public justification and explanation of the standards is suggested to win general acceptance of the framework.

It is now up to the CICA to evaluate the recommendations of the Stamp Report and develop a truly Canadian conceptual framework. The report is successful in listing major conceptual problems in developing any framework.

Reactions to the report have been mixed. It has been perceived as an opinion document: "In the final analysis, *Corporate Reporting* is an opinion document. It is not, nor do I believe it attempts to be, a classic inquiry type research study. Rather, it is based on the informed opinion of a group of experienced and capable accountants."[48] It has also been characterized as confusing, while finally opting for a socioeconomic-political world view: "We might conclude that the Stamp Report, though arriving at many blind alleys, going through several iterations, and making several detours, does arrive at a position on a world view that might prove to be very fruitful in the development of public accounting theory and standards—

the socioeconomic-political world view."[49] Finally, practitioners found the study's recommendations to be either impractical or too costly to implement.[50]

### British Efforts

In July 1976, the Accounting Standards Steering Committee of the Institute of Chartered Accountants in England and Wales published *The Corporate Report*, a discussion paper intended as a first step toward a major review of users, purposes, and methods of modern financial reporting in the United Kingdom.[51] The paper contained several major findings and recommendations.

First, the basic philosophy and starting point of *The Corporate Report* is that financial statements should be appropriate to their expected use by the potential users. In other words, they should attempt to satisfy the information needs of users. Second, the report assigns responsibility for reporting to the "economic entity" having an impact on society through its activities. Economic entities are described as limited companies (listed and unlisted), pension schemes, charitable and other trusts, not-for-profit organizations, noncommercially oriented central government departments and agencies, and national industries and other commercially oriented public-sector bodies.[52]

Third, the report defines *users* as those having a reasonable right to information and whose information needs should be recognized by corporate reports. The users are further identified as the equity-investor group, the loan-creditor group, the government, and the public.[53] Fourth, to satisfy the fundamental objectives of annual reports outlined in the basic philosophy, seven desirable characteristics of annual reports are cited — namely, that the corporate report be relevant, understandable, reliable, complete, objective, timely, and comparable. Fifth, after documenting the limitations of current reporting practices, *The Corporate Report* suggests the need for the following additional statements:

1. A *statement of value added,* showing how the benefits of the efforts of an enterprise are shared among employees, providers of capital, the state, and reinvestment. Exhibit 1.2 is an example of a statement of value added.

2. An *employment report,* showing the size and composition of the workforce relying on the enterprise for its livelihood, the work contribution of employees, and the benefits earned.

3. A *statement of money exchange with government,* showing the financial relationship between the enterprise and the state.

4. A *statement of transactions in foreign currency,* showing the direct dealings between the United Kingdom and other countries.

**Exhibit 1.2**
**A Manufacturing Company Statement of Value Added**

|                                                          | Year to Dec. 31, 1994, thousands of pounds |
| -------------------------------------------------------- | ------------------------------------------ |
| Turnover                                                 | £100.00                                    |
| Bought-in material and services                          | 60.00                                      |
| Value added                                              | £ 40.00                                    |
| Applied the following way                                |                                            |
| To pay employees, wages pensions and fringe benefits     | 25.9                                       |
| To pay providers or capital                              |                                            |
| Interest on loans                                        | 0.8                                        |
| Dividends to shareholders                                | 0.9                                        |
|                                                          | 1.7                                        |
| To pay government                                        |                                            |
| Corporation tax payable                                  | 7.6                                        |
| To provide for maintenance and expansion of assets       |                                            |
| Depreciation                                             | 2.0                                        |
| Retained profits                                         | 2.8                                        |
|                                                          | 4.8                                        |
| Value added                                              | £ 40.00                                    |

5. A *statement of future prospects,* showing likely future profit, employment, and investment levels.

6. A *statement of corporate objectives,* showing management policy and medium-term strategic targets.

Finally, after assessing six measurement bases (historical cost, purchasing power, replacement cost, net realizable value, value to the firm, and net present value) against three criteria (theoretical acceptability, utility, and practicality), the report rejected the use of historical cost in favor of current values (accompanied by the use of general-index adjustment).

## CONCLUSIONS

In spite of the basic differences among accounting systems internationally, an effort is being made toward a harmonization of accounting systems and the development of conceptual frameworks coordinated by a single international unit to guide in the production of better accounting results from an international perspective.

## APPENDIX:
## FINANCIAL ENGINEERING

The complex reality of today's markets, including increased iterate-rate volatility, frequency of tax and regulatory changes, deregulation of the financial-services industry, and increased investment-banking competition, demands a large amount of financial innovation. It is the objective of financial engineering to provide such innovation. As defined by Finnerty: "Financial engineering involves the design, the development, and the implementation of innovative financial instruments and processes, and the formation of creative solutions to problems in finance."[54] Miller,[55] Silber,[56-58] and Van Horne[59] identified 11 factors responsible for financial innovation. Exhibit A.1 identifies examples of financial innovations and the 11 factors primarily responsible for them.

These innovations can be classified as debt innovations (Exhibit A.2), preferred-stock innovations (Exhibit A.3), convertible-debt or preferred-stock innovations (Exhibit A.4), and common-equity innovations (Exhibit A.5). These innovations do not necessarily fit the conventional definitions of debt, equity, and hedging instruments; they are hybrids of the conventional instruments. Exhibit A.6 provides a glossary of selected financial instruments. The challenge to the accounting profession is to create special or different accounting for these instruments.

Other financial innovations include the following:

*Shogun bonds* — Foreign-currency bonds issued publicly in Japan by nonresidents, not to be confused with Geisha bonds, issued privately.

*Puttable bonds* — Bonds that provide the investor with an option to sell them back to the company.

*Commodity-indexed bonds* — Bonds for which the interest rate is tied to the price of a particular commodity.

*Hara-kiri swap* — A transaction in which a Japanese firm issues dollar bonds and then exchanges the proceeds with a Japanese bank for yen-denominated debt at a certain exchange and interest rate.

*Dual-currency bonds* — Bonds for which the investor receives interest payments in one currency and principal in another.

*Currency-option bonds* — Bonds for which the investor can choose the currency in which interest and/or principal is paid.[60]

**Exhibit A.1**

**Factors Primarily Responsible for Financial Innovations**

| Innovation | Factors Primarily Responsible | Innovation | Factors Primarily Responsible |
|---|---|---|---|
| *Consumer-Type Financial Instruments* | | | |
| Broker cash management accounts | 7 | Money market mutual funds | 6,7 |
| Municipal bond funds | 2,4,6 | Money market accounts | 6,7 |
| All-saver certificates | 6,7 | NOW accounts | 6,7 |
| Equity access account | 1,6,8 | Bull/Bear CDs | 2 |
| Debit card | 2,7,11 | IRA/Keogh accounts | 1,6 |
| Tuition futures | 4,8 | Universal or variable life insurance | 1,7,8 |
| Variable or adjustable rate mortgages | 7 | Convertible mortgages or reduction option loans | 2,7 |
| *Securities* | | | |
| Deep discount/zero coupon bonds | 1,4,7 | Stripped debt securities | 1,4,7 |
| Floating rate notes | 4,5,7 | Floating rate, rating sensitive notes | 3,4,5,7 |
| Floating rate tax-exempt notes | 4,5,7 | Auction rate notes/debentures | 2,3,4,7 |
| Real yield securities | 2,4,5,8 | Dollar BILS | 4,7 |
| Putable-extendible notes | 2,3,4 | Increasing rate notes | 3 |
| Interest rate reset notes | 3 | Annuity notes | 11 |
| Extendible notes | 2,4 | Variable coupon/rate renewable notes | 2,4,6 |
| Putable/adjustable tender bonds | 2,4,7 | Variable duration notes | 4,7 |
| Euronotes/Euro-commercial paper | 2,4 | Universal commercial paper | 4 |
| Medium term notes | 2 | Negotiable CDs | 2,5 |
| Mortgage-backed bonds | 4 | Mortgage pass-throughs | 2,4,5 |
| Collateralized mortgage obligations | 2,4,5 | Stripped mortgage-backed securities | 4 |
| Receivable-backed securities | 4,5 | Real estate-backed bonds | 4,5 |
| Letter of credit/surety bond credit support | 4,11 | Yield curve/maximum rate notes | 4,6,7 |
| Interest rate swaps | 4,6,7 | Currency swaps | 4,6 |
| Interest rate caps/floors/collars | 4,7 | Remarketed reset notes | 2,3,4 |
| Foreign-currency-denominated bonds | 4,7 | Eurocurrency bonds | 7 |
| Dual currency bonds | 4,6 | Indexed currency option notes | |
| Commodity-linked bonds | 4,6,8 | Principal exchange rate linked securities | 4,6,7 |

*(Continued on next page)*

**Exhibit A.1** (continued)

| Innovation | Factors Primarily Responsible |
|---|---|
| Gold loans | 4,8 |
| Exchange-traded options | 4,9 |
| Interest rate futures | 4,7,9 |
| Options on futures contracts | 4,7,9 |
| Warrants to purchase bonds | 4,7 |
| Convertible adjustable preferred stock | 1,4,5,7 |
| Remarketed preferred stock | 1,4,5,7,11 |
| Single point adjustable rate stock | 1,2,4,5,7 |
| Variable cumulative preferred stock | 1,2,3,4,5,7 |
| Adjustable rate convertible debt | 1,10 |
| Putable convertible bonds | 3,4,7 |
| Synthetic convertible debt | 1,10 |
| Convertible reset debentures | 3 |
| Master limited partnership | 1 |
| Americus trust | 4,6 |
| Putable common stock | 3,4,10 |
| High-yield (junk) bonds | 2,5,7,9 |
| Foreign currency futures | 4,9,11 |
| Stock index futures | 4,8,9 |
| Forward rate agreements | 4,7 |
| Adjustable rate preferred stock | 1,4,5,6,7 |
| Auction rate preferred stock | 1,4,5,7 |
| Indexed floating rate preferred stock | 1,4,5,7 |
| Stated rate auction preferred stock | 1,4,5,7 |
| Convertible exchangeable preferred | 1,3,4,5,7 |
| Zero coupon convertible debt | 1,2,10 |
| Mandatory convertible/equity contract notes | 1,11 |
| Exchangeable auction preferred | 1,6 |
| Participating bonds | 1,2,4,5,7 |
| Additional class(es) of common stock | 3,4 |
| Paired common stock | 11 |
| | 4 |

*Financial Processes*

| Innovation | Factors Primarily Responsible |
|---|---|
| Shelf registration | 2,6,7 |
| Discount brokerage | 2,6 |
| Point-of-sale terminals | 11 |
| Electronic funds transfer/ automated clearing houses | 7,11 |
| Direct public sale of securities | 2,6 |
| Automated teller machines | 2,11 |
| Electronic security trading | 2,11 |
| CHIPS (same day settlement) | 7,11 |
| Cash management/sweep accounts | 7,11 |

*Financial Strategies/Solutions*

| Innovation | Factors Primarily Responsible |
|---|---|
| More efficient bond call strategies | 7,9 |
| Stock-for-debt swaps | 1,7,10 |
| Preferred dividend rolls | 1 |
| Leveraged buyout structuring | 1,9,11 |
| Project finance/lease/ asset-based financial structuring | 4 |
| Debt-for-debt exchanges | 1,7,10 |
| In-substance defeasance | 1,7,10 |
| Hedged dividend capture | 1 |
| Corporate restructuring | 1,9,11 |

*Note:* 1, tax advantages; 2, reduced transaction costs; 3, reduced agency costs; 4, risk reallocation; 5, increased liquidity; 6, regulatory or legislative factors; 7, level and volatility of interest rates; 8, level and volatility of prices; 9, academic work; 10, accounting benefits; and 11, technological developments and other factors.

*Source:* J. D. Finnerty, "Financial Engineering in Corporate Finance: An Overview," *Financial Management* (Winter 1988): 17. Reprinted with permission.

**Exhibit A.2**
**Selected Debt Innovations**

| Security | Distinguishing Characteristics | Risk Reallocation/ Yield Reduction | Enhanced Liquidity | Reduction in Agency Costs | Reduction in Transaction Costs | Tax Arbitrage | Other Benefits |
|---|---|---|---|---|---|---|---|
| Adjustable Rate Notes and Floating Rate Notes | Coupon rate floats with some index, such as the 91-day Treasury bill rate. | Issuer exposed to floating interest rate risk but initial rate is lower than for fixed-rate issue. | Price remains closer to par than the price of a fixed-rate note of the same maturity. | | | | |
| Auction Rate Notes and Debentures | Interest rate reset by Dutch auction at the end of each interest period. | Coupon based on length of interest period, not on final maturity. | Designed to trade closer to par value than a floating rate note with a fixed interest rate formula. | Interest rate each period is determined in the marketplace, rather than by the issuer or the issuer's investment banker. | Intended to have lower transaction costs than repeatedly rolling over shorter maturity securities. | | |
| Bonds Linked to Commodity Price or Index | Interest and/or principal linked to a specified commodity price or index. | Issuer assumes commodity price or index risk in return for lower (minimum) coupon. Can serve as a hedge if the issuer produces the particular commodity. | | | | | Attractive to investors who would like to speculate in commodity options but cannot, for regulatory or other reasons, purchase commodity options directly. |
| Collateralized Mortgage Obligations (CMOs) and Real Estate Mortgage Investment Conduits (REMICs) | Mortgage payment stream is divided into several classes which are prioritized in terms of their right to receive principal payments. | Reduction in prepayment risk to classes with prepayment priority. Designed to appeal to different classes of investors; sum of the parts can exceed the whole. | More liquid than individual mortgages. | | Most investors could not achieve the same degree of prepayment risk reduction as cheaply on their own. | | |
| Commercial Real Estate-Backed Bonds | Nonrecourse bonds serviced and backed by a specified piece (or portfolio) of real estate. | Reduced yield due to greater liquidity. | More liquid than individual mortgages. | | | | Appeals to investors who like to lend against real estate properties. |

*(Continued on next page )*

27

# Exhibit A.2 (continued)

| Security | Distinguishing Characteristics | Risk Reallocation/ Yield Reduction | Enhanced Liquidity | Reduction in Agency Costs | Reduction in Transaction Costs | Tax Arbitrage | Other Benefits |
|---|---|---|---|---|---|---|---|
| Credit-Enhanced Debt Securities | Issuer's obligation to pay is backed by an irrevocable letter of credit or a surety bond. | Stronger credit rating of the letter of credit or surety bond issuer leads to lower yield, which can more than offset letter of credit or surety bond fees. | | | | | Enables a privately held company to borrow publicly while preserving confidentiality of financial information. |
| Dollar BILS | Floating rate zero coupon note the effective interest rate on which is determined retrospectively based on the change in the value of a specified index that measures the total return on long-term, high-grade corporate bonds. | Issuer assumes reinvestment risk. | | | | | Useful for hedging and immunization purposes because Dollar BILS have a zero duration when duration is measured with respect to the specified index. |
| Dual Currency Bonds | Interest payable in U.S. dollars but principal payable in a currency other than U.S. dollars. | Issuer has foreign currency risk with respect to principal repayment obligation. Currency swap can hedge this risk and lead, in some cases, to yield reduction. | | | | | Euroyen-dollar dual currency bonds popular with Japanese investors who are subject to regulatory restrictions and desire income in dollars without principal risk. |
| Euronotes and Euro-commercial Paper | Euro-commercial paper is similar to U.S. commercial paper. | Elimination of inter-mediary brings savings that lender and borrower can share. | | | Corporations invest in each other's paper directly rather than through an intermediary. | | |
| Extendible Notes | Interest rate adjusts every 2-3 years to a new interest rate the issuer establishes, at which time note holder has the option to put the notes back to the issuer if the new rate is unacceptable. | Coupon based on 2-3 year put date, not on final maturity. | | Investor has a put option, which provides protection against deterioration in credit quality or below-market coupon rate. | Lower transaction costs than issuing 2- or 3-year notes and rolling them over. | | |

| | | | | |
|---|---|---|---|---|
| Floating Rate Rating Sensitive Notes | Coupon rate resets quarterly based on a spread over LIBOR. Spread increases if the issuer's debt rating declines. | Issuer exposed to floating interest rate risk but initial rate is lower than for fixed-rate issue. | Price remains closer to par than the price of a fixed-rate note of the same maturity. | Investor protected against deterioration in the issuer's credit quality because of increase in coupon rate when rating declines. |
| Floating Rate Tax-Exempt Revenue Bonds | Coupon rate floats with some index, such as the 60-day high-grade commercial paper rate. | Issuer exposed to floating interest rate risk but initial rate is lower than for fixed-rate issue. Effectively, tax-exempt commercial paper. | | Investor does not have to pay income tax on the interest payments but issuer gets to deduct them. |
| Increasing Rate Notes | Coupon rate increases by specified amounts at specified intervals. | Defers portion of interest expense to later years, which increases duration. | When such notes are issued in connection with a bridge financing, the step-up in coupon rate compensates investors for the issuer's failure to redeem the notes on schedule. | |
| Indexed Currency Option Notes Principal Exchange Rate Linked Securities | Issuer pays reduced principal at maturity if specified foreign currency appreciates sufficiently relative to the U.S. dollar. | Investor assumes foreign currency risk by effectively selling the issuer a call option denominated in the foreign currency. | | Attractive to investors who would like to speculate in foreign currencies but cannot, for regulatory or other reasons, purchase or sell currency options directly. |

*(Continued on next page)*

**Exhibit A.2** (continued)

| Security | Distinguishing Characteristics | Risk Reallocation Yield Reduction | Enhanced Liquidity | Reduction in Agency Costs | Reduction in Transaction Costs | Tax Arbitrage | Other Benefits |
|---|---|---|---|---|---|---|---|
| Interest Rate Caps, Floors, and Collars | Investor who writes an interest rate cap (floor collar) contract agrees to make payments to the contract purchaser when a specified interest rate exceeds the specified cap (falls below the floor, falls outside the collar range). | Seller assumes the risk that interest rates may rise above the cap (fall below the floor, fall outside the collar range.) | | | | | |
| Interest Rate Reset Notes | Interest rate is reset 3 years after issuance to the greater of (i) the initial rate and (ii) a rate sufficient to give the notes a market value equal to 101% of their face amount. | Reduced (initial) yield due to the reduction in agency costs. | | Investor is compensated for a deterioration in the issuer's credit standing within 3 years of issuance. | | | |
| Interest Rate Swaps | Two entities agree to swap interest rate payment obligations, typically fixed rate for floating rate. | Effective vehicle for transferring interest rate risk from one party to another. Also, parties to a swap can realize a net benefit if they enjoy comparative advantages in different international credit markets. | | | | | Interest rate swaps are often designed to take advantage of special opportunities in particular markets outside the issuer's traditional market or to circumvent regulatory restrictions. |
| Medium-Term Notes | Notes are sold in varying amounts and in varying maturities on an agency basis. | Issuer bears market price risk during the marketing process. | | | Agents' commissions are lower than underwriting spreads. | | |
| Mortgage Pass-Through Certificates | Investor buys an undivided interest in a pool of mortgages. | Reduced yield due to the benefit to the investor of diversification and greater liquidity. | More liquid than individual mortgages. | | Most investors could not achieve the same degree of diversification as cheaply on their own. | | |

30

| Security | | | | | | |
|---|---|---|---|---|---|---|
| Negotiable Certificates of Deposit | Certificates of deposit are registered and sold to the public on an agency basis. | | More liquid than non-negotiable CDs. | | Agents' commissions are lower than underwriting spreads. | |
| Putable Bonds and Adjustable Tender Securities | Issuer can periodically reset the terms, in effect rolling over debt without having to redeem it until the final maturity. | Coupon based on whether fixed or floating rate and on the length of the interest rate period selected, not on final maturity. Issuer bears market price risk during the marketing process. | | Investor has a put option, which provides protection against deterioration in credit quality or below-market coupon rate. | Lower transaction costs than having to perform a series of refundings. | |
| Putable-Extendible Notes | At the end of each interest period, the issuer may elect to redeem the notes at par or to extend the maturity on terms the issuer proposes, at which time the note holder can put the notes back to the issuer if the new terms are unacceptable. Investors also have series of put options during initial interest period. | Coupon based on length of interest interval, not on final maturity. | | Put options protect against deterioration in issuer's credit standing and also against issuer setting below-market coupon rate or other terms that might work to investor's disadvantage. | | |
| Real Yield Securities | Coupon rate resets quarterly to the greater of (i) change in consumer price index plus the "Real Yield Spread" (3.0% in the first such issue) and (ii) the Real Yield Spread, in each case on a semiannual-equivalent basis. | Issuer exposed to inflation risk, which may be hedged in the CPI futures market. | Real yield securities could become more liquid than CPI futures, which tend to trade in significant volume only around the monthly CPI announcement date. | | Investors obtain a long-dated inflation hedging instrument that they could not create as cheaply on their own. | Real yield securities have a longer duration than alternative inflation hedging instruments. |

*(Continued on next page)*

**Exhibit A.2** (continued)

| Security | Distinguishing Characteristics | Risk Reallocation/ Yield Reduction | Enhanced Liquidity | Reduction in Agency Costs | Reduction in Transaction Costs | Tax Arbitrage | Other Benefits |
|---|---|---|---|---|---|---|---|
| Receivable Pay-Through Securities | Investor buys an undivided interest in a pool of receivables. | Reduced yield due to the benefit to the investor of diversification and greater liquidity. Significantly cheaper for issuer than pledging receivables to a bank. | More liquid than individual receivables. | | Security purchasers could not achieve the same degree of diversification as cheaply on their own. | | |
| Remarketed Reset Notes | Interest rate reset at the end of each interest period in a rate the remarketing agent determines will make the notes worth par. If issuer and remarketing agent can not agree on rate, then the coupon rate is determined by formula which dictates a higher rate the lower the issuer's credit standing. | Coupon based on length of interest period, not on final maturity. | Designed to trade closer to par value than a floating-rate note with a fixed interest rate formula. | Investors have a put option, which protects against the issuer and remarketing agent agreeing to set a below-market coupon rate, and the flexible interest rate formula protects investors against deterioration in the issuer's credit standing. | Intended to have lower transaction costs than auction rate notes and debentures, which require periodic Dutch auctions. | | |
| Stripped Mortgage-Backed Securities | Mortgage payment stream subdivided into two classes, (i) one with below-market coupon and the other with above-market coupon or (ii) one receiving interest only and the other receiving principal only from mortgage pools. | Securities have unique option characteristics that make them useful for hedging purposes. Designed to appeal to different classes of investors; sum of the parts can exceed the whole. | | | | | |
| Stripped Treasury or Municipal Securities | Coupons separated from corpus to create a series of zero coupon bonds that can be sold separately. | Yield curve arbitrage: sum of the parts can exceed the whole. | | | | | |

| Instrument | Description | | |
|---|---|---|---|
| Variable Coupon Renewable Notes | Coupon rate varies weekly and equals a fixed spread over the 91-day T-bill rate. Each 91 days the maturity extends another 91 days. If put option is exercised, spread is reduced. | Coupon based on 1-year termination date, not on final maturity. | Lower transaction costs than issuing 1-year note and rolling it over. | Designed to appeal to money market mutual funds, which face tight investment restrictions, and to discourage put to issuer. |
| Variable Rate Renewable Notes | Coupon rate varies monthly and equals a fixed spread over the 1-month commercial paper rate. Each quarter the maturity automatically extends an additional quarter unless the the investor elects to terminate the extension. | Coupon based on 1-year termination date, not on final maturity. | Lower transaction costs than issuing 1-year note and rolling it over. | Designed to appeal to money market mutual funds, which face tight investment restrictions. |
| Warrants to Purchase Debt Securities | Warrant with 1-5 years to expiration to buy intermediate-term or long-term bonds. | Issuer is effectively selling a covered call option, which can afford investors opportunities not available in the traditional options markets. | | |
| Yield Curve Notes and Maximum Notes | Interest rate equals a specified rate minus LIBOR. | Might reduce yield relative to conventional debt when coupled with an interest rate swap against LIBOR. | Useful for hedging and immunization purposes because of very long duration. | |
| Zero Coupon Bonds (sometimes issued in series) | Non-interest-bearing. Payment in one lump sum at maturity. | Issuer assumes reinvestment risk. Issues sold in Japan carried below-taxable market yields reflecting their tax advantage over conventional debt issues. | Straight-line amortization of original issue discount pre-TEFRA. Japanese investors realize significant tax savings. | |

*Source:* J. D. Finnerty, "Financial Engineering in Corporate Finance: An Overview," *Financial Management* (Winter 1988): 19–22. Reprinted with permission.

**Exhibit A.3**

**Selected Preferred-Stock Innovations**

| Security | Distinguishing Characteristics | Risk Reallocation/ Yield Reduction | Enhanced Liquidity | Reduction in Agency Costs | Reduction in Transaction Costs | Tax Arbitrage | Other Benefits |
|---|---|---|---|---|---|---|---|
| Adjustable Rate Preferred Stock | Quarterly dividend rate reset each quarter based on maximum of 3-month T-bill, 10-year Treasury, and 20-year Treasury rates plus or minus a specified spread. | Issuer bears more interest rate risk than a fixed-rate preferred would involve. Lower yield than commercial paper. | Security is designed to trade near its par value. | | | Designed to enable short-term corporate investors to take advantage of 70% dividends received deduction. | |
| Auction Rate Preferred Stock (MMP DARTS AMPS STAR) | Dividend rate reset by Dutch auction every 49 days (subject to a minimum rate of 110%, or under certain circumstances 125%, of the 60-day "AA" Composite Commercial Paper Rate). Dividend is paid at the end of each dividend period. | Issuer bears more interest rate risk than a fixed-rate preferred would involve. Lower yield than commercial paper. | Security is designed to provide greater liquidity than convertible adjustable preferred stock. | Dividend rate each period is determined in the marketplace, which provides protection against deterioration in issuer's credit standing (protection is limited by the dividend rate cap). | | Designed to enable short-term corporate investors to take advantage of 70% dividends received deduction. | |
| Convertible Adjustable Preferred Stock | Issue convertible on dividend payment dates into variable number of the issuer's common shares, subject to a cap, equal in market value to the par value of the preferred. | Issuer bears more interest rate risk than a fixed-rate preferred would involve. Lower yield than commercial paper. | Security is designed to provide greater liquidity than adjustable rate preferred stock (due to the conversion feature). | | | Designed to enable short-term corporate investors to take advantage of 70% dividends received deduction. | |

| Security | Description | Interest Rate Risk | Trading Value | Maximum Dividend Rate | Transaction Cost Savings | Tax Advantage | Other |
|---|---|---|---|---|---|---|---|
| Remarketed Preferred Stock (SABRES) | Perpetual preferred stock with a dividend rate that resets at the end of each dividend period to a rate the remarketing agent determines will make the preferred stock worth par (subject to a maximum rate of 110%, or under certain circumstances 125%, of the 60-day "AA" Composite Commercial Paper Rate). Dividend periods may be of any length, even 1 day. Different shares of a single issue may have different periods and different dividend rates. | Issuer bears more interest rate risk than a fixed-rate preferred would involve. Lower yield than commercial paper. | Security is designed to trade near its par value. | | | Designed to enable short-term corporate investors to take advantage of 70% dividends received deduction. | Remarketed preferred stock offers greater flexibility in setting the terms of the issue than auction rate preferred stock, which requires a Dutch auction for potentially the entire issue once every 49 days. |
| Single Point Adjustable Rate Stock | Dividend rate reset every 49 days as a specified percentage of the high-grade commercial paper rate. | Issuer bears more interest rate risk than a fixed-rate preferred would involve. Lower yield than commercial paper. | Security is designed to trade near its par value. | | Security is designed to save on recurring transaction costs associated with auction rate preferred stock. | Designed to enable short-term corporate investors to take advantage of 70% dividends received deduction. | |
| Stated Rate Auction Preferred Stock | Initial dividend period of several years during which the dividend rate is fixed. Thereafter the issuer can elect to have the dividend rate reset every 49 days by Dutch auction. | Issuer bears more interest rate risk than a fixed-rate preferred would involve. | Security is designed to trade near its par value after the initial dividend period has elapsed and the Dutch auctions determine the dividend rate. | The maximum permitted dividend rate, expressed as a percentage of the 60-day "AA" Composite Commercial Paper Rate, increases according to a specified schedule if the preferred stock's credit rating falls. | | Designed so as eventually to enable short-term corporate investors to take advantage of 70% dividends received deduction. | |
| Variable Cumulative Preferred Stock | At the end of any dividend period the issuer can select between the auction method and the remarketing method to have the dividend rate reset. | Issuer bears more interest rate risk than a fixed-rate preferred would involve. Lower yield than commercial paper. | Security is designed to trade near its par value. | The maximum permitted dividend rate, expressed as a percentage of the 60-day "AA" Composite Commercial Paper Rate, increases according to a specified schedule if the preferred stock's credit rating falls. | Security is designed to save on transaction costs the issuer would otherwise incur if it wanted to change from auction to remarketing reset or vice versa. | Designed to enable short-term corporate investors to take advantage of 70% dividends received deduction. | Security is designed to enable the issuer to select at the end of each dividend period the method of rate reset it prefers. |

*Source:* J. D. Finnerty, "Financial Engineering in Corporate Finance: An Overview," *Financial Management* (Winter 1988): 26. Reprinted with permission.

# Exhibit A.4
## Selected Convertible-Debt/Preferred-Stock Innovations

| Security | Distinguishing Characteristics | Risk Reallocation/ Yield Reduction | Enhanced Liquidity | Reduction in Agency Costs | Reduction in Transaction Costs | Tax Arbitrage | Other Benefits |
|---|---|---|---|---|---|---|---|
| Adjustable Rate Convertible Debt | Debt the interest rate on which varies directly with the dividend rate on the underlying common stock. No conversion premium. | | | | | Effectively, tax deductible common equity. Security has since been ruled equity by the IRS. | Portion of the issue carried as equity on the issuer's balance sheet. |
| Convertible Exchangeable Preferred Stock | Convertible preferred stock that is exchangeable, at the issuer's option, for convertible debt with identical rate and identical conversion terms. | | | | No need to reissue convertible security as debt—just exchange it—when the issuer becomes a taxpayer. | Issuer can exchange debt for the preferred when it becomes taxable with interest rate the same as the dividend rate and without any change in conversion features. | Appears as equity on the issuer's balance sheet until it is exchanged for convertible debt. |
| Convertible Reset Debentures | Convertible bond the interest rate on which must be adjusted upward, if necessary, by an amount sufficient to give the debentures a market value equal to their face amount 2 years after issuance. | | | Investor is protected against a deterioration in the issuer's financial prospects within 2 years of issuance. | | | |
| Debt with Mandatory Common Stock Purchase Contracts | Notes with contracts that obligate note purchasers to buy sufficient common stock from the issuer to retire the issue in full by its scheduled maturity date. | | | | | Notes provide a stream of interest tax shields, which (true) equity does not. | Commercial bank holding companies have issued it because it counted as "primary capital" for regulatory purposes. |

| | | | | |
|---|---|---|---|---|
| Exchangeable Auction Preferred Stock | Auction rate preferred stock that is exchangeable on any dividend payment date, at the option of the issuer, for auction rate notes, the interest rate on which is reset by Dutch auction every 35 days. | Issuer bears more interest rate risk than a fixed-rate instrument would involve.<br><br>Security is designed to trade near its par value. | Issuance of auction rate notes involves no underwriting commissions. | Issuer can exchange notes for the preferred when it becomes taxable.<br><br>Appears as equity on the issuer's balance sheet until it is exchanged for auction rate notes. |
| Synthetic Convertible Debt | Debt and warrants package structured in such a way as to mirror a traditional convertible debt issue. | | In effect, warrant proceeds are tax deductible.<br><br>Warrants go on the balance sheet as equity. | |
| Zero Coupon Convertible Debt | Non-interest-bearing convertible debt issue. | | If issue converts, the issuer will have sold, in effect, tax deductible equity.<br><br>If holders convert, entire debt service stream is converted to common equity. | |

*Source:* J. D. Finnerty, "Financial Engineering in Corporate Finance: An Overview," *Financial Management* (Winter 1988): 28. Reprinted with permission.

# Exhibit A.5
## Selected Common-Equity Innovations

| Security | Distinguishing Characteristics | Risk Reallocation/ Yield Reduction | Enhanced Liquidity | Reduction in Agency Costs | Reduction in Transaction Costs | Tax Arbitrage | Other Benefits |
|---|---|---|---|---|---|---|---|
| Additional Class(es) of Common Stock | A company issues a second class of common stock on which dividends on which are tied to the earnings of a specified subsidiary. | | | | | | Establishes separate market value for the subsidiary while assuring the parent 100% voting control. Useful for employee compensation programs for subsidiary. |
| Americus Trust | Outstanding shares of a particular common stock are contributed to a five-year unit investment trust. Units may be separated into a PRIME component, which embodies full dividend and voting rights in the underlying share and permits limited capital appreciation, and a SCORE component, which provides full capital appreciation above a stated price. | Stream of annual total returns on a share of stock is separated into (*i*) a dividend stream (with limited capital appreciation potential) and (*ii*) a (residual) capital appreciation stream. | | | | PRIME component would appeal to corporate investors who can take advantage of the 70% dividends received deduction. SCORE component would appeal to capital-gain-oriented individual investors. | PRIME component resembles participating preferred stock if the issuer's common stock dividend rate is stable. SCORE component is a longer-dated call option than the ones customarily traded in the options market. |
| Master Limited Partnership | A business is given the legal form of a partnership but is otherwise structured, and is traded publicly, like a corporation. | | | | | Eliminates a layer of taxation because partnerships are not taxable entities. | |
| Puttable Common Stock | Issuer sells a new issue of common stock along with rights to put the stock back to the issuer on a specified date at a specified place. | Issuer sells investors a put option, which investors will exercise if the company's share price decreases. | | The put option reduces agency costs associated with a new share issue that are brought on by informational asymmetries. | | | Equivalent under certain conditions to convertible bonds but can be recorded as equity on the balance sheet so long as the company's payment obligation under the put option can be settled in common stock. |

*Source:* J. D. Finnerty, "Financial Engineering in Corporate Finance: An Overview," *Financial Management* (Winter 1988): 29. Reprinted with permission.

## Exhibit A.6
## Glossary of Selected Financial Instruments

### DEBT INSTRUMENTS

**Commercial paper:** Unsecured short-term (up to 270 days) obligations issued through brokers or directly. The interest is usually discounted.
- **Universal commercial paper:** Foreign currency denominated commercial paper that trades and settles in the United States.

**Convertible bonds:** Debt securities that are convertible into the stock of the issuer at a specified price at the option of the holder.
- **Carrot and stick bonds:** Carrots have a low conversion premium to encourage early conversion, and sticks allow the issuer to call the bond at a specified premium if the common stock is trading at a specified percentage above the strike price.
- **Convertible bonds with a premium put:** Convertible bonds issued at face value with a put entitling the bondholder to redeem the bonds for more than their face value.

**Debt with equity warrants:** Bonds issued with warrants for the purchase of shares. The warrants are separately tradeable.

**Dual-currency bonds:** Bonds that are denominated and pay interest in one currency and are redeemable in another currency—thus allowing interest rate arbitrage between two markets.
- **COPS** (covered option securities): Short-term debt that gives the issuer an option to repay the principal and interest in U.S. dollars or a mutually acceptable foreign currency.
- **ECU bonds** (European currency unit bonds): A Eurobond denominated in a basket of currencies of the 10 countries that constitute the European Community. The bonds pay interest and principal in ECUs or in any of the 10 currencies at the option of the holder.
- **ICONs** (indexed currency option notes): A bond denominated and paying interest in one currency with redemption value linked to the exchange rate of another currency.
- **PERLS** (principal exchange-rate-linked securities): Securities paying interest and principal in dollars but with principal payments linked to the exchange rate between the dollar and a second currency.

**Flip-flop notes:** An instrument that allows investors to switch between two types of securities—for example, to switch from a long-term bond to a short-term fixed-rate note.

**FRNs** (floating rate notes): Debt instruments that feature periodic interest rate adjustments.
- **Capped floater:** An FRN with an interest rate ceiling.
- **Convertible FRNs:** The issuer can convert the FRNs into long-term fixed-rate bonds.
- **Drop-lock FRNs:** The FRNs automatically convert to fixed-rate bonds when short-term interest rates fall below a specified level.
- **Minimax FRNs:** FRNs with upper and lower interest limits—that is, a ceiling and a floor.

**Indexed debt instruments:** Instruments with guaranteed and contingent payments, the latter being linked to an index or prices of certain commodities (oil or gold, for example).
- **Bull and bear bonds:** Bonds linked to upward and downward movements in a designated index. Bulls yield more in a rising market; bears yield more in a falling market.
- **SPINs** (Standard and Poor's indexed notes): A debt instrument featuring interest payments linked to the performance of the Standard and Poor's stock indexes.

**Put bonds:** Bonds that the investor can put (or tender) back to issuer after a specified period.

**Stripped government securities:** A type of zero-coupon bond, these securities represent long-term Treasury bonds "stripped" of semiannual interest coupons by an investment banker who resells these coupons and an interest in the principal payments. Investment banks market these stripped securities under such registered acronyms as
- **CATs:** certificates of accrual on Treasury certificates.
- **COUGRs:** certificates of government receipts.
- **STAGS:** sterling transferable accruing government securities.
- **STRIPS:** separate trading of registered interest and principal of securities.
- **TIGRs:** Treasury investment growth certificates.

*(Continued on next page)*

39

## Exhibit A.6 (continued)

■ **ZEBRAs:** zero coupon eurosterling bearer or registered accruing certificates.

**Zero-coupon bonds:** A bond that's sold at a deep discount from its face value. It carries no interest coupon, but investors receive the gradual appreciation to face value.
■ **LYONs** (liquid yield option notes): Zero-coupon bonds that are convertible into the issuer's common stock.

### ASSET-BACKED SECURITIES

**CMOs** (collateralized mortgage obligations): Debt obligations that are backed by a pool of whole mortgages or mortgage-backed securities such as Ginnie Maes.

**Mortgage-backed securities:** A participation in an organized pool of residential mortgages, including Ginnie Maes (Government National Mortgage Association), Fannie Maes (Federal National Mortgage Association) and Freddie Macs (Federal Home Loan Mortgage Corporation).

**Securitized receivables:** Debt securities collateralized by a pool of receivables. They include
■ **CARDs** (certificates of amortizing revolving debts) backed by credit card debt.
■ **CARs** (certificates of automobile receivables) backed by automobile loans.
■ **CLEOs** (collateralized lease equipment obligations) backed by leasing receivables.
■ **FRENDS** (floating rate enhanced debt securities) backed by LBO loan participations.

### EQUITY INSTRUMENTS

**MMP** (money market preferred stock or dutch-auction preferred stock): Preferred stock featuring dividends that are reset at a dutch auction—that is, an auction in which the securities are sold at the lowest yield necessary to sell the entire issue. Several investment banks have issued these instruments under such registered names as
■ **CAMPS:** cumulative auction market preferred stock.
■ **CMPS:** capital market preferred stock.
■ **Convertible MMP stock:** MMPs that can be converted into common stock.
■ **DARTS:** dutch-auction rate transferable securities.
■ **FRAPS:** fixed-rate auction preferred stock.
■ **MAPS:** market auction preferred stock.
■ **STARS:** short-term auction rate cumulative preferred stock.
■ **STRAPS:** stated rate auction preferred stock.

**PIK (pay in kind) preferred stock:** Dividends are "paid" in additional shares of preferred stock.
■ **Exchangeable PIK preferred stock:** The issuer can convert the PIK stock into debt.

### HEDGING INSTRUMENTS

**Butterfly spread:** Options strategy involving two calls and two puts on the same or different markets, with several maturity dates.

**Calendar spread:** Options strategy that involves buying and selling options on the same security with different maturities.

**Cancelable forward exchange contracts:** The holder has the unilateral right to cancel the contract at maturity.

**CIRCUS:** Combined currency and interest rate swap.

**Convertible option contracts:** A foreign currency option that converts to a forward contract if the forward exchange rate falls below a trigger price.

**Cross-hedging:** Hedging one exposure with an instrument pegged to another market or index.

**Cylinder options:** A combined call option and put option on currency.
■ **Range forwards:** A forward exchange contract specifying a range of exchange rates within which currencies will be exchanged at maturity.
■ **ZCRO** (zero cost ratio option): A cylinder option with a put written in an amount offsetting the call premium.

**OPOSSMS** (options to purchase or sell specified mortgage-backed securities).

**Perpendicular spread:** Options strategy using options with the same maturities but different strike prices.

**Swaption:** An option to enter or be forced to enter a swap.

**Synthetic instruments:** Two or more transactions that have the effect of a financial instrument. For example, a fixed-rate bond combined with an interest rate swap can result in a synthetic floating rate instrument.

**Zero-coupon swap:** A swap of zero-coupon debt into floating rate debt.

---

*Source:* J. E. Stewart, "The Challenges of the Hedge Accounting," *Journal of Accountancy* (November 1989): 59–60. Reprinted with permission.

## NOTES

1. T. Atlas, "Global Markets Make Partners Out of Rivals," *The Chicago Tribune,* April 25, 1989, sec. 1, p. 18; O. Kenishi, *Triad Power: The Coming Shape of Global Competition* (New York: Free Press, 1985), 66–68.

2. F. Washington and D. Pauly, "Driving Toward A World Car?," *Newsweek,* May 1, 1989, 48–49.

3. B. Balassa, *The Theory of Economic Integration* (Homewood, IL: Irwin, 1961), 1.

4. R. Waldman, *Managed Trade: The Competition Between Nations* (Cambridge, MA: Ballinger, 1986), 13–18. Another interesting factor is the intense bidding war conducted by governments eager to attract companies and ready to use the government image of givebacks, grants, tax holidays, and subsidies as incentives. For a good presentation of this subject, see R. Weigand, "International Investment: Weighing the Incentives," *Harvard Business Review* (July/August 1983): 146–152.

5. R. E. Yates, "Wherever Japan's At, It's There for the Long Haul," *Chicago Tribune,* April 24, 1989, p. 1.

6. S. Franklin, "Turks Bullish on Stock Market," *Chicago Tribune,* February 20, 1989, p. 17.

7. Central Intelligence Agency, *CIA Handbook of Economic Statistics* (Washington, DC: CIA, 1988), 117–119.

8. Ibid.

9. M. Porter, *The Competitive Advantage of Nations* (New York: Free Press, 1989), 98–110.

10. Ibid.

11. Ibid.

12. W. Leslie, "The Realities of 'Friday the 13th,'" *New York Times,* (October 22, 1989), p. 2 and p. 6.

13. J. Beaty and R. Hornick, "A Torrent of Dirty Dollars," *Time,* December 18, 1989, 50.

14. M. Qureshi, "Pragmatic and Academic Bases of International Accounting," *Management International Review 2* (1979): 61–68.

15. T. R. Weirich, C. G. Avery, and H. R. Anderson, "International Accounting: Varying Definitions," *International Accounting, Education and Research* (Fall 1971): 79–87.

16. Ibid., 9.

17. Qureshi, "Pragmatic and Academic Bases of International Accounting," 62.

18. Weirich, Avery, and Anderson, "International Accounting: Varying Definitions," 79–87.

19. Ibid.

20. K. B. Berg, G. G. Mueller, and L. M. Walker, "Annual Reports Go International," *Journal of Accountancy* (August 1967): 16–77.

21. G. G. Mueller and L. M. Walker, "The Coming of Age of Transnational Financial Reporting," *Journal of Accountancy* (July 1976): 5–9.

22. Accountants International Study Group, *International Financial Reporting,* London: AISG, 1975, para. 39.

23. G. G. Mueller, "To International Significance of Financial Statements," *Illinois CPA* (Spring 1965): 1–10.

24. "Current Composites Cited in Audits of Multinationals," *Journal of Accountancy* (January 1984): 36.

25. Ibid.

26. Ibid.

27. R. L. May, "The Harmonization of International Auditing Standards," in *Internationalization in the Accounting Profession,* ed. W. J. Brennan (Toronto: CICA, 1979), 63–64.

28. H.-M. W. Schoenfeld, "International Accounting: Development, Issues, and Future Directions," *Journal of International Business Studies* (Fall 1981): 83–84.

29. S. J. Gray, J. C. Shaw, and B. McSweeney, "Accounting Standards and Multinational Corporations," *Journal of International Business Studies* (Spring 1981): 121–36.

30. Mueller and Walker, "The Coming of Age," 4.

31. Ibid., 128–129.

32. F. D. S. Choi, "Multinational Challenges for Managerial Accountants," *Journal of Contemporary Business* (Autumn 1975): 10.

33. J. Cummings and W. L. Rogers, "Development in International Accounting," *CPA Journal* (May 1978): 12.

34. S. J. Gray, J. C. Shaw, and B. McSweeney, "Accounting Standards and Multinational Corporations," 130.

35. J. A. Wilson, "The Need for Standardization of International Accounting," *Touche Ross Tempo* (Winter 1969): 40.

36. E. W. Macrae, "Impediments to a Free International Market in Accounting and the Effects on International Accounting Firms," in *The International World of Accounting: Challenges and Opportunities,* ed. J. C. Burton (New York: Arthur Young, 1981), 150.

37. L. J. Seidler, "Technical Issues in International Accounting," in *Multinational Accounting: A Research Framework for the Eighties,* ed. F. D. S. Choi (Ann Arbor, MI: UMI Research Press, 1981), 41.

38. SFAC. Financial Accounting Standards Board, *Conceptual Framework for Financial Accounting and Reporting: Elements of Financial Statements and Their Measurement,* Stamford, CT: FASB, December 2, 1976, 2.

39. Financial Accounting Standards Board, *Scope and Implications of the Conceptual Framework Project,* Stamford, CT: FASB, December 2, 1976, 6–8.

40. American Institute of Certified Public Accountants, *Basic Concepts and Accounting Principles Underlying Financial Statements of Business Enterprises,* Accounting Principles Board Statement No. 4 (New York: AICPA, 1970).

41. Financial Accounting Standards Board, *Report of the Study Group on the Objectives of Financial Statements.* (New York: AICPA, 1973).

42. Financial Accounting Standards Board, *Conceptual Framework for Financial Accounting and Reporting.* (Stamford, CT: FASB, 1976).

43. FASB, "Objectives of Financial Reporting by Business Enterprises," *Concepts Statement No. 1* (Stamford, CT: FASB, 1978).

44. SFAC 4. FASB, "Objectives of Financial Reporting by Nonbusiness Organizations" *Concepts Statement No. 4* (Stamford, CT: FASB, 1975).

45. SFAC 3. FASB, "Elements of Financial Statements of Business Enterprises" (Stamford, CT: FASB, 1980).

46. SFAS 33. FASB, *Statement No. 33*, "Financial Reporting and Changing Prices," (Stamford, CT: FASB, 1979).

47. E. Stamp, *Corporate Reporting: Its Future Evolution* (Toronto: CICA, 1980).

48. T. R. Archibald, "A Research Perspective on *Corporate Reporting: Its Future Evolution*," in *Research to Support Standard Setting in Financial Accounting: A Canadian Perspective,* ed. S. Basu and J. A. Milburn (Toronto: Clarkson Gordon Foundation, 1982), 229.

49. J. F. Dewhirst, "An Evaluation of *Corporate Reporting: Its Future Evolution* Based on Different World Views," in Basu and Milburn, *Research to Support Standard Setting,* 253.

50. R. W. Park, "Is *Corporate Reporting* Asking Too Much?" *Chartered Accountant* (December 1981): 34–37.

51. Accounting Standards Steering Committee, *The Corporate Report* (London: Institute of Chartered Accountants in England and Wales, 1975), 50.

52. Ibid., 16.

53. Ibid., 17.

54. J. D. Finnerty, "Financial Engineering in Corporate Finance: An Overview," *Financial Management* (Winter 1988): 14.

55. M. H. Miller, "Financial Innovations: The Last Twenty Years and the Next," *Journal of Financial and Quantitative Analysis* (December 1986):459–471.

56. W. L. Silber, (ed.), *Financial Innovation* (Lexington, MA: Lexington Books, 1975), 15–18.

57. W. L. Silber, "Innovation, Competition, and New Contract Design in Futures Markets," *Journal of Futures Market* 2 (1981): 123–156.

58. W. L. Silber, "The Process of Financial Innovation," *American Economic Review* (May 1983): 89–95.

59. J. C. Van Horne, "Of Financial Innovations and Excess," *Journal of Finance* (July 1985): 621–631.

60. M. A. Czinkota, R. Rivoli,and A. I. Ronkainen, *International Business* (Chicago: Dryden Press, 1989), 53.

## BIBLIOGRAPHY

AlHashim, D. D. "Accounting Control through Purposive Uniformity: An International Perspective." *International Journal of Accounting Education and Research* 8 (Spring 1973): 21–32.

_____. "Regulation of Financial Accounting: An International Perspective." *International Journal of Accounting Education and Research* 16 (Fall 1980): 47–62.

Beaty, J., and R. Hornick, "A Torrent of Dirty Dollars." *Time,* December 18, 1989, 50.

Belkaoui, A., A. Kahl, and R. Peyrard. "Information Needs of Financial Analysts: An International Comparison." *International Journal of Accounting Education and Research* 13 (Fall 1977): 9–12.

Benson, Sir H. "The Story of International Accounting Standards" *Accountancy* 87 (July 1976): 34–39.

Black, F. "The Ins and Outs of Foreign Investment" In *International Financial Management: Theory and Application,* edited by D. R. Lessard, 1–15. New York: Wiley, 1985.

Brown, J. G. "The Development of International Accounting Standards." *The Woman CPA* 39 (October 1977): 9–12.

Chetkovich, M. N. "An Appeal for Unity in Establishing Financial Accounting Standards." *International Journal of Accounting Education and Research* 8 (Fall 1972): 34–39.

Choi, F. D. S. "A Cluster Approach to Accounting Harmonization." *Management Accounting* 63 (August 1981): 9–12.

Corbett, P. G. "International Accounting Standards: The Impact on Practicing Firms." *Accountant* 176 (May 26, 1977): 602–603.

_____. "Why International Accounting Standards?" *CA Magazine* 111 (July 1978): 36–39.

Cowperthwaite, G. H. "Prospectus for International Harmonization." *CA Magazine* 108 (June 1976): 22–31.

Cummings, J. P. "The International Accounting Standards Committee: Current and Future Developments," *International Journal of Accounting Education and Research* 11 (Fall 1975): 31–37.

_____. "The International Accounting Standards Committee—Its Purpose and Status." *CPA Journal* 44 (September 1974): 50–53.

Cummings, J. P., and M. N. Chetkovich. "World Accounting Enters a New Era." *Journal of Accountancy* 145 (April 1978): 52–62.

Cummings, J. P., and W. L. Rogers. "Developments in International Accounting." *CPA Journal* 48 (May 1978): 15–19.

DaCosta, R. C., J. C. Bourgeois, and W. M. Lawson. "A Classification of International Financial Accounting Practices." *International Journal of Accounting Education and Research* 13 (Spring 1978): 73–86.

Daniels, J. D., and L. R. Radebaugh. *International Business: Environments and Operations.* Reading, MA: Addison-Wesley, 1989.

Enthoven, A. J. H. *Social and Political Impact of Multinationals on Third World Countries (and Its Accounting Implications).* Dallas, TX: Center for International Accounting Development, University of Texas at Dallas, 1976.

Heckscher, E. *Mercantilism.* London: George Allen & Unwin, 1935.

Kenishi, O. *Triad Power: The Coming Shape of Global Competition.* New York: Free Press, 1985.

# 2

# ACCOUNTING FOR FOREIGN-CURRENCY TRANSACTIONS, FUTURES CONTRACTS, AND OTHER FINANCIAL INSTRUMENTS

## INTRODUCTION

A crucial problem facing multinational corporations is how to account for foreign-currency transactions, futures contracts, interest-rate swaps, and other financial transactions. The financial-engineering phenomenon has spurred new financial instruments combining various attractive features. These instruments need new accounting methods. Statement of Financial Accounting Standard No. 52 (SFAS 52), *Foreign Currency Translation,* deals with foreign-currency transactions and futures involving foreign currency. SFAS 80, *Accounting for Futures Contracts,* deals with other futures. Various exposure drafts have been issued to deal with the growing area of new instruments. This chapter discusses each of the preceding issues as they have been treated in the professional accounting literature.

## THE WORLD OF FOREIGN EXCHANGE

Each country has its own national currency. Therefore, *foreign exchange* refers to the trade of national currency for that of another country. Each national currency has its own relative value or exchange rate. An exchange rate of a currency initially is determined as a function of its direct or indirect precious-metal content or by the reserves of other currencies held in its central bank to be used as a support for its international exchangeability.

To facilitate the determination of the values of foreign exchange and its sales and purchases, foreign-exchange markets have been organized. These markets include mainly the foreign-exchange traders of commercial banks, the International Money Market Division of the Chicago Mercantile Exchange, which specializes in trading currency futures, and so-called exchange clubs, such as The Hague Club and the Paris Club. These markets establish foreign exchange as an economic commodity whose value is subject to the laws of supply and demand. Basically, the foreign-exchange market determines the rate at which one national currency is exchanged for another national currency. The resulting exchange rates are the basis for the exchange prices used for international business transactions. Within these foreign exchange markets is the forward market, used to hedge against the exchange-rate risks arising from holding open-ended account balances.

There are basically two types of foreign-exchange rates: the spot rate and the forward rate. The *spot rate* is the rate quoted for currency transactions to be delivered within two days; it is determined by trade flows, inflation, seasonal demands for a currency, and arbitrage. The *forward rate* is the rate quoted for forward-exchange contracts. These are contracts between a foreign-exchange trader and a customer, or between two foreign-exchange traders, that specify the delivery of a certain sum in foreign currency at a future date and at a given rate. Various reasons motivate the use of a forward contract: to hedge a transaction, to speculate on currency movements, to hedge a net investment in a foreign entity, and to hedge a foreign-currency commitment. The designated rate in the forward contracts is the *forward rate.*

The forward rate may be equal to or different from the spot rate at the time the contract is made. The difference between the two rates is known as the *spread.* If the forward rate is superior to the spot rate, it is selling at a premium. The discount and the premium normally are quoted at the number of points above or below the spot rate. They may also be quoted in annualized-percentage terms computed as follows:

$$\text{Premium (discount)} = \left(\frac{FR - SR}{SR}\right)\left(\frac{12}{N}\right)$$

where
  $PR$ = forward rate on the day the contract is entered into
  $SR$ = spot rate on the same day
  $N$ = number of months forward

The formula above may be used as a way of determining the forward rate. Assuming the premium or discount is due to the interest-rate differential between two countries, the local country (LC) and the foreign country (FC), then

$$rLC - rFC = \left(\frac{FR - SR}{SR}\right)\left(\frac{12}{N}\right)$$

and

$$FR = SR\,(rLC - rFC)\left(\frac{N}{12}\right) + SR$$

where
$rLC$ = interest rate in the local country
$rFC$ = interest rate in the foreign country

## ACCOUNTING FOR FOREIGN-CURRENCY TRANSACTIONS

Various corporation transactions require the flow of money worldwide. These global transactions include the import or export of merchandise, the sale or purchase of services, the payment or receipt of dividends, royalties, and management fees, and borrowing and lending money; they are called *foreign-currency transactions* because they require settlement in a currency other than the functional currency of the reporting entity. The functional currency of an entity is the currency used in the economic environment in which that entity operates. For a corporation based in the United States, accounting for foreign-currency transactions is covered in SFAS 52. This chapter divides the process of accounting for foreign transactions into two major categories: accounting for foreign-currency transactions that are not the result of forward-exchange contracts and accounting for foreign-currency transactions involving forward-exchange contracts.

### Foreign-Currency Transactions Not Involving Forward-Exchange Contracts

For those foreign currency transactions not involving forward-exchange contracts, the following treatments apply:

1. At the time of the transaction, the asset, liability, revenue, or expense is recorded in the functional currency of the recording entity by use of the current exchange rate on the date of the transaction.

2. At the balance-sheet date and at the date of the settlement of the foreign-currency translation, recorded balances in the foreign-currency transaction accounts are adjusted to reflect the current exchange rate.

3. With two exceptions, gains and losses resulting from the restatement are reflected in the current period's income statement.

4. The two exceptions are foreign-currency transactions that are the result of an economic hedge of a net investment in a foreign entity, and long-term, intercompany foreign-currency transactions when the entities to the transaction are consolidated, combined, or accounted for by the equity method in the reporting enterprise's financial statements. In both cases, the gains and losses are reported as translation adjustments in a separate component of the stockholders' equity account.

The two examples that follow illustrate these treatments. In Example 1, the treatment of transaction gains and losses in current net income is discussed in relation to the export and import of goods. Example 2 uses an intercompany foreign-currency transaction to illustrate the treatment of transaction gains and losses and translation adjustments to stockholders' equity.

*Example 1: Foreign-Exchange Transactions Involving*
*Import or Export of Goods*

Let us suppose the following events: On December 21, 19X3, the American National Company sold merchandise to a foreign supplier — the Foreign National Company — billed and valued for FC1,000,000, at "net 30" terms. Information about exchange rates between the U.S. dollar and the foreign currency (FC) of the seller is as follows:

December 21, 19X3: FC1 = $.50

December 31, 19X3: FC1 = $.55

January 20, 19X4: FC1 = $.45

The entries for this foreign-exchange transaction follow.
    At the date of foreign-exchange transaction, December 21, 19X3,

| | | |
|---|---|---|
| Accounts Receivable | $500,000 | |
| Sales | | $500,000 |

to record the purchase of goods for $500,000 (FC1,000,00 × $50).
    At the balance-sheet date, December 31, 19X3,

| | | |
|---|---|---|
| Accounts Receivable | $500,000 | |
| Exchange Gain | | $50,000 |

to record the exchange gain equal to FC1,000,000 × ($.55 − $.50). This exchange gain will be included in the 19X3 income statement of American National Company as a nonoperating item.
    At the date of the settlement, January 20, 19X4,

| Cash | $450,000 | |
| Exchange Loss | 100,000 | |
| Accounts Receivable | | $550,000 |

to record the amount received on settlement, equal to FC1,000,000 × $.45, and the exchange loss, equal to FC1,000,000 × ($.55 − $.45).

This exchange loss will be included in the 19X4 income statement of American National Company as a nonoperating item.

### Example 2: Foreign-Exchange Transactions Involving Intercompany Items

Let us hypothesize further these additional events: On December 21, 19X3, the American National Company made an advance of FC1,000,000 to the Other National Company, which is a subsidiary of the American National Company. This advance is considered to be long-term in nature. Information about the exchange rates between the U.S. dollar and the foreign currency of the subsidiary is as follows:

December 21, 19X3: FC1 = $.50

December 31, 19X3: FC1 = $.55

The entries for this foreign exchange transaction follow.

At the date of the foreign-exchange transaction, December 21, 19X3,

| Investment in Other National Company | $500,000 | |
| Cash | | $500,000 |

At the balance-sheet date, no exchange gains and losses are recognized in the current net income, but instead enter into the determination of the translation adjustment as a component of stockholders' equity, as determined by the following:

Amount Used in Translation Adjustment = FC1,000,000 ($.55 − $.50) = $50,000

### Foreign-Currency Transactions Involving Forward-Exchange Contracts

A *forward-exchange contract* is defined as an agreement to exchange different currencies at a specified future date and at a specified rate (the forward rate). Firms enter in a forward-exchange contract with a third-party broker to guarantee a fixed exchange price for the transaction. Three adjustments have to be computed and accounted for.

The first adjustment is the gain or loss (whether or not deferred) on a forward contract. It is equal to the foreign-currency amount of the forward contract multiplied by the difference between the spot rate at the balance-sheet date and the spot rate at the inception of the forward contract (or the spot rate last used to measure a gain or loss on that contract for an earlier period). The second adjustment is the discount or premium on a forward contract. This discount is equal to the foreign-currency amount of the contract multiplied by the difference between the contracted forward rate and the spot rate at the contract inception date.

The third adjustment is the gain or loss on a speculative forward contract, which is equal to the foreign-currency amount of the contract multiplied by the difference between the forward rate available for the remaining maturity of the contract and the contract forward rate (or the forward rate last used to measure a gain or loss on that contract for an earlier period).

The accounting treatment for a foreign-currency transaction involving foreign-exchange contracts can be handled in different manners, depending on whether the forward-exchange contract is intended as a hedge of an identifiable foreign-currency commitment, a hedge of an exposed net-asset or liability position, or a hedge of a foreign-currency speculation.

A forward-exchange contract is considered a hedge of an identifiable foreign-currency commitment if (1) the foreign-currency transaction is designated as, and is effective as, a hedge of a foreign-currency commitment and (2) the foreign-currency commitment is firm. In such a case, the gain on the forward contract will be deferred and accounted for in the cost basis of the object of the foreign-currency commitment. Any loss is recognized currently rather than deferred. In addition, the discount or premium on a forward contract will be deferred and included in the cost basis.

A forward-exchange contract that serves as a hedge of an exposed net-asset or liability position is accounted for in a different manner. The gain or loss is recognized in the current accounting period, while the discount or premium is accounted for separately over the life of the contract.

A forward-exchange contract that serves as a hedge of foreign-currency speculation is also accounted for differently, with all gains and losses, premiums, and discounts recognized currently.

The examples that follow involve the hedge of an identifiable foreign-currency commitment, the hedge of an exposed net-asset or liability position, and the hedge of a foreign-currency speculation to illustrate these treatments.

*Example 1: Hedge of an Identifiable Foreign-Currency Commitment*

Let us suppose the following events: On December 1, 19X3, the American National Company agreed to buy merchandise from a foreign supplier — the Foreign National Company — for FC200,000, at "net 90" terms.

Also on December 1, 19X3, the American National Company entered into a forward-exchange contract for the delivery of FC2,000,000 in 90 days. Information about the exchange rates between the U.S. dollar and the foreign currency of the seller is as follows:

December 1, 19X3, Forward Rate: FC1 = $.50

December 1, 19X3, Spot Rate: FC1 = $.45

December 31, 19X3, Spot Rate: FC1 eq $.55

March 1, 19X4, Spot Rate: FC1 = $.60

Because the contract qualifies as an identifiable foreign-currency commitment, the entries appear in the following manner:

At the date of the inception of the forward-exchange contract, December 1, 19X3,

| | | |
|---|---|---|
| Foreign Currency Receivable from Exchange Broker | $90,000 | |
| Premium on Forward-Exchange Contract | 10,000 | |
| Payable to Exchange Broker | | $100,000 |

to record the receivable and payable relating to the forward exchange contract. The premium is equal to ($.50 − $.40) × FC200,000.

At the balance-sheet date, December 31, 19X3,

| | | |
|---|---|---|
| Foreign Currency Receivable from Exchange Broker | $20,000 | |
| Deferred Gain on Forward-Exchange Contract | | $20,000 |

to record the gain from the forward exchange contract. The gain is equal to ($.55 − $.45) × FC200,000.

At the date of the settlement, March 1, 19X4, there are three entries.

1. To record the gain from the forward-exchange contract,

| | | |
|---|---|---|
| Foreign Currency Receivable from Exchange Broker | $10,000 | |
| Deferred Gain on Forward-Exchange Contract | | $10,000 |

where the gain equals ($.60 − $.55) × 200,000.

2. To record the payment of the obligation to the exchange broker and the receipt of the foreign currency,

| | | |
|---|---|---|
| Payable to Exchange Broker | $100,000 | |
| Cash | | $100,000 |
| Foreign Currency | 120,000 | |
| Foreign Currency Receivable from Exchange Broker | | 120,000 |

3. To record the cost of the merchandise received and the payment of the foreign currency to the supplier,

| | | |
|---|---|---|
| Deferred Gain on Forward-Exchange Contract | $30,000 | |
| Equipment | 100,000 | |
| Foreign Currency | | $120,000 |
| Premium on Forward-Exchange Contract | | 10,000 |

*Example 2: Hedge of an Exposed Net-Asset or Liability Position*

Let us suppose the following events: On December 1, 19X3, to hedge against an exposed liability position, the American National Company entered into a forward-exchange contract with an exchange broker for the delivery of FC2,000,000 in 90 days.

Information about the exchange rates between the U.S. dollar and the foreign currency of the seller is as follows:

December 1, 19X3, Forward Rate: FC = $.48

December 1, 19X3, Spot Rate: FC = $.45

December 31, 19X3, Spot Rate: FC = $.55

March 1, 19X4, Spot Rate: FC = $.60

Because the contract qualifies as a hedge of an exposed-liability position, the entries will be as follows:

At the date of the inception of the forward-exchange contract, December 1, 19X3,

| | |
|---|---|
| Foreign Currency Receivable from Exchange Broker | $90,000 |

Premium on Forward Exchange
   Contract                    6,000
      Payable to Exchange Broker          $96,000

to record the receivables and payables dating to the forward contract.

At the balance-sheet date, December 31, 19X3, the gain from the forward-exchange contract and the amortization of premium is recognized by the two entries that follow.

1.

Foreign Currency Receivable
   from Exchange Broker         $20,000
      Gain on Forward-
          Exchange Contract          $20,000

2.

Amortization of Premium on
   Forward-Exchange Contract    $2,000
      Premium on
         Forward-Exchange
         Contract              $2,000

At the date of settlement, March 1, 19X4, there are three entries.
1. To recognize the gain from the forward-exchange contract,

Foreign Currency Receivable
   from Exchange Broker         $10,000
      Gain on Forward-
          Exchange Contract          $10,000

where the gain equals ($.60 − $.55) × FC200,000.

2. To record the payment of the obligation to the exchange broker and the receipt of the foreign currency,

Payable to Exchange Broker    $96,000
   Cash                       $96,000
Foreign Currency          120,000
   Foreign Currency
      Receivable from
      Exchange Broker          120,000

3. To record the amortization of the premium,

Amortization of Premium
   on Forward-Exchange
   Contract                                    $4,000
     Premium on Forward-
      Exchange Contract                                    $4,000

*Example 3: Hedge of a Foreign-Currency Speculation*

Let us suppose the following events: On December 1, 19X3, to speculate in the foreign-currency market, the American National Company entered into a forward-exchange contract with an exchange broker for the delivery of FC200,000 in 60 days. Information about the exchange rates between the U.S. dollar and the foreign currency is as follows:

December 1, 19X3, 60-day Forward Rate: FC1 = $.50

December 31, 19X3, 30-day Forward Rate: FC1 = $.55

January 30, 19X4, Spot Rate: FC1 = $.60

Because the contract qualifies as foreign-currency speculation, the entries will be as follows:

At the date of the inception of the forward-exchange contract, December 1, 19X3,

Foreign Currency
   Receivable from
   Exchange Broker                                    $100,000
     Payable to Exchange
      Broker                                    $100,000

to record the receivable and payable relating to the forward contract.

At the balance-sheet date, December 31, 19X3,

Foreign Currency
   Receivable from
   Exchange Broker                                    $10,000
     Gain on Forward-
      Exchange Contract                                    $10,000

to record the gain on the foreign-exchange contract. The gain is computed as ($.55 − .50) × FC200,000.

At the date of settlement, January 30, 19X4, there are three entries.

1. To recognize the gain from the forward-exchange contract,

Foreign Currency
Receivable from
Exchange Broker                 $10,000
    Gain on Forward-
        Exchange Contract                          $10,000

where the gain equals ($.60 − .55) × FC200,000

2. To record the payment of the obligation to the exchange broker and the receipt of foreign currency,

Payable to Exchange
Broker                          $100,000
    Cash                                       $100,000
Foreign Currency                 120,000
    Foreign Currency
    Receivable from
    Exchange Broker                             120,000

3. To record the sale of foreign currency,

Cash                            $160,000
    Foreign Currency                           $120,000

## ACCOUNTING FOR FUTURES CONTRACTS

### Background

A variety of commodities are traded on various exchanges around the world. The number and originality of these commodities are on the increase due to the innovativeness of the marketplace and the growth of financial engineering in the global economy. Examples of these commodities and securities include metals (gold, silver, platinum, copper, zinc, lead, etc.), meats (pork bellies, turkeys, cattle, etc.), grains (wheat, barley, oats, corn, etc.), unique items (eggs, soybeans, plywood, and cotton), and financial instruments (bonds and notes, commercial paper, treasury bills, GNMA mortgages). Both spot contracts and futures contracts are used for trading in these commodities, but the name of the game is mainly in futures contracts. By definition, *futures contracts* are exchange-traded contracts for future delivery of a standardized quantity of an item at a specified future date and at a specified price.

Accounting for futures contracts is covered in SFAS 80, *Accounting for Futures Contracts,* issued in August 1984. It does not, however, cover foreign-currency, forward-placement, or delayed-delivery contracts.

Foreign-currency futures contracts, discussed above in this chapter, are covered in SFAS 52, *Foreign Currency Translation.*

Common characteristics of all forward contracts with an exchange broker are (1) the need for an initial margin deposit, paid to the worker, that represents a small proportion of the futures contract, (2) the need to readjust the deposit as the market value of the futures contract changes, and (3) the need to close out the account by either receiving or delivering the item, paying or receiving cash, or entering into an offsetting contract. The change in the market value of the contract is equal to the contract's quoted market price.

The accounting for futures contracts differs depending on whether or not the contract is accounted for as a hedge and, if it is a hedge, whether the hedged item is carried at market value, whether it is a hedge of an existing asset or liability position or a firm commitment, or if the contract is a hedge of an anticipated transaction.

### Futures Contracts Not
### Accounted for as a Hedge

When the transaction does not qualify as a hedge because it does not relate to a hedged item (such as an asset or liability position, a firm commitment, or an anticipated transaction), it is accounted for as a speculation in futures contracts. In such a case, (1) the provisions of the Accounting Principles Board (APB) Opinion No. 30 are followed, and the gain or loss on the contract that is equal to the change in contract market price times the contract size is charged to income in periods of change in value of the contract, and (2) the payables to a futures broker are classified as a current asset until the closing of the contract.

The following example illustrates the accounting for futures contracts not accounted for as hedges:

On October 1, 19X1, the Kamilis Futures Company purchases 100 February 1, 19X2, soybean futures contracts. The quoted market price at the date of purchase is $5.80 a bushel; each contract covers 5000 bushels. The initial margin deposit is $40,000. At the end of Year 1, the quoted market price of the soybean contract is $5.60 a bushel. The contract is closed on February 1, 19X2, when the quoted market price is $5.30 a bushel.

The entries for the futures-contract transaction are as follows:

1. At the inception of the contract on October 1, 19X1,

| | | |
|---|---|---|
| Deposit with Futures Broker | $40,000 | |
| Cash | | $40,000 |

to record the initial margin deposit when the contract is executed.

2. At the end of Year 1,

| | | |
|---|---|---|
| Loss on Futures Contracts | $100,000 | |
| Payable to Futures Broker | | $100,000 |

to recognize losses on futures contracts of $.20 per bushel ($5.80 − $5.60) on 500,000 bushels (5000 × 100).

3. At the expiration of the contract on February 1, 19X2,

| | | |
|---|---|---|
| Payable to Futures Broker | $100,000 | |
| Loss on Futures Contract | 150,000 | |
| Cash | | $250,000 |

to record the total loss on the contract, which is figured as ($5.60 − 5.30) × 500,000, and the payment to the broker.

| | | |
|---|---|---|
| Cash | $40,000 | |
| Deposit with Futures Broker | | $40,000 |

to record the return of the margin deposit by the broker.

### Hedge Criteria Set by SFAS 80

The accounting for futures contracts that qualify as hedges is different from the accounting for futures contracts that do not qualify as hedges. To qualify as a hedge according to SFAS 80, the contract must meet the following criteria:

1. The contract must be related to and designated as a hedge of identifiable assets, liabilities, firm commitments, or anticipated transactions.

2. The hedged item must expose the firm to the risks of changes in price or interest rates. The determination of price risk is to be done on a decentralized basis when the firm is unable to do so at the firm level.

3. The changes in the market value of a futures contract must be highly correlated during the life of the contract with the changes in the fair value of the hedged items. The correlation must last if changes in the market value of the futures contract essentially offset changes in the fair value of the hedged item or the hedged item's interest expense or interest income.

After qualifying as a hedge by meeting the criteria above, the accounting for futures contracts for each type of hedge item depends on whether the hedged item is reported at market value, whether it is a hedge of an existing asset or liability position or a firm commitment, and whether it is a hedge of an anticipated transaction.

### Futures-Contract Accounted for as a Hedge When Hedged Item Is Carried at Market Value

If a futures contract qualifies as a hedge and the hedged items are reported at fair market value, both the changes in the value of the hedged asset and the related futures contract must be recognized in the same accounting period. With regard to the unrealized change of the fair value of the item, firms use one of two options: either (1) change it to net income or (2) maintain it in a separate stockholders' equity account until sale or disposition of the hedged item. The treatment of the changes in the market value of the related futures contract follows the option chosen for the changes in the fair market value of the hedged item. If the latter is changed to income, the changes in the market value of the related futures contract is also changed to income in the period in which the market value changes. If the changes in the fair market value of the hedged item is charged to a separated stockholders' equity account, the changes in the market value of the futures contract is also maintained in a stockholders' equity account until disposition of the related item.

The following example illustrates the accounting for a futures contract accounted for as a hedge when the hedged item is carried at market value: On November 1, 19X1, Gold Management, Inc. has a gold inventory of 20,000 troy ounces, carried at a market value of $400 per ounce. The company expects to sell the gold in February 19X2, and sells 200 futures contracts of 100 troy ounces of gold each at a price of $400 per ounce to be delivered at the time of sale. A $140,000 deposit is required by the broker. At the end of Year 1, the market price of gold is $420. In February of 19X2, the company sells the entire gold inventory at $450 per ounce and closes out the futures contracts at the same price. The entries for the futures contracts transactions are as follows:

1. At the inception of the contract on November 1, 19X1,

| | | |
|---|---|---|
| Deposit with the Futures Broker | $140,000 | |
| Cash | | $140,000 |

to make a record of the initial margin deposit when the contract is executed.
2. At the end of Year 1,

| | | |
|---|---|---|
| Gold Inventory | $400,000 | |
| Unrealized Gain on Market Increase of Gold | | $400,000 |

to recognize the changes in the fair market value of the gold inventory, which equals ($420 − 400) × (20,000 troy ounces) = $400,000.

| | | |
|---|---|---|
| Loss on Futures Contract | $400,000 | |
| Payable to Futures | | |
| Broker | | $400,000 |

to recognize the loss on futures contracts, which equals ($420 − $400) × (20,000 troy ounces) = $400,000.

3. At the expiration of the contract in February 19X2,

| | | |
|---|---|---|
| Cash | $9,000,000 | |
| Gold Inventory | | $400,000 |
| Gain on Market Increase | | |
| in Gold | | 600,000 |

to recognize the sale of the gold at $420 per ounce and the realization of a gain in the market increase in gold of $600,000, which is computed as ($450 − 420) × (20,000).

| | | |
|---|---|---|
| Payable to Futures Broker | $400,000 | |
| Loss on Futures Contracts | 600,000 | |
| Cash | | $860,000 |
| Deposit with Futures | | |
| Broker | | 140,000 |

*Futures Contract Accounted for as a Hedge of an Existing Asset or Liability Position or a Firm Commitment*

When a futures contract is accounted for as a hedge and the hedged item is not carried at market value, the futures contract is accounted for as a hedge of an existing asset or liability position, a firm commitment, or an anticipated transaction. This section deals with hedges of an existing asset or liability or a firm commitment.

If the contract is a hedge of an existing asset or liability position, any changes in the market value of the futures contract is accounted for as an adjustment of the carrying value of the hedged item. If the contract is a hedge of a firm commitment, the changes in the market value of the contract are included in the measurement of the transaction satisfying the commitment. If there is a difference between the contract price and the value of the hedged item and two conditions are met, the difference between the contract price and the fair value of the hedged item is accounted for as a discount or premium to be amortized as income over the life of the contract. The two conditions that need to be met are that (1) the hedged item is deliverable under contract and (2) the futures contract and the hedged item will be kept by the firm until the date of the delivery of the futures contract. If the two conditions are not met, then the difference between the contract price and the value of the hedged item is accounted for in the same manner as changes in contract value.

The following example illustrates accounting for futures contracts accounted for as hedges of an existing asset or liability position: On November 1, 19X1, Kelly Soybeans, Inc. has a soybean inventory of 20,000 bushels, carried at a cost of $5.00 per bushel. The firm intends to sell the whole inventory by February 19X2. The firm sells four February 19X2 futures contracts in November 19X1 at a price of $5.50 per bushel. A $5,000 deposit is required by the broker. At the end of Year 1, the market price of soybeans is $6.10 per bushel. In February 19X2, the company sells the whole inventory at $5.30 per bushel and closes out the four futures contracts at the same price. The entries for the futures contracts transactions are as follows:

1. At the inception of the contract on November 1, 19X1,

| | | |
|---|---|---|
| Deposit with the Futures Broker | $5,000 | |
| Cash | | $5,000 |

to make a record of the initial margin deposit when the contract is executed.

2. At the end of Year 1,

| | | |
|---|---|---|
| Deferred Loss on Futures Contract | $12,000 | |
| Payable to Futures Broker | | $12,000 |

to recognize the change in the market value of the contracts, which is calculated as ($6.10 − $5.50) × (20,000) = $12,000, and carry the deferred loss on futures contracts as a current asset.

3. At the expiration of the contract in February 19X2,

| | | |
|---|---|---|
| Cash | $33,000 | |
| Payable to Futures Broker | 12,000 | |
| Deferred Gain on Futures Contracts | | $40,000 |
| Deposit with Futures Broker | | 5,000 |

to recognize, at the expiration of the contract, (1) the deferred gain on futures contracts, which is equal to ($5.50 − 5.30) × 20,000, and (2) the cash received from the broker ($5,000 deposit − 12,000 deferred loss to the broker + 40,000 gain on futures contracts).

| Deferred Gain on Futures | | |
|---|---|---|
| Contracts | $40,000 | |
| Deferred Loss on | | |
| Futures Contracts | | $12,000 |
| Inventory | | 28,000 |

to make an adjustment in the carrying value of the hedged item.

| Cash | $106,000 | |
|---|---|---|
| Cost of Sales | 72,000 | |
| Sales | | $106,000 |
| Inventory | | 72,000 |

to recognize the sale of the inventory (20,000 × $5.30) and the expensing of the cost of inventory ($100,000 − 28,000).

### Futures Contract Accounted for as a Hedge of an Anticipated Transaction

As stated above, when a futures contract is accounted for as a hedge, the hedge may be for an anticipated transaction that the firm intends or expects to enter into, but is not legally required to do so. Therefore, in such a situation, the futures contract does not relate to a firm's existing assets, liabilities, or commitment. To qualify as a hedge of an anticipated transaction the following criteria need to be met: the terms and characteristics of the transactions are identifiable, and the anticipated transaction is possible. If the two conditions are not met, the gain or loss on the contract is charged to income in the period of change in the market value of the contract. If the two conditions are met, the hedge qualifies as a hedge of an anticipated transaction and the following situations are possible: (1) if it is probable that the quantity of the anticipated transaction is less than the hedge, then the gains and losses on the contract in excess of the anticipated transaction are charged to income; (2) if the hedge is closed prior to the completion of the transaction, the changes in value are accumulated, carried forward, and included in the anticipated transaction, and (3) if the hedge is not closed prior to the completion of the transaction, the change in market value of the contract is accounted for in the same manner as the anticipated transaction.

The following example illustrates the accounting for a futures contract accounted for as a hedge of an anticipated transaction: The Zribi Manufacturing Company uses gold in its finishing process. In October 19X1, their decision is to acquire 20,000 troy ounces of gold at $400 per ounce. A $140,000 deposit is required by the broker. On February 1, 19X2, the Zribi Manufacturing Company acquires 20,000 troy ounces of gold for $420 per ounce and closes out the futures contract. The end of the fiscal year for the company is March 30. The entries for the futures contract transaction are as follows:

1. At the inception of the contract on October 1, 19X1,

| | | |
|---|---|---|
| Deposit with Futures Broker | $140,000 | |
| Cash | | $140,000 |

2. At the expiration of the contract on February 1, 19X2,

| | | |
|---|---|---|
| Cash | $540,000 | |
| Deposit with Futures Broker | | $140,000 |
| Deferred Gain on Futures Contract | | 400,000 |

to recognize the deferred gain on the futures contract, which is equal to ($420 − 400) × (20,000), and the cash received from the broker ($400,000 + 140,000).

| | | |
|---|---|---|
| Deferred Gains on Futures Contract | $ 400,000 | |
| Raw Materials Inventory (Gold) | 8,000,000 | |
| Cash | | $8,400,000 |

## INTEREST-RATE SWAPS

### Background

An interest-rate swap is an agreement between two parties for an exchange of a given interest rate for a different interest rate to be applied to the same, agreed-upon currency amount. The exchange may be from a fixed to a floating rate, from a floating to a fixed rate, or from a floating-rate index to a different index. The party paying the fixed rate is known as the *fixed-rate payer,* while the party paying the variable rate is known as the *floating-rate payer.* The floating-rate payment is generally based on the London Interbank-Offered Rate (LIBOR), the Treasury-bill rate, the commercial-paper composite rate, the price rate, the certificate-of-deposit (CD) composite rate, the federal-funds rate, or the I. I. Kenny rate. The interest swap takes place because of differential information and institutional restrictions across national boundaries. As stated by Bricksler and Chen:

For example in contrast to the U.S. Corporate bond market, there is virtually no registration or disclosure requirement for issuing new corporate bonds in the Eurobond market. As a segment, it takes much less time to place a new bond issue in the Eurobond markets. However, issuing a new bond in the Eurobond markets requires a large underwriting cost and a larger credit premium. Thus, it is generally more difficult for a relatively small and unknown bank or business firm to issue new bonds in the Eurobond markets. In the floating-rate market, the U.S. short term interest rates are usually lower than those in the European markets due, in part, to the presence of government insurance on deposits.[1]

As an example, suppose that company XYZ has $100 million of noncallable bonds outstanding that carry a fixed rate of 14% and have 6 years to maturity. The company elects to enter into an interest-rate swap with a bank under which it agrees to pay the price rate of $9\frac{1}{2}\%$ plus 50 basis points and to receive 13% from a fixed-rate payer. The company benefits from the swap as it obtains a net floating-rate cost of 11% and an economic gain of 3 percentage points on the cost of borrowed funds.

For an additional example, assume that a AAA-rated firm is able to obtain fixed-rate financing at the lowest available market rate of 8%, while a BBB-rated firm would have to pay 12% for fixed-rate financing (assuming that it could obtain it at all). The AAA-rated firm has a "comparative-credit advantage." However, the spread of the floating-rate financing available in the capital market is not nearly as wide; the AAA-rated firm can borrow at the prime rate, while the BBB-rated firm can borrow at the prime rate plus 3%. If Firm A agrees to pay Firm B prime plus 2.5% in exchange for Firm B paying Firm A an 11% fixed rate for the fixed-rate debt it swapped to Firm B, since Firm A's cost on the fixed-rate debt was only 8%, it is receiving 300 basis points (3%) over its cost. The net gain from the swap for Firm A is 50 basis points (0.5%), computed by deducting the 250 basis points the firm is paying over its normal cost of borrowing at floating rates (prime) from the 300 basis points it made by swapping the fixed-rate debt to Firm B (11% − 8%). Firm B will receive prime plus 2.5% for the floating-rate debt transferred to Firm A, for which it paid prime plus 3%, but will pay only 11% for the fixed-rate debt, which would normally have cost it 12%. The net savings to Firm B is also 50 basis points, or 0.5%.

Hedging and speculation with regard to interest-rate or currency-value fluctuations can be obtained by a swap. For example, if Firm A believes interest rates will rise, while Firm B believes they will fall, then Firm A will be willing to trade its variable-rate interest payments for Firm B's fixed-rate interest payments. And, if Firm A expects significant devaluation of the dollar will occur, it will seek to swap its dollar-based interest payments for interest payments based on what it considers to be a more stable currency.

The swaps are termed *unmatched* when the company entering the swap has no other asset or liability related to the swap transaction. The motivations are generally speculative. "The swap agreement may have been entered into for the speculative purpose or to hedge the enterprise's overall exposure to interest rate risk (so-called macro-hedging) or as a temporary position before establishing a matched, hedged or offsetting position."[2]

Basically, in an unmatched, or speculative position, the interest-rate swap serves to create interest-rate risk, and the user expects to gain from favorable changes in interest rates. In a *matched,* or *linked* swap, the interest-rate swap is specifically linked to an asset or liability.

Some swaps may be unmatched but are still considered to be hedged if the firm in some way reduces or eliminates the risk posed by the agreement. An example involves offsetting the interest-rate risk in an unmatched swap position by purchasing or selling Treasury securities.[3]

The swap can be hedged if the firm takes any position that offsets the interest-rate risk in an unmatched swap. Another swap, called the *offsetting swap,* occurs when an intermediary arranges two swap positions that counterbalance each other, thus maintaining a "matched look" of swaps and eliminating interest-rate risk. The intermediary retains the credit risk if either part should default. Other types of swaps include the following:

1. *Commodity Swap.* Similar to the basis swap, except that one of the indexes is tied to a commodity (i.e., silver)

2. *Basis Swap.* Floating-rate debt is exchanged for floating-rate debt based on a different index (i.e., T-bill vs. LIBOR)

3. *Circus Swap.* Fixed-rate debt is swapped for floating-rate debt valued in a different currency (i.e., yen vs. dollars)

4. *Reverse Swap.* If interest rates change so that the company could profit or escape loss by terminating the swap, it can enter into another swap that reverses or "unwinds" the original swap

5. *Asset Swap.* Converts a fixed-rate asset into a floating-rate asset (or vice versa) by creating a synthetic floating-rate note through a swap

6. *Amortizing Swap.* Notional principle decreases over the term of the swap

7. *Options on Swaps* or *Swap Options.* Give the purchaser of the option the right (but not the obligation) to enter into an interest-rate swap at predetermined rates

8. *Forward Swaps.* Swaps that become effective at some future time

Advantages of interest rate swaps include the following:

*Confidentiality.* The swap is a "silent" form of financing

*New funding source.* Fixed-rate funding is obtained without resorting to the public- or private-capital markets

*Flexibility.* A swap contract can be sold or assigned to another party at any time

*Reduction of interest-rate sensitivity.* Corporations often arrange interest-rate swaps to match debt costs against projected revenues

*Interest-rate management.* Interest-rate swaps allow a company to manage its interest-rate exposure actively by switching from fixed-rate to floating-rate debt and back again, depending on its forecast of interest rates or hedging needs

*"Cash out" convenience.* Companies can use interest-rate swaps to "cash out" of older, fixed-rate debt when they have realized substantial gains due to a change in interest rates[4]

Other advantages of interest-rate swapping include its ability (1) to provide inexpensive fixed-rate financing for firms with poor credit ratings, (2) to hedge against interest-rate exposure by converting floating-rate debt to fixed-rate debt with a renegotiation of the debt instrument, (3) to lock in a denied interest rate, or (4) to benefit from market imperfections by securing a low, fixed, or floating rate. Banks also take advantage of interest swapping in order to close the maturity gaps between the assets and liabilities on their balance sheets and eliminate interest-rate exposure during a period, to raise low-cost funds not otherwise available, or to manage the risk of swapping a floating-rate debt based on one index with a floating-rate debt based on a more advantageous index.

There are, however, some risks involved in interest-rate swaps: a credit risk, caused when the counterparty required to make payments under the interest-rate swap fails to do so; a market risk, which may occur due to changing interest rates; or a market-liquidity risk, which can occur because most interest-rate swaps are over-the-counter contracts with limited liquidity.

### Accounting for Interest-Rate Swaps

There are a diversity of approaches used in the reporting of interest-rate swap transactions due to the absence of official pronouncements from the FASB. The examples that follow present several alternatives for accounting for interest-rate swaps.

*Unmatched Interest-Rate Swap with No Change
in Market Interest Rate*

On January 1, 19X1, the XYZ Company enters into an unmatched interest-rate swap with the RST Corporation. The deal involves the exchange of a 3-year series of fixed payments of $20,000 at 10% on a $200,000 bond issue for a 3-year series of variable payments, currently at 8% for the same amount of debt.

January 1:

| | | |
|---|---|---|
| Swap-Payment Receivable | $60,000 | |
|     Swap-Payment Liability | | $48,000 |
|     Preferred Gain | | 12,000 |

December 31:

| | | |
|---|---|---|
| Interest Expense | $20,000 | |
|     Interest Payable | | $20,000 |

December 31:

| | | |
|---|---|---|
| Deferred Gain | $4,000 | |
|     Realized Gain | | $4,000 |

Various approaches may be used in accounting for the deferred gains or losses recognized at the inception of the swap, including:

They can be systematically written off over the life of the swap, or only the gain is systematically written off and any loss is immediately recognized. Under the better method, recoveries of any previously recognized losses are recorded up to the amount of the realized loss; beyond this point, recoveries are recorded as deferred gains. Alternatively, both the gain or loss can be maintained in a deferred account until the swap agreement expires. At that time, the realized amount of the gain or loss is recognized. This deferred account is considered an adjustment to the stockholders' equity until expiration of the swap. A variation of the last alternative is to defer any gain as part of the stockholders' equity but to recognize any loss as a realized loss in the current income statement. In this case, later gains from changes in the market rate interest are limited in the amounts recognized to the total of past realized losses. Beyond that point, gains are deferred until the expiration of the swap agreement.[5]

### Unmatched Interest Swap with an Increase in the Market Interest Rate

Let us assume that the interest rate for the preceding example increased to 12%. The following entries are made in the first year.

January 1:

| | | |
|---|---|---|
| Swap-Payment Receivable | $60,000 | |
|     Swap-Payment Liability | | $48,000 |
|     Deferred Gain | | 12,000 |

December 31:

| | | |
|---|---|---|
| Interest Expense | $20,000 | |
|     Interest Payable | | $20,000 |

December 31:

| | | |
|---|---|---|
| Deferred Expense | $12,000 | |
| Loss on Interest Swap | 12,000 | |
|     Swap-Payment Liability | | $24,000 |

to recognize the increase of the swap-payment liability to $72,000 ($200,000 × 12% × 3) and a loss on the interest swap equal to ($72,000 − $60,000).

*Matched Interest-Rate Swap with No Change in Market Interest Rate*

Let us assume that, in the original example concerning the XYZ Company, a matched swap occurs and the swap is an integral part of the original debt. Instead of a deferred gain, a deferred interest will be recognized because the swap payments are linked to the interest expense of the underlying debt. The following entries are made the first year.

January 1:

| | | |
|---|---|---|
| Swap-Payment Receivable | $60,000 | |
|     Swap-Payment Liability | | $48,000 |
|     Deferred Interest | | 12,000 |

December 31:

| | | |
|---|---|---|
| Interest Expense | $20,000 | |
|     Interest Payable | | $20,000 |

December 31:

| | | |
|---|---|---|
| Deferred Interest | $4,000 | |
|     Interest Expense | | $4,000 |

*Matched Interest-Rate Swap with an Increase in the Market Interest Rate*

Using the original example, let us assume that the swap is matched and that the interest rate increases to 12%. The following entries are made in the first year.

January 1:

| | | |
|---|---|---|
| Swap-Payment Receivable | $60,000 | |
|     Swap-Payment Liability | | $48,000 |
|     Deferred Interest | | 12,000 |

December 31:

| | | |
|---|---|---|
| Interest Expense | $20,000 | |
| Interest Payable | | $20,000 |

December 31:

| | | |
|---|---|---|
| Deferred Interest | $24,000 | |
| Swap-Payment Liability | | $24,000 |

December 31:

| | | |
|---|---|---|
| Interest Expense | $4,000 | |
| Deferred Interest | | $4,000 |

to write off the deferred interest over the 3-year period.

## A LOT REMAINS TO BE DONE

SFAS 52, *Foreign Currency Translation,* covers hedge accounting for foreign-currency forward-exchange contracts, futures contracts, and interest-rate swaps. SFAS 80, *Accounting for Futures Contracts,* covers all types of exchange-traded futures except foreign currency. Neither statement covers the multitude of new instruments and transactions (such as interest-rate forwards, all types of options, and interest-rate swaps). An exception is the accounting for options or common stocks covered by SFAS 12, *Accounting for Certain Marketable Securities.*

Obviously, a lot remains to be done in terms of solving some of the conflicts existing between SFAS 52 and SFAS 80,[6] providing accounting solutions for some of the new products resulting from the emerging phenomenon of financial engineering (see the Appendix to Chapter 1), and resolving some of the issues connected with these new products, such as off-balance-sheet financing, primitive recognition of gains, unjustifiable deferral of losses, and inadequate disclosure of risks.[7]

To deal with these issues, in November 1987 the FASB issued an exposure draft, *Disclosures about Financial Instruments,* that would have required all financial instruments to provide disclosures about credit risks, contractual futures, cash receipts and payments, interest rates, and current market values. Because of the response of its constituents, the FASB decided to focus first on off-balance-sheet risk and concentration of credit risk. In July 1989, it issued a revised exposure draft, *Disclosures of Information about Financial Instruments with Off-Balance-Sheet Risk and Financial Instruments with Concentration of Credit Risk.*

The project's intention was to provide an answer to such questions as the following:

- Should financial assets be considered sold if there's recourse or other continuing involvement with them? Should financial liabilities be considered settled when assets are dedicated to settle them? Under what other circumstances should related assets and liabilities be derecognized, not recognized or offset?

- What should the accounting be for financial instruments and transactions that seek to transfer market and credit risk—for example, futures contracts, interest rate swaps, options, forward commitments, nonrecourse arrangements, and financial guarantees—and for the underlying assets or liabilities to which the risk-transferring items are related?

- How should financial instruments be measured—for example, at market value, at amortized original cost, or at the lower of cost or market?[8]

Summaries of the major provisions of the 1987 and 1989 FASB exposure drafts are given in Exhibit 2.1. Effective with the 1989 calendar-year reporting, firms need to include the extent, nature, and terms of financial instruments with off-balance-sheet risk and maximum-credit risk. The disclosure of information about collateral and concentrations of credit risk is necessary in financial statements for fiscal years ending after June 15, 1990. Exhibit 2.2 provides a sample disclosure about financial instruments with off-balance-sheet risk.

Basically, the statement proposed by the FASB exposure drafts will require all entries to disclose the following information about financial instruments with off-balance-sheet risk:

- The face, contract, or notational principal amount and the amount recognized in the statement of financial position

- The nature and terms of the instruments and a discussion of the credit, market, and liquidity risks, and related accounting policies

- The accounting loss the entity would incur if any counterparty to the financial instrument failed to perform

- The entity's policy for requiring collateral or other security on financial instruments it accepts and a description of collateral on instruments presently held

The accounting loss from a financial instrument includes four risks, namely

1. A credit risk, or the possibility of loss from the failure of another party to perform according to the terms of a contract

**Exhibit 2.1**
**Summary of the Major Provisions of the 1987 and 1989 FASB Exposure Drafts**

|  | 1987 exposure draft | 1989 revised exposure draft |
|---|---|---|
| **Definition of a financial instrument** | Contract driven—emphasis on future receipt, delivery or exchange of cash or other financial instrument that ultimately results in cash. | Same as 1987 ED. |
| **Financial instrument with off-balance-sheet risk** | Not defined. | Financial instrument with risk of accounting loss in excess of amount recognized in balance sheet. |
| **Scope** | All financial instruments. | Principally financial instruments with off-balance-sheet risk but also all financial instruments with concentrations of credit risk. |
| **Financial instruments excluded** | No exclusions. | ■ Insurance contracts other than financial guarantees and investment contracts.<br>■ Lease contracts.<br>■ Take-or-pay and throughput contracts.<br>■ Pensions and other forms of deferred compensation.<br>■ Extinguished debt and related assets held in trust. |
| **Disclosure proposals:** |  |  |
| Nature and terms | — | Information about nature and terms of financial instruments with off-balance-sheet risk and a discussion of the related credit, market and liquidity risk and accounting policy. |
| Extent of involvement | — | Contract or notional principal amount of financial instruments with off-balance-sheet risk and related amount recognized in the balance sheet. |
| Credit risk | Maximum credit risk. | Amount of loss due to counterparty failure (maximum credit risk) and information about collateral for financial instruments with off-balance-sheet credit risk. |
|  | Probable credit loss. | — |
|  | Reasonably possible credit loss. | — |
|  | Credit risk concentration—information about shared activity or region, and information about credit risk, as noted above, by area of significant concentration. | Credit risk concentration—information about shared activity, region or economic characteristic, and information about credit risk, as noted above, by area of significant concentration. |
|  | Numerical threshold for individual concentrations. | No numerical threshold specified for individual concentration. |
| Market risk | Effective interest rates, contractual repricing or maturity dates. | — |
|  | Separate disclosure of above for market risk concentrations involving foreign currencies. | — |
| Liquidity risk | Contractual future cash receipts and payments. | Narrative discussion only (see requirements under "nature and terms"). |
|  | Separate disclosure of above for liquidity risk concentrations involving foreign currencies. |  |
| Market value | Current market value. | Disclosed only if market value is the measure of (a) maximum credit risk for a financial instrument with off-balance-sheet credit risk or (b) the amount recognized in the balance sheet for a financial instrument with off-balance-sheet risk. |

*Source:* J. L. Amble, "The FASB's New ED on Disclosure," *Journal of Accounting* (November 1989): 66. Reprinted with permission.

2. A market risk, or the possibility that future changes in market prices may make a financial instrument less valuable or more onerous

3. A liquidity risk, or the possibility that an entity may be obligated to pay cash that it may not have available

4. A risk of theft or physical loss

Financial instruments that have off-balance-sheet risk, or risk of accounting loss (credit, market, or liquidity risk) that exceeds the amount recognized, if any, in the statement of financial position are shown in Exhibit 2.3.

In the 1989 exposure draft, the FASB also provided a definition of a financial instrument that distinguishes between instruments that entail one party's right to receive and another party's obligation to deliver and those instruments that entail rights and obligations to an exchange. It defined a financial instrument as cash, evidence of an ownership interest in an equity, or a contract that is both (1) a (recognized or unrecognized) contractual right of one entity to either receive cash or another financial instrument from another entity or exchange other financial instruments on potentially favorable terms with another entity, and (2) a (recognized or unrecognized) contractual obligation of another entity to either deliver cash or another financial instrument from another entity or exchange other financial instruments on potentially unfavorable terms with another entity.[9] This definition resulted in six tentatively identified, fundamental financial instruments (see Exhibit 2.4). These instruments need to be analyzed to determine their economic substance and to develop consistent accounting standards thoroughly; according to Bullen, Wilkins, and Woods:

The approach is based on the premise that all financial instruments are made up of a few different "building blocks"—fundamental financial instruments—and that determining how to recognize and measure those fundamental instruments is the key to reaching consistent solutions for the accounting issues raised by other, more complex instruments and by various relationships between instruments.[10]

Disclosure of information about financial instruments that is important to investors, creditors, and others who use financial reports, is warranted, especially information about credit risk, future cash receipts and payments, interest rates, and market values. Examples of short-term cuts disclosing future contractual cash receipts and payments of financial instruments, interest-rate information, and foreign-currency future contractual cash receipts and payments are shown in Exhibits 2.5, 2.6, and 2.7, respectively.

## CONCLUSIONS

This chapter deals with the problems of accounting for foreign-currency transactions, futures contracts, and interest-rate swaps. A great deal remains to be done by the standards-setting bodies in dealing with accounting for myriad innovative financial instruments and off-balance-sheet financing.

**Exhibit 2.2**
**Sample Disclosure about Financial Instruments with Off-Balance-Sheet Risk**

Here's an example of how S&C Bank might disclose information about its off-balance-sheet risk. S&C is a party in these financial instruments with off-balance-sheet risk:

- Commitments to extend credit.

- Standby letters of credit and financial guarantees.

- Interest rate swap agreements.

S&C Bank has no significant concentrations of credit risk with any individual or groups of counterparties. The information present is not comparative. This is permitted in the year of implementation; for all subsequent years, the information would be presented on a comparative basis.

S&C might disclose the following:

*Note A: Summary of accounting policies*
*Interest rate swap agreements*
S&C Bank is an intermediary in the interest rate swap market. As an intermediary, the bank maintains a portfolio of generally

matched offsetting swap agreements. Those swaps are accounted for at market value, with changes in value reflected in noninterest income. At inception of a swap, the portion of the compensation related to credit risk and ongoing servicing is deferred and recognized as income over the term of the swap agreement.

*Note B: Financial instruments with off-balance-sheet risk*
The bank is a party to financial instruments with off-balance-sheet risk in the normal course of business to meet the financing needs of its customers. These financial instruments include commitments to extend credit, standby letters of credit and financial guarantees and interest rate swap agreements. Those instruments involve to varying degrees elements of credit, interest rate or liquidity risk in excess of the amount recognized in the statement of financial position. The contract or notional amounts of those instruments express the extent of involvement the bank has in particular classes of financial instruments.

S&C's exposure to credit loss from nonperformance by the other party to the financial instruments for commitments to extend credit and standby letters of credit and financial guarantees written is represented by the contractual amount of those instruments. The bank uses the same credit policies in making commitments and conditional obligations as it does for on-balance-sheet instruments. For interest rate swap transactions, the exposure to credit loss is much less than the contract or notional amounts. S&C controls the credit risk of its interest rate swap agreements through credit approvals, limits and monitoring procedures.

Unless noted otherwise, the bank does not require collateral or other security to support financial instruments with off-balance-sheet credit risk.

72

| | Contract or notional amount |
|---|---|
| Financial instruments whose contract amounts represent credit risk: | |
| Commitments to extend credit | $XX |
| Standby letters of credit and financial guarantees written | XX |
| Financial instruments whose notional amounts do not represent credit risk: | |
| Interest rate swap agreements | XX |

Commitments to extend credit are legally binding agreements to lend to customers. Commitments generally have fixed expiration dates or other termination clauses and may require payment of fees. Since many of the commitments are expected to expire without being drawn upon, the total commitment amounts do not necessarily represent future liquidity requirements. The amount recognized as a liability in the statement of financial position at December 31, 19XX, for deferred fees on those commitments was $XX. The bank evaluates each customer's creditworthiness on a case-by-case basis. The amount of collateral obtained if deemed necessary by S&C on extension of credit is based on management's credit assessment of the counterparty. Collateral held varies but may include accounts receivable; inventory; property, plant and equipment; and existing income-producing commercial properties.

Standby letters of credit and financial guarantees written are conditional commitments issued by the bank guaranteeing performance by a customer to a third party. Those guarantees are issued primarily to support public and private borrowing arrangements, including commercial paper, bond financing and

similar transactions. The credit risk involved in issuing letters of credit is essentially the same as that involved in extending loan facilities to customers. S&C holds marketable securities as collateral supporting those commitments. The extent of collateral held for those commitments varies from X% to XX%; the average amount collateralized is XX%. The amount recognized in the statement of financial position at December 31, 19XX, as a liability for credit loss and a liability for fees received for standby letters of credit and financial guarantees written approximated $XX.

Interest rate swap transactions generally involve exchanges of fixed and floating rate interest payment obligations without exchanges of the underlying principal amounts. S&C Bank enters into the interest rate swap market as an intermediary in arranging interest rate swap transactions for customers. The bank, as a principal in the exchange of interest payments between the parties, is exposed to loss if one of the parties defaults. The bank performs normal credit reviews on its swap customers and minimizes its exposure to the interest rate risk inherent in intermediated swaps by entering into offsetting swap positions so that the risks essentially counterbalance each other.

Entering into interest rate swap agreements involves not only the risk of dealing with counterparties and their ability to meet the terms of the contracts but also the interest rate risk associated with unmatched positions. Notional principal amounts often are used to express the volume of these transactions but do not represent the much smaller amounts potentially subject to credit risk. Amounts recognized in the statement of financial position as assets and liabilities for swap agreements entered into as an intermediary approximated $XX and $XX, respectively, which represent the market value of those instruments.

*Source:* J. L. Amble, "The FASB's New ED on Disclosure," *Journal of Accounting* (November 1989): 69. Reprinted with permission.

### Exhibit 2.3
### Off-Balance-Sheet (OBS) Risk

| Financial Instrument | Holder[a] OBS Risk[d] | CR | MR | LR | Issuer[b] OBS Risk[d] | CR | MR | LR |
|---|---|---|---|---|---|---|---|---|
| **Traditional items:** | | | | | | | | |
| Cash | No | | | | | | | |
| Foreign currency | No | | | | | | | |
| Time deposits (non-interest bearing, fixed rate, or variable rate) | No | | | | No | | | |
| Bonds carried at amortized cost (fixed or variable rate bonds, with or without a cap) | No | | | | No | | | |
| Bonds carried at market (in trading accounts, fixed or variable rate bonds, with or without a cap) | No | | | | No | | | |
| Convertible bonds (convertible into stock of the issuer at a specified price at option of the holder; callable at a premium to face at option of the issuer) | No | | | | No | | | |
| Accounts and notes receivable/payable (non-interest bearing, fixed rate, or variable rate) | No | | | | No | | | |
| Pledge of a contribution: | | | | | | | | |
|   Unconditional pledge receivable/payable | No | | | | No | | | |
|   Conditional pledge received/made | No | | | | Yes | | | X |
| Loans (fixed or variable rate, with or without a cap) | No | | | | No | | | |
| Refundable (margin) deposits | No | | | | No | | | |
| Accrued expenses receivable/payable (wages, etc.) | No | | | | No | | | |
| Obligations receivable/payable in foreign currency | No | | | | No | | | |
| Common stock (equity investments—cost method or equity method)[e] | No | | | | No | | | |
| Preferred stock (convertible or participating) | No | | | | No | | | |
| Preferred stock (noncovertible or nonparticipating) | No | | | | No | | | |
| Cash dividends declared | No | | | | No | | | |

Note: *Off-balance-sheet risk* refers to *risk of accounting loss* (credit, market, or liquidity risk) that exceeds the amount recognized, if any, in the statement of financial position.

[a]Holder includes buyer and investor.

[b]Issuer includes seller, borrower, and writer.

[c]An "X" in any of the columns (CR, MR, or LR) denotes the presence of the respective off-balance-sheet risk. The types of risk included are:

1. *Credit risk* (CR)—the possibility of loss, even if remote, from the failure of another party to perform according to the terms of a contract
2. *Market risk* (MR)—the possibility that future changes in market prices may make a financial instrument less valuable or more onerous
3. *Liquidity risk* (LR)—the possibility that an entity may be obligated to pay cash that it may not have available.

[d]A "Yes" in this column denotes the presence of off-balance-sheet risk; a "No" denotes no off-balance-sheet risk.

[e]Many joint ventures or other equity method investments are accompanied by guarantees of the debt of the investee. Debt guarantees of this nature present off-balance-sheet credit and liquidity risk and should be evaluated with other financial guarantees.

|  | Holder | | | | Issuer | | | |
|---|---|---|---|---|---|---|---|---|
|  | | Type of Risk | | | | Type of Risk | | |
|  | OBS Risk | CR | MR | LR | OBS Risk | CR | MR | LR |
| Innovative items: | | | | | | | | |
| Increasing rate debt | No | | | | No | | | |
| Variable coupon redeemable notes | No | | | | No | | | |
| Collateralized mortgage obligations (CMOs): | | | | | | | | |
| CMO accounted for as a borrowing by issuer | No | | | | No | | | |
| CMO accounted for as a sale by issuer | No | | | | No[f] | | | |
| Transfer of receivables: | | | | | | | | |
| Investor has recourse to the issuer at or below the receivable carrying amount— accounted for as a borrowing by issuer | No | | | | No | | | |
| Investor has recourse to the issuer— accounted for as a sale by issuer | No | | | | Yes | X | | |
| Investor has no recourse to the issuer— accounted for as a sale by issuer | No | | | | No | | | |
| Securitized receivables | Same as transfer of receivables with recourse | | | | | | | |
| (Reverse) Repurchase agreements: | | | | | | | | |
| Accounted for as a borrowing by issuer | No | | | | No | | | |
| Accounted for as a sale by issuer | No | | | | Yes | X | X | X |
| Put option on stock (premium paid up front): | | | | | | | | |
| Writer—covered option | No | | | | Yes | | X | |
| Writer—naked option | No | | | | Yes | | X | X |
| Put option on interest rate contracts with credit risk and foreign currency (premium paid up front): | | | | | | | | |
| Writer—covered option | No | | | | Yes | X | X | |
| Writer—naked option | No | | | | Yes | X | X | X |
| Call option on stock, foreign currency, or interest rate contracts (premium paid up front): | | | | | | | | |
| Writer—covered option | No | | | | Yes | | X | |
| Writer—naked option | No | | | | Yes | | X | X |
| Loan commitments: | | | | | | | | |
| Fixed rate | No | | | | Yes | X | X | X |
| Variable rate | No | | | | Yes | X | | X |
| Interest rate caps | No | | | | Yes | | X | X |
| Interest rate floors | No | | | | Yes | | X | X |
| Financial guarantees | No | | | | Yes | X | | X |
| Note issuance facilities at floating rates | No | | | | Yes | X | | X |
| Letters of credit (also standby letters of credit) at floating rates | No | | | | Yes | X | | X |

---
[f] The "issuer" refers to both the trust and sponsor.

**Exhibit 2.3** (continued)

| | Both Counterparties[g] | | | |
| | | Type of Risk | | |
| | OBS Risk | CR | MR | LR |
|---|---|---|---|---|
| Interest rate swaps—cash basis: | | | | |
|   In a gain position | Yes | X | X | X |
|   In a loss position | Yes | | X | X |
|   Gain or loss position netted | Yes | X | X | X |
| Interest rate swaps—marked to market: | | | | |
|   In a gain position | Yes | | X | X |
|   In a loss position | Yes | | X | X |
|   Gain or loss position netted | Yes | X | X | X |
| Currency swaps | Same as interest rate swaps | | | |
| Forward contracts—hedges (marked to market and gain or loss deferred— Statement 52 or 80 accounting): | | | | |
|   In a gain position | Yes | | X | X |
|   In a loss position | Yes | | X | X |
|   Gain or loss position netted | Yes | X | X | X |
| Forward contracts—Statement 80 accounting not followed: | | | | |
|   In a gain position | Yes | X | X | X |
|   In a loss position | Yes | | X | X |
|   Gain or loss position netted | Yes | X | X | X |
| Forward contracts—nonhedges (marked to market—Statement 80 accounting): | | | | |
|   In a gain position | Yes | | X | X |
|   In a loss position | Yes | | X | X |
|   Gain or loss position netted | Yes | X | X | X |
| Financial futures—hedges (marked to market and gain or loss deferred— Statement 52 or 80 accounting): | | | | |
|   In a gain position | Yes | | X | X |
|   In a loss position | Yes | | X | X |
|   Multiple contracts settled net | Yes | | X | X |
| Financial futures—nonhedges (marked to market—Statement 80 accounting): | | | | |
|   In a gain position | Yes | | X | X |
|   In a loss position | Yes | | X | X |
|   Multiple contracts settled net | Yes | | X | X |

[g]Swaps, forwards, and futures are two-sided transactions; therefore, the "holder" and "issuer" categories are not applicable. Risks are assessed in terms of the position held by the entity.

*Source:* Financial Accounting Standards Board, *Disclosure of Information about Financial Instruments with Off-Balance-Sheet Risk and Financial Instruments with Concentration of Credit Risk,* Exposure Draft, (Norwalk, CT: FASB, 1989): 19, 21, 23. Reprinted with permission.

**Exhibit 2.4**
**Six Tentatively Identified Fundamental Financial Instruments**

**Unconditional receivable (payable).** An unqualified right (obligation) to receive (deliver) cash or another financial asset on or before a specified date or on demand. These contracts entail a future one-way transfer of one or more financial assets. Examples are trade accounts, notes, loans and bonds receivable (payable).

**Conditional receivable (payable).** A right (obligation) to receive (deliver) cash or another financial asset dependent on the occurrence of an event beyond the control of either party to the contract. These contracts entail a potential one-way transfer of one or more assets. Examples include interest rate caps and floors, insurance contracts without subrogation rights and compensation promised to a third party if a transaction or other event occurs.

**Forward contract.** An unconditional right and obligation to exchange financial instruments. Examples include forward purchase and sale contracts, futures contracts and repurchase agreements that obligate both

parties to a future exchange of financial instruments. (Forward and futures contracts for the purchase or sale of metals, grain or other goods do not qualify as financial instruments because the items to be exchanged are not both financial instruments.)

**Option.** A right (obligation) to exchange other financial instruments on potentially favorable (unfavorable) terms that is conditional on the occurrence of an event within the control of one party to the contract. Most commonly, the conditional event is an option holder's decision to exercise the right to demand the exchange. Examples include warrants, loan commitments and exchange-traded and other put or call options. Bonds or stocks with attached warrants, mortgages that allow the borrower to prepay and convertible bonds are examples of compound financial instruments containing options.

**Guarantee or other conditional exchange.** A right (obligation) to exchange financial instruments on potentially fa-

vorable (unfavorable) terms that is conditional on the occurrence of an event outside the control of either party. Examples include performance bonds, letters of credit and all other contracts for which the obligor, on occurrence of a specified event, would receive the subrogation or other rights to another financial instrument in exchange for its delivery of a financial instrument.

**Equity instrument.** An ownership interest in an equity. It typically entitles its holder to a pro rata share of any distributions made to that class of holders but only entails a right (obligation) to receive (deliver) cash or other financial instrument assets on the entity's liquidation. Examples include common stock and partnership interests.

This set of fundamental instruments is being reexamined as the recognition and measurement phase proceeds. Some categories might be combined if analysis shows they should be accounted for similarly, while others might have to be divided.

*Source:* H. G. Bullen, R. C. Wilkins, and C. C. Woods III, "The Fundamental Financial Instrument Approach," *Journal of Accounting* (November 1989): 73. Reprinted with permission.

## Exhibit 2.5
### Future Contractual Cash Receipts and Payments of Financial Instruments (in thousands)

| | [Optional] Within 91 Days | After 91 Days but within 1 Year | After 1 Year through 5 Years | After 5 Years | Total | [Optional] Less: Future Interest Portion | [Optional] Plus: Items without Maturities | Present Balance |
|---|---|---|---|---|---|---|---|---|
| **Financial assets on balance sheet:** | | | | | | | | |
| Cash equiv. (deposits, fed. funds) | $ 807,400 | $ 8,200 | $ 7,200 | $ 2,000 | $ 824,800 | $ 5,700 | — | $ 819,100 |
| Investment securities | 617,400 | 1,779,100 | 1,132,500 | 673,500 | 4,202,500 | 748,000 | $315,000 | 3,769,500 |
| Loans, leases, other receivables | 753,400 | 1,396,900 | 2,406,600 | 2,092,800 | 6,649,700 | 1,546,700 | — | 5,103,000 |
| Other assets | 80,000 | 20,000 | — | — | 100,000 | — | — | 100,000 |
| Total financial assets | 2,258,200 | 3,204,200 | 3,546,300 | 2,768,300 | 11,777,000 | 2,300,400 | 315,000 | 9,791,600 |
| **Financial liabilities on balance sheet:** | | | | | | | | |
| Deposits | (6,385,200) | (2,085,500) | (198,100) | (53,100) | (8,721,900) | (247,600) | — | (8,474,300) |
| Borrowed funds | (130,900) | (105,800) | — | — | (236,700) | (8,800) | — | (227,900) |
| Long-term debt | (11,800) | (128,100) | (702,600) | (53,300) | (895,800) | (195,800) | — | (700,000) |
| Other liabilities | (45,300) | (60,000) | — | — | (105,300) | — | — | (105,300) |
| Total financial liabilities | (6,573,200) | (2,379,400) | (900,700) | (106,400) | (9,959,700) | (452,200) | — | (9,507,500) |
| Preferred stock | (1,200) | (3,400) | (18,400) | — | (23,000) | (23,000) | (50,000) | (50,000) |
| **Off-balance-sheet financial items:** | | | | | | | | |
| Interest rate swaps | (800) | (2,500) | (12,900) | (6,000) | 22,200 | (22,200) | — | — |
| Currency swaps & forwards | — | — | — | — | — | — | — | — |
| Operating lease obligations | (2,100) | (6,400) | (31,500) | (9,800) | (49,800) | — | — | (49,800) |
| Total off-balance-sheet items | (1,300) | (3,900) | (18,600) | (3,800) | (27,600) | 22,200 | — | (49,800) |

Notes that might accompany this schedule:

a. Future contractual cash flows—Amounts include interest, principal, and any other future cash receipts or payments resulting from the financial instruments, reflected in the period in which they are contracted to occur. Actual cash flows are likely to be different because of options and other contingent features included in many of the instruments, including rights allowing the Company or the counterparty to sell or settle the instruments before contracted maturity.

b. Instruments not reflected—Totals exclude trading portfolio assets or liabilities. Also, contingent loan commitments and other options and contingencies that, if exercised or otherwise put into effect, could result in significant cash payments or receipts are excluded from this schedule.

c. Floating-rate items—The schedule assumes no changes from present market rates of interest during the contractual terms of floating-rate investment securities, loans, and deposits or from present dividend rates on preferred stock.

d. Items without maturities—Because future contractual interest receipts from perpetual floating-rate notes and dividend payments on preferred stock continue indefinitely, they are included in the early time intervals but have been omitted from the after-five-years time interval.

*Source:* Financial Accounting Standards Board, *Disclosure about Financial Instruments*, Exposure Draft, (Norwalk, CT: FASB, November 30, 1987): 25. Reprinted with permission.

Exhibit 2.6

Interest-Rate Information – Schedule of Financial Instruments Repricing or Maturing during Periods, Indicating Their Effective Interest Rates (dollars in thousands)

| | [Optional] Within 91 Days $ | % | After 91 Days but within 1 Year $ | % | After 1 Year through 5 Years $ | % | After 5 Years $ | % | Subtotal $ | % | [Optional] Non-interest Bearing $ | Total $ |
|---|---|---|---|---|---|---|---|---|---|---|---|---|
| **Financial assets on balance sheet:** | | | | | | | | | | | | |
| Cash equiv. (deposits, fed. funds) | 245,000 | 5.0 | 7,500 | 6.5 | 6,000 | 6.8 | 1,500 | 6.0 | 260,000 | 5.1 | 559,100 | 819,100 |
| Investment securities | 560,000 | 5.5 | 1,630,000 | 6.0 | 833,500 | 6.3 | 746,000 | 6.5 | 3,769,500 | 6.1 | — | 3,769,500 |
| Loans, leases, other receivables | 3,055,900 | 9.0 | 1,168,200 | 10.0 | 440,900 | 11.0 | 414,300 | 12.0 | 5,079,300 | 9.6 | 23,700 | 5,103,000 |
| Other assets | | | | | | | | | | | 100,000 | 100,000 |
| Total financial assets | 3,860,900 | 7.9 | 2,805,700 | 7.6 | 1,280,400 | 7.9 | 1,161,800 | 8.5 | 9,108,800 | 7.9 | 682,800 | 9,791,600 |
| **Financial liabilities on balance sheet:** | | | | | | | | | | | | |
| Deposits | (4,928,000) | 6.0 | (1,945,600) | 6.3 | (120,700) | 6.5 | (39,300) | 7.0 | (7,033,600) | 6.1 | (1,440,700) | (8,474,300) |
| Borrowed funds | (126,900) | 7.5 | (101,000) | 6.3 | | | | | (227,900) | 7.0 | — | (227,900) |
| Long-term debt | (100,000) | 6.0 | (100,000) | 6.3 | (500,000) | 6.5 | | | (700,000) | 8.0 | — | (700,000) |
| Other liabilities | | | | | | | | | | | (105,300) | (105,300) |
| Total financial liabilities | (5,154,900) | 6.0 | (2,146,600) | 6.3 | (620,700) | 6.5 | (39,300) | 7.0 | (7,961,500) | 6.1 | (1,546,000) | (9,507,500) |
| Preferred stock: [optional]* | (50,000) | 9.2 | | | | | | | (50,000) | 9.2 | — | (50,000) |
| **Off-balance-sheet financial items:** | | | | | | | | | | | | |
| Interest rate swaps | 800,000 | 6.4 | | | (300,000) | 6.5 | (500,000) | 7.0 | | | — | — |
| Currency swaps & forwards | | | | | | | | | | | — | — |
| Operating lease obligations | | | | | | | | | | | (49,800) | (49,800) |
| Total net | (544,000) | | 659,100 | | 359,700 | | 622,500 | | 1,097,300 | | (913,000) | 184,300 |
| Cumulative net | (544,000) | | 115,100 | | 474,800 | | 1,097,300 | | 1,097,300 | | 184,300 | 184,300 |

*The preferred stock has been included because the Company considers its effects when evaluating the overall interest rate position.

Notes that might accompany this schedule:

a. Time intervals and percentages—Fixed-rate instruments are shown in the period during which the instruments are contracted to mature. Floating- or adjustable-rate instruments are shown in the period in which the rate adjusts to a market rate in accordance with the contract terms. Percentages represent the weighted-average effective interest rates of the financial instruments that mature or reprice in the periods indicated.

b. Instruments not reflected—Totals exclude trading portfolio assets or liabilities. Also excluded are contingent loan commitments and other options and contingencies that, if exercised by the Company or by counterparties, or otherwise put into effect, could significantly change the interest rate position.

c. Floating-rate loans—Floating-rate loans of $2,655,000 are included in the Within-91-Days interval. Floating rates are generally determined by a fixed percentage over the current LIBOR. The fixed differential can range from 1 to 3.5 percent. Also, the bank has capped $500,000 of its floating-rate loans, which are included in the Within-91-Days interval, at 50 basis points above present rates.

d. Interest rate position—The interest rate schedule indicates only a one-day position. Major changes in position can be, and are, made promptly as market outlooks change. In addition, significant variations in rate sensitivity may exist within the periods presented.

*Source:* Financial Accounting Standards Board, *Disclosure about Financial Instruments*, Exposure Draft, (Norwalk, CT: FASB, November 30, 1987): 35. Reprinted with permission.

Exhibit 2.7
Foreign-Currency Future Contractual Cash Receipts and Payments (in thousands)

(Translated into U.S. Dollars at Year-End Rate)

| | [Optional] Within 91 Days | After 91 Days but within 1 Year | After 1 Year through 5 Years | After 5 Years | Total | [Optional] Less: Future Interest Portion | Plus: Items without Maturities | Present Balance |
|---|---|---|---|---|---|---|---|---|
| **Pounds sterling:** | | | | | | | | |
| Financial assets on balance sheet | $ 269,200 | $362,200 | $197,000 | $377,400 | $1,205,800 | $243,900 | $225,000 | $1,186,900 |
| Financial liabilities on balance sheet | (1,100,000) | (456,600) | (356,200) | — | (1,912,800) | (105,300) | — | (1,807,500) |
| Off-balance-sheet financial items | 238,700 | 184,000 | 45,000 | 10,200 | 477,900 | 27,200 | — | 450,700 |
| Net total | $ (592,100) | $ 89,600 | $(114,200) | $387,600 | $ (229,100) | $165,800 | $225,000 | $ (169,900) |
| **Japanese yen:** | | | | | | | | |
| Financial assets on balance sheet | $ 241,000 | $ 39,000 | $ 226,200 | $188,000 | $ 694,200 | $106,700 | $ — | $ 587,500 |
| Financial liabilities on balance sheet | (363,000) | (40,000) | (2,500) | — | (405,500) | (6,700) | — | (398,800) |
| Off-balance-sheet financial items | 221,300 | 93,000 | 17,000 | (10,000) | 321,300 | 9,000 | — | 312,300 |
| Net total | $ 99,300 | $ 92,000 | $ 240,700 | $178,000 | $ 610,000 | $109,000 | $ 0 | $ 501,000 |

**Foreign Currency Interest Rate Information**

| | [Optional] Within 91 Days $ | % | After 91 Days but within 1 Year $ | % | After 1 Year through 5 Years $ | % | After 5 Years $ | % | Subtotal $ | % | [Optional] Non-interest Bearing $ | Total $ |
|---|---|---|---|---|---|---|---|---|---|---|---|---|
| **Financial assets on balance sheet:** | | | | | | | | | | | | |
| Pounds sterling | 338,500 | 8.7 | 766,700 | 8.6 | 35,700 | 12.6 | 26,500 | 13.8 | 1,167,400 | 8.9 | 19,500 | 1,186,900 |
| Japanese yen | 335,100 | 4.4 | 145,700 | 5.0 | 106,700 | 8.0 | — | | 587,500 | 5.2 | — | 587,500 |
| **Financial liabilities on balance sheet:** | | | | | | | | | | | | |
| Pounds sterling | (1,325,700) | 7.6 | (232,600) | 8.3 | (249,200) | 8.2 | — | | (1,807,500) | 7.8 | — | (1,807,500) |
| Japanese yen | (358,000) | 4.7 | (40,800) | 4.1 | — | | — | | (398,800) | 4.6 | — | (398,800) |
| **Off-balance-sheet financial items:** | | | | | | | | | | | | |
| Pounds sterling | 450,700 | 8.9 | — | | — | | — | | 450,700 | 8.9 | — | 450,700 |
| Japanese yen | 312,300 | 4.3 | — | | — | | — | | 312,300 | 4.3 | — | 312,300 |

Notes that might accompany this schedule:

a. Foreign currency—The company also has financial instruments denominated in several other currencies, none significant in relation to overall amounts.

b. Off-balance-sheet financial items—Items are principally currency swaps and forward foreign exchange contracts

*Source:* Financial Accounting Standards Board, *Disclosure about Financial Instruments*, Exposure Draft, (Norwalk, CT: FASB, November 30, 1987): 39. Reprinted with permission.

## NOTES

1. J. Bricksler and A. H. Chen, "An Economic Analysis of Interest Rate Swaps," *Journal of Finance* (July 1986): 646.
2. K. Wishon and L. S. Chevalier, "Interest Rate Swaps – Your Rate or Mine?" *Journal of Accounting* (September 1985): 74.
3. Ibid., 24.
4. A. J. R. Gambino, "Cash Management, Interest Rate Swaps, Risk Management Addressed by CPAs in Industry," *Journal of Accounting* (August 1985): 66, 68.
5. W. B. Riley and G. S. Smith, "Interest Rate Swaps: Disclosure and Recognition," *CPA Journal* (January 1987): 68.
6. J. E. Stewart, "The Challenges of Hedge Accounting," *Journal of Accountancy* (November 1989): 48–56.
7. C. C. Woods III, "An Overview of the FASB's Financial Instruments Project," *Journal of Accountancy* (November 1989): 43–47.
8. Ibid., 44.
9. H. G. Bullen, R. C. Wilkins, and C. C. Woods III, "The Fundamental Financial Instrument Approach," *Journal of Accountancy* (November 1989): 72.
10. Ibid., 71.

## BIBLIOGRAPHY

Amble, J. L. "The FASB's New ED in Disclosure." *Journal of Accountancy* (November 1989): 63–70.

Bricksler, J., and A. H. Chen. "An Economic Analysis of Interest Rate Swaps." *Journal of Finance* (July 1986): 15–35, 646.

Bullen, H. G., R. C. Wilkins, and C. C. Woods III. "The Fundamental Financial Instrument Approach." *Journal of Accountancy* (November 1989): 71–78.

Gambino, A. J. "Cash Management, Interest Rate Swaps, Risk Management Addressed by CPAs in Industry." *Journal of Accountancy* (August 1985): 66–69.

Stewart, J. E. "The Challenges of Hedge Accounting." *Journal of Accountancy* (November 1989): 48–56.

Wishon, K., and L. S. Chevalier. "Interest Rate Swaps: Your Rate or Mine?" *Journal of Accountancy* (September 1985): 74–79.

Woods, C. C., III. "An Overview of the FASB's Financial Instruments Project." *Journal of Accountancy* (November 1989): 43–47.

# 3

# MANAGING TRANSLATION EXPOSURE

## INTRODUCTION

Chapters 1 and 2 elaborate on the problems and techniques associated with managing economic and transaction exposures. This chapter continues with the topic of foreign-exchange risk management and elaborates on the problems and techniques used to define, compute, and manage translation exposure.[1] Before the issues of managing translation exposure are presented, the chapter covers the various methods of translation as well as the official accounting pronouncements concerning the issue.

## TRANSLATION METHODS

### Current–Noncurrent Translation Method

Under the current–noncurrent method of translation, current assets and liabilities are translated at the current exchange rate (the actual exchange rate in effect at the balance-sheet date) and noncurrent assets and liabilities are translated at historical exchange rates (the rates in effect when the assets were acquired and liabilities were incurred). Income-statement items are translated at the average exchange rate, except for depreciation and amortization charges, which are translated at the historical rates in effect when the assets were acquired.

The current–noncurrent method, described fully in Chapter 12 of the AICPA's Accounting Research Bulletin No. 43,[2] was in popular use in the United States until its replacement by SFAS No. 8 (SFAS 8), *Accounting for the Translation of Foreign Currency Transactions and Foreign Cur-*

*rency Financial Statements.* The current–noncurrent method suffered from a basic limitation: the assumptions that accounts should be grouped first according to maturity and then translated according to that maturity lacks conceptual justification. Balance-sheet presentation according to maturity does not justify it as a choice of a translation rate.

### Monetary–Nonmonetary Translation Method

Under the monetary–nonmonetary method of translation, monetary assets and liabilities are translated at current rates, while nonmonetary assets and liabilities are translated at historical rates. Income-statement items are translated in the same manner as in the current–noncurrent method. Basically, monetary assets and liabilities are those representing rights to receive obligations to pay a fixed number of foreign-currency units. Examples of monetary assets and liabilities include cash, receivables, payables, and long-term debt. Examples of nonmonetary assets and liabilities include fixed assets, long-term investment, and inventories.

The monetary–nonmonetary method was introduced by Hepworth as a way of correcting some of the limitations of the current–noncurrent method.[3] The rationale behind the method was that monetary assets and liabilities represent fixed amounts of money the parent-currency equivalent of which changes each time the exchange rate changes. The method gained immediate acceptance. First, the National Association of Accountants (NAA) published a monograph that praised the relevance of the monetary–nonmonetary method.[4] Second, the Accounting Principles Board (APB) gave official recognition to the method in APB Opinion No. 6 by allowing long-term debt to be translated at current rates.[5]

It is evident, however, that the monetary–nonmonetary method suffers from the same conceptual limitation as the current–noncurrent method. In effect, the monetary–nonmonetary classification scheme does not present any conceptual ground for the choice of the translation rates. A criticism of the method, given in SFAS 8, follows:

No comprehensive principle of translation can be derived solely from the monetary–nonmonetary distinction. Nonmonetary assets and liabilities are measured on different bases (for example, past prices or current prices) under different circumstances, and translation at a past rate does not always fit. Translating nonmonetary items at a past rate produces reasonable results if the items are stated at historical cost but not if they are stated at current market price in foreign currency.[6]

### Current-Rate Translation Method

Under the current-rate method of translation, all assets and liabilities are translated at the current exchange rate. The method was introduced and supported first by the Institute of Chartered Accountants in England and

Wales in their 1968 Statement No. 25.[7] It was also heavily advocated by Parkinson in a study performed under the auspices of the CICA's Accounting and Auditing Research Committee.[8]

The principal advantage of the current-rate method is that, in the translation of accounts, it reflects the economic situation and perspective of the local country. Basically, the ratios and relationships existing in a local currency do not change after translation to the parent currency. The maintenance of the local perspective after translation is seen as a positive factor.

A problem arising from the use of the current-rate method is in the choice between the market exchange rate and the official exchange rate. The problem is aggravated by the degree of fluctuation in currency values in a world of floating exchange rates. One way to get out of this dilemma, according to Parkinson, is to use a standard bookkeeping rate that will approximate actual exchange rates:

As a general rule, the accounts of a foreign subsidiary should be translated to Canadian currency at bookkeeping rates of exchange which need only approximate actual rates for converting the foreign currency. Once established, a bookkeeping rate should not be changed until, because of changes in actual exchange rates, it becomes clearly inappropriate; a new translation rate should be selected as soon as practical after a currency revaluation, as distinct from a mere currency fluctuation.[9]

A better choice for translation would be the market exchange rate quoted for spot transactions in the country where the accounts to be translated originate, given that it is readily available and that it gives a better measure of the economic value of the local currency. Choi and Mueller see an exception to the use of the free-market rate where specific exchange controls are in effect:

For instance, if a Latin American subsidiary of a United States parent has received permission to import certain goods from the United States at a favorable rate and has set aside certain cash funds to do so, the earmarked funds should be translated to dollars at the special preference rate. The current year-end free-market rate should, of course, be applied to the balance of the foreign cash account. This procedure has the effect of translating portions of a foreign currency cash account at two or more different translation rates. Nothing is wrong as long as economic reality is properly and fully reflected thereby.[10]

A second problem that may arise from the use of the of current-rate method is the possibility of having "abnormal" exchange gains and losses when the foreign currency is subject to strong fluctuation. A third problem arises from the use of foreign currency rather than the parent currency as the unit of measure. The parent firm may object to the situation, while the subsidiary may argue that the local perspective allows it to see the same relationships in parent-currency units as seen in the local currency. The situation is basically a plus from the point of view of the subsidiary and a minus from the parent's point of view.

Finally, the current-rate method may be considered a partial departure from the cost principle. In effect, it becomes a revaluation of assets expressed in foreign currencies, while those assets expressed in local currencies are kept at cost.

### Temporal Translation Method

The temporal method was first introduced by Lorensen in the AICPA Accounting Research Study No. 12.[11] The purpose of the method is to use translation as a measurement process that does not change the attribute of the item being measured, but changes only the unit of measure. Basically, accounts carried at past exchange rates are translated at historical rates, while accounts carried at current purchase prices, sale exchange prices, or future exchange prices are translated at current rates. Thus, under the temporal method, both current and noncurrent cash, receivables, and payables are translated at current rates. Other assets and liabilities are translated at either the current rate or their historical rates, depending upon whether they are carried at current values or historical values. In other words, the temporal method retains the accounting valuation basis used to measure the foreign-currency items. It should be noted that similar results may be obtained under both the monetary–nonmonetary and the temporal methods if the historical cost-valuation basis is applied to all accounts. It should also be noted that the temporal method may be adapted to all other forms of asset-valuation bases, such as replacement cost, net realizable value, or discounted cash flows. Finally, the temporal method appears to avoid most of the limitations of the other translation methods. A comprehensive tabulation of the rates for the translation of balance-sheet items under the current method, the current–noncurrent method, the monetary–nonmonetary method, and the temporal method is presented in Exhibit 3.1.

### Financial Statement Effects

Exhibits 3.2–3.5 are provided to illustrate the application of translation methods. A simple balance-sheet example of the year-end balance for a foreign subsidiary of a U.S. firm is given in Exhibit 3.2.[12] Relevant exchange rates applicable to the translation of the balance sheet in Exhibit 3.2 appear in Exhibit 3.3.

Exhibit 3.4 illustrates the balance sheet of the foreign subsidiary after translation, using each of the translation methods discussed in this chapter. The different translation methods offer a rich variety of results. In addition, Exhibit 3.5 shows the different balance-sheet exposures to foreign-exchange risks that occur with use of the four translation methods.

**Exhibit 3.1**
**Rates Used to Translate Assets and Liabilities**

| Balance Sheet Accounts* | Current Rate Method | Current-Noncurrent Method | Monetary-Nonmonetary Method | Temporal Method |
|---|---|---|---|---|
| Assets | | | | |
| Cash | c | c | c | c |
| Marketable equity securities: | | | | |
| Carried at cost | c | c | h | h |
| Carried at current market price | c | c | h | c |
| Accounts and Notes Receivables | c | c | c | c |
| Inventories: | | | | |
| Carried at cost | c | c | h | h |
| Current at market | c | c | h | c |
| Prepaid Expenses | c | c | h | h |
| Property, Plant and Equipment | c | h | h | h |
| Accumulated Depreciation | c | h | h | h |
| Other Intangible Assets | c | h | h | h |
| Liabilities and Equities | | | | |
| Accounts and Notes Payable | c | c | c | c |
| Bonds Payable or Other Long-Term Debt | c | h | c | c |
| Common Stock | h | h | h | h |
| Paid-in surplus | h | h | h | h |
| Retained Earnings | amount used to balance the balance sheet | | | |

**Exhibit 3.2**
**Year-End Balance Sheet, Foreign Subsidiary of U.S. Firm**

| Assets | | | Liabilities and Equities | | |
|---|---|---|---|---|---|
| Cash | FC | 2,000 | Accounts Payable | FC | 3,000 |
| Accounts Receivable | | 3,000 | Long-term debt | | 6,000 |
| Marketable Equity Securities (at cost) | | 8,000 | Common Stock | | 9,000 |
| | | | Retained Earnings | | 7,000 |
| Inventories (at market) | | 7,000 | | | |
| Property, Plant and Equipment | | 5,000 | | | |
| | FC | 25,000 | | FC | 25,000 |

**Exhibit 3.3**
**Relevant Exchange Rates for the Translation of Balance Sheet in Exhibit 3.2**

| | |
|---|---|
| Current Exchange Rate (End of the Year) | FC 1 = $1.60 |
| Historical Exchange Rate for the Marketable Equity Securities | FC 1 = $1.80 |
| Historical Exchange Rate for Inventories (End of the Year) | FC 1 = $1.90 |
| Historical Exchange Rate for Property, Plant and Equipment | FC 1 = $2.30 |
| Historical Exchange Rate for Long-Term Debt | FC 1 = $2.30 |
| Historical Exchange Rate for Common Stock | FC 1 = $2.30 |
| Historical Exchange Rate for Inventories (Beginning of the Year) | FC 1 = $2.40 |
| Average Current Exchange Rate | FC 1 = $2.00 |

The wide array of results and exposures resulting from the different translation methods may call for a choice of one of the methods, based on conceptual reasons and in order to provide some uniformity in the translation process for multinational companies. This choice has been made over the years and has included each of the translation methods. More recently, official pronouncements in the United States, England, and Canada have selected either the temporal method or the current-rate method for various conceptual and practical reasons. The official positions concerning foreign-currency translation in the United States, Great Britain, and Canada are examined below.

## OFFICIAL POSITIONS ON FOREIGN-CURRENCY TRANSLATION

### The U.S. Position

As mentioned above, Accounting Research Study No. 12 recommended the use of the temporal method of foreign-currency translation. In October 1975, the FASB issued SFAS 8, *Accounting for the Translation of Foreign Currency Transactions and Foreign Currency Financial Statements,* which also recommended the use of the temporal method. According to SFAS 8: "For the purpose of preparing an enterprise's financial statements, the objective of translation is to measure and express (a) in dollars and (b) in conformity with U.S. generally accepted accounting principles (GAAP) the assets, liabilities, revenue, or expenses that are measured or denominated in foreign currency."[13] The temporal method advocated by SFAS 8 was unique, however, in that foreign-exchange gains and losses were to be recognized in the income statement in the period in which they occurred. SFAS 8 generated a lot of debate and criticism, especially with regard to the translation of inventory and long-term debt and the recognition of exchange gains and losses. For example, the 1978 Exxon *Annual Report* mentions the problem as follows:

**Exhibit 3.4**
**Balance Sheet from Exhibit 3.2 Expressed in U.S. Currency**

| Balance Sheet Items | Current Rate Method | | Current Noncurrent Method | | Monetary Nonmonetary Method | | Temporal Method | |
|---|---|---|---|---|---|---|---|---|
| | Rate | $ | Rate | $ | Rate | $ | Rate | $ |
| **Assets** | | | | | | | | |
| Cash | $1.60 | $ 3,200 | $1.60 | $ 3,200 | $1.60 | $3,200 | $1.60 | $3,200 |
| Accounts Receivable | 1.60 | 4,800 | 1.60 | 4,800 | 1.60 | 4,800 | 1.60 | 4,800 |
| Marketable Equity Securities (cost) | 1.60 | 12,800 | 1.60 | 12,800 | 1.80 | 14,400 | 1.80 | 14,400 |
| Inventories (market) | 1.60 | 11,200 | 1.60 | 11,200 | 2.40 | 16,800 | 1.60 | 11,200 |
| Property, Plant and Equipment | 1.60 | 8,000 | 2.30 | 11,500 | 2.30 | 11,500 | 2.30 | 11,500 |
| TOTAL | | $40,000 | | $43,500 | | $50,700 | | $45,100 |
| **Liabilities and Equities** | | | | | | | | |
| Accounts Payable | 1.60 | $ 4,800 | 1.60 | $ 4,800 | 1.60 | $ 4,800 | 1.60 | $ 4,800 |
| Long-Term Debt | 1.60 | 9,600 | 2.30 | 13,800 | 1.60 | | | |
| Common Stock | 1.60 | 14,400 | 2.30 | 20,700* | 2.30 | | | |
| Retained Earnings | | 11,200* | | 4,200* | | | | |
| TOTAL | | $40,000 | | $43,500 | | $50,700 | | $45,102 |

*Exchange gains and losses are included in the income figure.

**Exhibit 3.5**
**Balance-Sheet Exposure to Foreign-Exchange Risk**

|  | Current Rate Method | Current Noncurrent Method | Monetary Nonmonetary Method | Temporal Method |
|---|---|---|---|---|
| Cash | FC 2,000 | FC 2,000 | FC 2,000 | FC 2,000 |
| Accounts Receivable | 3,000 | 3,000 | 3,000 | 3,000 |
| Marketable Equity Securities (cost) | 8,000 | 8,000 | -- | |
| Inventories (market) | 7,000 | 7,000 | -- | 7,000 |
| Property, Plant and Equipment | 5,000 | -- | -- | -- |
| Total | FC 25,000 | FC 20,000 | FC 5,000 | FC 12,000 |
| | | | | |
| Accounts Payable | FC 3,000 | FC 3,000 | FC 3,000 | FC 3,000 |
| Long-Term Debt | 6,000 | -- | 6,000 | 6,000 |
| Common Stock | 9,000 | -- | -- | -- |
| Total | FC 18,000 | FC 3,000 | FC 9,000 | FC 9,000 |

Under these presently prescribed accounting procedures, essentially all of Exxon's foreign liabilities, including short-term and long-term debt obligations, are measured in terms of year-end exchange rates. As the dollar has weakened, these liabilities, translated at the year-end rates of exchange, are equivalent to greater U.S. dollar obligations. In contrast, a relatively small portion of the corporation's foreign assets—essentially only cash, marketable securities and receivables—are measured using year-end exchange rates. The balance of the corporation's foreign assets—mainly inventory, plant and equipment—are not included in the calculation and continue to be measured in terms of their equivalent dollar value at the time these assets were acquired. As a consequence of using the Standard No. 8 definition, Exxon continued to show a net liability exposure which creates currency translation losses during periods of U.S. dollar weakness.[14]

In December 1981, in reaction to these criticisms and debate, the FASB issued SFAS 52.[15] According to SFAS 52, foreign-currency financial statements must be in conformity with GAAP before being translated to the reporting currency. Foreign-currency financial statements must be expressed and, if necessary, remeasured in the functional currency before being translated to the reporting currency. SFAS 52 provides some guidelines to be used in determining the functional currency. These guidelines are based on indicators of cash flow, sales price, sales market, expense, financing, and intercompany transactions and arrangements.

Basically, if the foreign operation's cash flows are usually in foreign currency and do not affect the parent's cash flows, if the sales price of its products depends on local conditions rather than on fluctuations in the exchange rates, if it has an active local sales market for its product, if most of its costs are incurred locally, if it services its debt obligations through local resources, and if it has little relationship with the parent company except for competitive advantages, then the functional currency is the parent company's currency.

The translation process may be divided into two categories. In the first category, the U.S. dollar is the functional currency, and the temporal method of SFAS 8 is used, with one major exception. According to SFAS 8, deferred taxes are translated using the historical exchange rates; under SFAS 52, they are translated using the current rate. In addition, the translation gains and losses are reported in the income statement as a nonoperating item. In the second category, the foreign currency is the functional currency, and the current method is used. In addition, the translation gains or losses are reported in the stockholders' equity section of the balance sheet as a translation adjustment. The translation rates for both categories given by SFAS 52 appear in Exhibit 3.6.

The only exception to the translation process above relates to the financial statements of a foreign entity in a country that has had cumulative inflation of approximately 100% or more over a 3-year period (high inflationary). In this case, the reporting currency is the functional currency.

### Illustration of the Translation Process under SFAS 52

As is noted above, the rates used under SFAS 52 to translate assets and liabilities depend on whether the U.S. dollar or the foreign currency is the functional currency. To illustrate the translation process under SFAS 52, it is desirable to examine both cases.

Let us assume that the first financial statements of a subsidiary, named the Foreign Company, for the period ending December 31, 19X1, are as shown in Exhibits 3.7, 3.8, and 3.9, and have been prepared in accordance with generally accepted accounting principles of the United States. To facilitate the translation process, selected foreign-exchange rates are provided in Exhibit 3.10. The translation process is examined first with the assumption that the foreign currency is the functional currency.

### Translation Process When the U.S. Dollar
### Is the Functional Currency

Exhibit 3.6 indicates when to use historical or current exchange rates when the U.S. dollar is the functional currency. When the exchange rates provided in Exhibit 3.10 are applied to the balance-sheet items of Exhibit 3.7, they result in the balance sheet for the Foreign Company shown in

# Exhibit 3.6
## Rates Used in the Translation of Balance-Sheet Items under SFAS 52

| | U.S. Dollar Is Functional Currency Translation | | Foreign Currency Is Functional Currency Translation | |
|---|---|---|---|---|
| | Rates | | Rates | |
| | Current | Historical | Current | Historical |
| **ASSETS** | | | | |
| Cash on hand and demand and time deposits | X | | X | |
| Marketable equity securities: | | | | |
| Carried at cost | | X | X | |
| Carried at current market price | X | | X | |
| Accounts and Notes Receivable and related unearned discount | X | | X | |
| Allowance for doubtful accounts and notes receivable | X | | X | |
| Inventories: | | | | |
| Carried at cost | | X | X | |
| Carried at current replacement price or current selling price | X | | X | |
| Carried at net realizable value | X | | X | |
| Carried at contract price (produced under fixed priced contracts) | X | | X | |
| Prepaid insurance, advertising, and rent | | X | X | |
| Refundable deposits | X | | X | |
| Advances to unconsolidated subsidiaries | X | | X | |
| Property, Plant and Equipment | | X | X | |
| Accumulated depreciation of property, plant, and equipment | | X | X | |
| Cash surrender value of life insurance | X | | X | |
| Patents, trademarks, licenses, and formulas | | X | X | |
| Goodwill | | X | X | |
| Other intangible assets | | X | X | |
| **LIABILITIES** | | | | |
| Accounts and notes payable and overdrafts | X | | X | |
| Accrued expenses payable | X | | X | |
| Accrued losses on firm purchase commitments | X | | X | |
| Refundable Deposits | X | | X | |
| Deferred Income | | X | X | |
| Bonds payable or other long-term debt | X | | X | |
| Unamortized premium or discount on bonds or notes payable | X | | X | |
| Convertible bonds payable | X | | X | |
| Accrued pension obligations | X | | X | |
| Obligations under warranties | X | | X | |

**Exhibit 3.7**
**Balance Sheet Expressed in Foreign Currency, Functional Currency Based on U.S. Dollar, Foreign Company, December 31, 19X1 (in thousands)**

| | 19X1 |
|---|---|
| Current Assets | |
| Cash | 478.15 |
| Accounts Receivable—Trade | 1,221.85 |
| Notes Receivable—Intercompany | 0 |
| Notes Receivable | 500.00 |
| Inventories | 3,950.25 |
| Prepaid Expenses | 0 |
| Accrued interest on notes receivable | 5.70 |
| Total Current Assets | 6,155.95 |
| Long-Term Notes Receivable | 3,000.00 |
| Property, Plant and Equipment | |
| Land | 8,500.00 |
| Buildings | 74,905.50 |
| Equipment | 16,313.00 |
| Total Property, Plant and Equipment | 99,718.50 |
| Accumulated depreciation | (5,632.60) |
| Net Property, Plant and Equipment | 94,085.90 |
| Total Assets | 103,241.85 |
| Current Liabilities | |
| Accounts payable | 1,814.00 |
| Accrued interest on long-term debt | 225.00 |
| Income tax payable | 383.25 |
| Dividends payable | 125.00 |
| Current portion of long-term debt | 1,250.00 |
| Total Current Liabilities | 3,797.25 |
| Long-Term Debt | 33,750.00 |
| Deferred Income Taxes | 548.10 |
| Stockholders' Equity | |
| Common Stock | 25,000.00 |
| Contributed capital in excess of par | 38,591.20 |
| Retained Earnings | 1,555.30 |
| Total Stockholders' Equity | 65,146.50 |
| Total Liabilities and Stockholders' Equity | 103,241.85 |

Exhibit 3.11. Although the translation of the balance-sheet items is straightforward, it is important to note that the retained-earnings figure is determined as a "plug" figure. The computation of retained earnings is made in the following manner:

**Exhibit 3.8**

**Income Statement Expressed in Foreign Currency, Functional Currency Based on U.S. Dollars, Foreign Company, December 31, 19X1 (in thousands)**

|  |  | 19X1 |
|---|---|---|
| Sales |  | 36,638.00 |
| Costs and expenses |  |  |
| Cost of goods sold: |  |  |
| Inventory—January 1 | 0.00 |  |
| Production costs | 24,982.80 |  |
| Goods available for sale | 24,982.80 |  |
| Inventory—December 31 | (3,950.25) |  |
| Cost of goods sold |  | 21,032.55 |
| General and Administrative |  | 4,122.50 |
| Advertising and selling |  | 2,335.75 |
| Depreciation |  | 5,632.60 |
| Total costs and expenses |  | 33,123.40 |
| Net income from operations |  | 3,514.60 |
| Other income (expenses) |  | (339.10) |
| Net income before taxes |  | 3,175.50 |
| Income Taxes |  |  |
| Current |  | 572.10 |
| Deferred |  | 548.10 |
| Total taxes |  | 1,120.20 |
| Net Income |  | 2,055.30 |

**Exhibit 3.9**

**Statement of Retained Earnings Expressed in Foreign Currency, Functional Currency Based on U.S. Dollar, Foreign Company, Years Ended December 31, 19X1 and 19X2 (in thousands)**

|  | 19X2 | 19X1 |
|---|---|---|
| Retained Earnings—January 1 | 1,555.30 | 0.00 |
| Add net income for the year | 1,429.60 | 2,055.30 |
| Deduct dividends for the year | (1,000.00) | (500.00) |
| Retained Earnings—December 31 | 1,984.90 | 1,555.30 |

| | |
|---|---|
| Total dollar value of assets translated | $206,170.22 |
| Total dollar value of liabilities and equities translated (other than retained earnings) | 202,869.11 |
| Retained earnings balance | 3,301.11 |

**Exhibit 3.10**
**Foreign-Currency Exchange Rates**

|  | U.S. Dollar Is Functional Currency | Foreign Currency Is Functional Currency |
|---|---|---|
|  | FC1 | FC1 |
|  | 19X1 | 19X1 |
| **Rates** | | |
| 1. Current rate at March 31 | $2.00 | NA |
| 2. Current rate at September 30 | $1.98 | NA |
| 3. Current rate at June 30 | $1.96 | NA |
| 4. Current rate at December 31 | $1.92 | $1.92 |
| 5. Average rate for the year | $1.964 | $1.964 |
| 6. Historical rate when stock was issued and land purchased | $2.04 | $2.04 |
| 7. Historical rate when property, plant and equipment were purchased | $2.00 | NA |
| 8. Average historical rate applicable to inventories on hand at December 31 | $1.94 | NA |

The translation of the income statement proceeds in three phases: the first phase determines the net income translated before finding the translation gains or losses, the second phase determines the translation gains or losses, and the third phase combines both results. The first phase of the income statement translation of the Foreign Company is shown in Exhibit 3.12. The second phase includes the determination of the translation gains or losses as a "plug" figure.[16] Using the results of the computation for retained earnings for December 31, 19X1 from above, the computation of the translation gains or losses is accomplished in the following manner:

| | |
|---|---|
| Retained earnings—January 1, 19X1 | $0.0000 |
| Add net income (see Exhibit 3.12) | 2,756.5298 |
| Minus retained earnings, December 31, 19X0 | 3,301.1100 |
| Translation gains | 544.5802 |

The third phase of the income statement translation incorporates the translation gains as a nonoperating item in the income statement (see Exhibit 3.13).

**Exhibit 3.11**

**Balance Sheet Expressed in U.S. Dollars, Functional Currency Based on U.S. Dollar, Foreign Company, December 31, 19X1 (in thousands)**

| | FC | Translation Rate | $ |
|---|---|---|---|
| **Current Assets** | | | |
| Cash | FC 478.15 | 1.92 | $ 918.048 |
| Accounts receivable—trade | 1,221.85 | 1.92 | 2,345.952 |
| Accounts receivable—intercompany | 0.00 | 1.92 | 0.00 |
| Notes receivable | 500.00 | 1.92 | 960.000 |
| Inventories | 3,950.25 | 1.94 | 7,663.485 |
| Prepaid expenses | 0.00 | 1.92 | 0.000 |
| Accrued interest on notes receivable | 5.70 | 1.92 | 10.944 |
| Total Current Assets | 6,155.95 | | $11,898.429 |
| | | | |
| Long Term Notes Receivable | 3,000.00 | 1.92 | 5,760.000 |
| **Property, Plant and Equipment** | | | |
| Land | 8,500.00 | 2.04 | 17,340.000 |
| Buildings | 74,905.50 | 2 | 149,811.000 |
| Equipment | 16,313.000 | 2 | 32,626.000 |
| Total Property, Plant and Equipment | 99,718.50 | | $199,777.000 |
| Accumulated depreciation | (5,632.60) | 2 | (11,265.200) |
| Net Property, Plant and Equipment | 94,085.90 | | $188,511.800 |
| | | | |
| **Total Assets** | 103,241.85 | | $206,170.220 |
| | | | |
| **Current Liabilities** | | | |
| Accounts payable | 1,814.00 | 1.92 | $ 3,482.88 |
| Accrued interest on long-term debt | 225.00 | 1.92 | 432.00 |
| Income tax payable | 383.25 | 1.92 | 735.84 |
| Dividends payable | 125.00 | 1.92 | 240.00 |
| Current portion of long-term debt | 1,250.00 | 1.92 | 2,400.00 |
| Total Current Liabilities | 3,797.25 | | 7,290.72 |
| | | | |
| Long-term debt | 33,750.00 | 1.92 | 64,800.00 |
| Deferred Income Taxes | 548.10 | 1.92 | 1,052.352 |
| **Stockholders' Equity** | | | |
| Common Stock | 25,000.00 | 2.04 | 51,000.00 |
| Contributed capital in excess of par | 38,591.20 | 2.04 | 78,726.048 |
| Retained Earnings | 1,555.30 | | 3,301.11 |
| Total Stockholders' Equity | 65,146.50 | | 133,027.15 |
| | | | |
| Total Liabilities and Stockholders' Equity | 103,241.85 | | $206,170.220 |

**Exhibit 3.12**
**Income Statement Translation before Gains and Losses, Expressed in U.S. Dollars, Functional Currency Based on U.S. Dollar, Foreign Company, December 31, 19X1 (in thousands)**

| | FC | Rate | $ |
|---|---|---|---|
| Sales | 36,638.00 | 1.964 | $71,957.032 |
| Costs and Expenses | | | |
| Costs of goods sold | | | |
| Inventory—January 1 | 0.00 | | 0.000 |
| Production costs | 24,982.80 | 1.964 | 49,066.219 |
| Goods available for sale | 24,982.80 | | 49,066.219 |
| Inventory (December 31 | (3,950.25) | 1.94 | (7,663.485) |
| Cost of goods sold | 21,032.55 | | 41,402.734 |
| General and Administrative | 4,122.50 | 1.964 | 8,096.59 |
| Advertising and Selling | 2,335.75 | 1.964 | 4,587.413 |
| Depreciation | 5,632.60 | 2 | 11,265.200 |
| Total costs and expenses | 33,123.40 | | 65,351.937 |
| Net income from operations | 3,514.60 | | 6,605.095 |
| Other Income (expenses) | (339.10) | 1.964 | (665.9924) |
| Net Income before taxes | 3,175.50 | | 5,939.1026 |
| Income taxes | | | |
| Current | 572.10 | 1.964 | 1,123.6044 |
| Deferred | 548.10 | 1.964 | 1,076.4684 |
| Total taxes | 1,120.20 | | 2,200.0728 |
| Net Income before dividends | 2,055.30 | | 3,739.0298 |
| Dividends | | | |
| 1st quarter | 125 | 2 | 250 |
| 2nd quarter | 125 | 1.98 | 247.50 |
| 3rd quarter | 125 | 1.96 | 245.00 |
| 4th quarter | 125 | 1.92 | 240.00 |
| Total dividends | 500 | | 982.50 |
| | 1,555.3 | | 2,756.5298 |

## Translation Process When the Foreign Currency Is the Functional Currency

When the foreign currency is the functional currency, SFAS 52 advises the use of the current method of translation. Basically, most balance-sheet accounts are translated using the current exchange rate and most revenues and expenses are translated using the average rate for the period; thus, the translation process is more straightforward. Exhibit 3.14 provides the income statement of the Foreign Company in U.S. dollars, and is based on the use of foreign currency as the functional currency. All income statement items have been translated using the average exchange rate of 1.964. Translation gains and losses do not appear in the income statement of Exhibit 3.14, but they are shown in the stockholders' equity section of the balance sheet provided in Exhibit 3.15. With the exception of common stock and

**Exhibit 3.13**
**Income Statement Expressed in U.S. Dollars, Functional Currency Based on U.S. Dollar, Foreign Company, December 31, 19X1 (in thousands)**

| | | |
|---|---|---|
| Sales | | $71,957.032 |
| Costs and expenses | | |
|    Cost of goods sold | | |
|       Inventory—January 1 | $ 0.00 | |
|       Production costs | 49,066.219 | |
|       Goods available for sale | 49,066.219 | |
|       Inventory, December 31 | (7,663.485) | |
|       Cost of goods sold | | 41,402.734 |
|    General and Administrative | | 8,096.590 |
|    Advertising and Selling | | 4,587.413 |
|    Depreciation | | 11,265.200 |
|       Total costs and expenses | | $65,351.937 |
| Net income from operations | | 6,605.095 |
| Nonoperating items | | |
|    Other income (expenses) | | (665.9924) |
|    Translation gain | | 554.5802 |
| Net income before taxes | | $ 6,493.6828 |
| Income taxes | | |
|    Current | | 1,123.6044 |
|    Deferred | | 1,076.4684 |
| Net income | | $ 4,293.61 |
| Add Retained Earnings—January 1, 19X1 | | 0.00 |
| Deduct Dividends for the year | | 982.50 |
| Retained Earnings—December 31, 19X1 | | $ 3,301.11 |

the contributed capital in excess of par, all balance-sheet items have been translated using the current exchange rate of 1.92. The common stock and contributed capital are translated at the historical rate of 2.04. The translation adjustment of ($7,698.8698) appears as a "plug" figure in Exhibit 3.15. For the sake of reconciling the figures and checking on the accuracy of the computation, the determination of the translation adjustment is shown in Exhibit 3.16.

## The Canadian Position

The Canadian position on foreign-currency translation is expressed in Section 1650 of the Accounting Standards Committee handbook.[17] The Canadian position does not use the term *functional currency,* but instead classifies foreign operations as either "integrated" or "self-sustaining." Whether a foreign operation is classified as integrated or self-sustaining depends on the exposure of the reporting firm to exchange-rate changes as determined by the economic facts and circumstances. Matters taken into consideration in the classification include essentially the same indicators as those used in SFAS 52, namely, cash-flow indicators, sales price indicators,

**Exhibit 3.14**
**Income Statement Expressed in U.S. Dollars, Functional Currency Based on Foreign Currency, Foreign Company, December 31, 19X1 (in thousands)**

|  | FC | Rate | $ |
|---|---|---|---|
| Sales | 36,638.00 | 1.964 | $71,957.032 |
| Costs and expenses |  |  |  |
| Inventory—January 1 | 0.00 | 1.964 | 0.00 |
| Production costs | 24,982.80 | 1.964 | 49,066.219 |
| Goods available for sale | 24,982.80 |  | 49,066.219 |
| Inventory—December 31 | (3,950.25) | 1.964 | (7,758.291) |
| Costs of goods sold | 21,032.55 |  | 41,307.928 |
| General and Administrative | 4,122.50 | 1.964 | 8,096.59 |
| Advertising and Selling | 2,335.75 | 1.964 | 4,587.413 |
| Depreciation | 5,632.60 | 1.964 | 11,062.426 |
| Total costs and expenses | 33,123.40 |  | 65,054.357 |
| Net income from operations | 3,514.60 |  | 6,902.675 |
| Other Income (expenses) | (339.10) | 1.964 | (665.9924) |
| Net income before taxes | 3,175.50 |  | 6,236.6826 |
| Income taxes |  |  |  |
| Current | 572.10 | 1.964 | 1,123.6044 |
| Deferred | 548.10 | 1.964 | 1,076.4684 |
| Total taxes | 1,120.20 |  | 2,200.0728 |
| Net income before dividends | 2,055.30 |  | 4,036.6098 |
| Deduct dividends | 500.00 |  | 982.50 |
| Retained Earnings—December 31 | 1,553.3 |  | 3,054.1098 |

and intercompany transactions and arrangement indicators. Basically, an *integrated* foreign operation is a foreign operation that is financially or operationally interdependent with the reporting firm such that the exposure to the exchange rate is similar to the exposure that would exist had the transactions and activities of the foreign operation been undertaken by the reporting enterprise. Similarly, a *self-sustaining* foreign operation is a foreign operation that is financially and operationally independent of the reporting firm such that the exposure to exchange-rate changes is limited to the reporting firm's net investment in the foreign operation.[18]

Given this difference between foreign operations, the Canadian position recommends that (1) foreign-currency-denominated transactions and related financial-statement items of the reporting firm are to be translated using the temporal method, as are financial statements of integrated foreign operations; (2) financial statements of self-sustaining foreign operations are to be translated using the current-rate method unless the economic environment of the foreign operation is highly inflationary, in which case the temporal method is used; (3) exchange gains and losses of the reporting firm that arise on translation or settlement of a foreign-currency-

**Exhibit 3.15**

**Balance Sheet Expressed in U.S. Dollars, Functional Currency Based on Foreign Currency, Foreign Company, December 31, 19X1, (in thousands)**

| | FC | Rate | $ |
|---|---|---|---|
| **Current Assets** | | | |
| Cash | 478.15 | 1.92 | $ 918.048 |
| Accounts receivable-trade | 1,221.85 | 1.92 | 2,345.952 |
| intercompany | 0.00 | 1.92 | 0.000 |
| Notes receivable | 500.00 | 1.92 | 960.000 |
| Inventories | 3,950.25 | 1.92 | 7,584.48 |
| Prepaid expenses | 0.00 | 1.92 | 0.00 |
| Accrued interest on notes receivable | 5.70 | 1.92 | 10.944 |
| Total Current Assets | 6,155.90 | | $ 11,819.424 |
| | | | |
| Long-Term Notes Receivable | 3,000.00 | 1.92 | 5,760.000 |
| Property, Plant and Equipment | | | |
| Land | 8,500.00 | 1.92 | 16,320.00 |
| Buildings | 74,905.50 | 1.92 | 143,818.56 |
| Equipment | 16,313.00 | 1.92 | 31,320.96 |
| Total Property, Plant and Equipment | 99,718.50 | | 191,459.52 |
| Accumulated depreciation | (5,632.60) | 1.92 | (10,814.592) |
| Net Property, Plant and Equipment | 94,085.90 | | 180,644.93 |
| Total Assets | 103,241.85 | | 198,224.35 |
| | | | |
| **Current Liabilities** | | | |
| Accounts payable | 1,814.00 | 1.92 | $ 3,482.88 |
| Accrued interest on long-term debt | 225.00 | 1.92 | 432.00 |
| Income tax payable | 383.25 | 1.92 | 735.84 |
| Dividends payable | 125.00 | 1.92 | 240.00 |
| Current portion of long-term debt | 1,250.00 | 1.92 | 2,400.00 |
| Total Current Liabilities | 3,797.25 | | $ 7,290.72 |
| | | | |
| Long-Term Debt | 33,750.00 | 1.92 | 64,800.00 |
| Deferred Income Taxes | 548.10 | 1.92 | 1,052.352 |
| Stockholders' Equity | | | |
| Common stock | 25,000.00 | 2.04 | 51,000.00 |
| Contributed capital in excess of par | 38,591.20 | 2.04 | 78,726.048 |
| Retained Earnings | 1,555.30 | | 3,054.1098 (1) |
| Translation Adjustment | | | (7,698.8698)(2) |
| Total Stockholders' Equity | 365,146.50 | | 125,081.28 |
| | | | |
| Total Liabilities and Stockholders' Equity | 103,241.85 | | 198,224.35 |

(1) See Exhibit 3.14.
(2) See Exhibit 3.16 for reconciliation of this result.

**Exhibit 3.16**
**Reconciliation of Translation Adjustment in Exhibit 3.15**

| | | |
|---|---|---|
| Total Assets—Foreign Currency | | 103,241.85 |
| Total Liabilities—Foreign Currency | | |
| Current | 3,797.25 | |
| Long-term debt | 33,750.00 | |
| Deferred income taxes | 548.10 | |
| Total Liabilities—Foreign Currency | 38,095.35 | 38,095.35 |
| Net Assets—Foreign Currency | | 65,146.50 |
| End of the Period Exchange Rate | | 1.92 |
| Net Assets in Dollars | | $125,081.28 |
| Stockholders' Equity Dollars | | |
| Common stock | $51,000.00 | |
| Contributed capital in | | |
| excess of par | 78,726.048 | |
| Retained Earnings | 3,054.1098 | |
| Total Stockholders' Equity in Dollars | $132,780.16 | $132,780.16 |
| Translation Adjustment | | 7,698.8698 |

denominated item or a nonmonetary item carried at market should be included in the determination of net income for the current period; (4) exchange gains and losses of the reporting firm relating to the translation of foreign-currency-denominated monetary items that have a fixed or ascertainable life extending beyond the end of the following fixed year should be deferred and amortized on a systematic basis over the remaining life of the monetary item;[19] (5) exchange gains or losses arising on the translation of financial statements of integrated foreign operations and on those of self-sustaining operations in highly inflationary environments are also deferred and amortized on a systematic basis over the remaining life of the monetary item; and (6) exchange gains and losses arising from the translation of the financial statements of a self-sustaining foreign operation should be deferred and included in a separate component of shareholders' equity.[20]

Two major differences arise in a comparison of the Canadian position with that of SFAS 52. First, in Canada, Section 1650 requires deferral and amortization of exchange gains and losses relating to long-term, foreign-currency-denominated monetary items of the reporting firm and adjustments arising on translation of long-term monetary items of integrated foreign operation, while SFAS 52 requires recognition of such amounts in the determination of net income. Second, Section 1650 requires translation of deferred income-tax balances of integrated foreign operations at historical rates, while SFAS 52 requires translation at current rates. These two differences force Canadian Securities and Exchange Commission (SEC) registrants to report still another difference between Canadian and U.S. generally accepted accounting principles.

### The British Position

The latest British position concerning foreign-currency translation is expressed in the Statement of Standard Accounting Practice No. 20 (SSAP 20), issued in April 1983.[21] According to SSAP 20, the objectives of translation are to produce results that generally are compatible with the effects of rate changes on a firm's cash flows and equity, and to ensure that the financial statements present a true and fair view of the results of management actions. To do so, a two-stage procedure is adopted, namely, preparation of the financial statement of an individual company and preparation of the consolidated financial statements.

#### Individual-Company Stage

For a company that undertakes transactions denominated in a foreign currency, the following guidelines are provided:

1. Translate transaction values in local currency at transition-date rates and use an average rate for periods where there is little fluctuation.

2. If there is a contracted rate, use that; if there is a matching forward contract covering the transaction, the rate specified in the contract should be used.

3. At balance-sheet date, monetary assets and liabilities denominated in a foreign currency are to be translated using that date's exchange rate or the rates specified by any binding contract.

4. All exchange gains and losses on either settled or unsettled transitions should be reported in the current income statement.

#### Consolidated-Financial-Statements Stage

The method used to translate financial statements for consolidation purposes should reflect the financial and operational relationships that existed between an investment company and its foreign enterprises. Basically, two methods may be used: either the closing-rate/net-investment method or the temporal method.

The closing-rate/net-investment method is used when the investment of a company is in the net worth of its foreign enterprise rather than a direct investment in the individual assets and liabilities of that enterprise. Under this method, financial-statement items should be translated at the closing rate or at an average rate for the period. Exchange differences are dealt with as adjustments to reserves.

The temporal method is used when the affairs of a foreign enterprise are interlinked so closely with those of the investing company that the dealings of the foreign enterprise may be regarded as being more dependent upon the economic environment of the investing company's currency than on its own reporting currency. The factors taken into account to determine whether the currency of the investing company is the dominant currency in the economic environment in which the foreign enterprise operates include (1) the extent to which cash flows of the enterprise have a direct impact upon those of the investing company, (2) the extent to which the functioning of the enterprise is dependent upon the investing company, (3) the currency in which the majority of the trading transactions are denominated, and (4) the major currency to which the operation is exposed in its financing structure.[22]

### The International Position

In 1983, the International Accounting Standards Committee issued International Accounting Standard 21 (IAS 21), *Accounting for the Effects of Changes of Foreign Exchange Rates.*[23] IAS 21 deals with accounting for transactions in foreign currencies in the financial statements of an enterprise and also with translation of financial statements of foreign-based operations into a single reporting currency for the purpose of including them in the financial statements of the parent firm. IAS 21's recommendations are very similar to those of SFAS 52. The major difference between them is that IAS 21 permits exchange gains and losses on long-term, foreign-currency monetary items to be deferred and amortized over the remaining lives of the related monetary items unless it is reasonable to expect that recurring exchange losses on the items will arise in the future.

## MANAGING TRANSLATION EXPOSURE

### Defining Translation Exposure

A translation exposure results from the periodic necessity of consolidating or aggregating the financial statements of parent companies and their subsidiaries. Before being consolidated with the parent's financial statements, the subsidiaries' financial statements have to be translated into the parent's currency. Translation exposure results from the possibility that a change in exchange rates will create an exchange gain or loss and, therefore, depends on the translation method and the exchange rate used for the translation of individual items in the balance sheet and income statement. The accounting or translation exposure may be stated in the following manner:

Translation Exposure = Foreign Assets − Foreign Liabilities Translated
at the Current Exchange Rate

Under the current-rate method, all accounts are translated at the exchange rate prevailing at the time of consolidation. In such cases, the translation exposure is equal to the net worth of the subsidiary as expressed in its local currency.

Under the current–noncurrent method, current assets and liabilities are translated at historical rates. In such cases, the translation exposure is equal to the difference between current assets and current liabilities, that is, the working capital.

Under the monetary–nonmonetary method, monetary assets and liabilities are translated at the current rate, while nonmonetary assets and liabilities are translated at historical rates. In such cases, the translation exposure is equal to the difference between the monetary assets and the monetary liabilities.

Under the temporal method, assets and liabilities are translated in a manner that retains their original measurement bases. Basically, cash, receivables, and payables are translated at the current rate. Assets carried at historical costs are translated at the historical rate, while assets carried at current costs are translated at the current rate. The method advocated by SFAS 8 deviates a little from the temporal method because foreign-currency-denominated, long-term debt must be translated at the current rate. In such a case, the translation exposure may be expressed in the following manner:

$$\text{Translation Exposure (using the temporal method)} = \left(\begin{array}{c}\text{Cash +}\\\text{Accounts}\\\text{Receivable}\end{array}\right) - \left(\begin{array}{c}\text{Accounts Payable +}\\\text{Long-Term Debt}\end{array}\right)$$

denominated in currencies other than the functional currency.

### Minimizing Translation Exposure: Balance Sheet Hedge

One way of minimizing translation exposure is try to reach a "monetary balance," where exposed assets are equal to exposed liabilities. This may be achieved by early declaration of dividends, prepayments of debits in foreign currencies, and settlement of other liabilities denominated in strong currencies. The objective is to reach a zero net translation exposure, where change in the exchange rate will affect the value of exposed assets in an equal but opposite direction to the change in value of exposed liabilities. If a firm uses the monetary–nonmonetary translation method, a monetary balance is reached when the exposed monetary assets are equal to the exposed monetary liabilities, which, under SFAS 52, is possible for a firm using the monetary–nonmonetary method of translation that has the dollar as its functional currency.

## Minimizing Translation Exposure: Contractual Hedges

Firms may elect to reduce translation exposure with a hedge in the forward, money, or option markets. The firm hedges the potential translation loss by selling local currency forward in an amount determined by the following formula:

$$\begin{array}{l}\text{Forward} \\ \text{Contract} = \\ \text{Size}\end{array} \frac{\text{Expected Translation Loss in Reporting Currency}}{\left(\begin{array}{c}\text{Forward Rate in} \\ \text{Reporting-Currency Units} \\ \text{per Local-Currency Units}\end{array}\right) - \left(\begin{array}{c}\text{Expected Future Spot Rate} \\ \text{in Reporting-Currency Units} \\ \text{per Local-Currency Units}\end{array}\right)}$$

Basically, the amount of foreign currency that may be sold forward is equal to the potential translation loss divided by the difference between the forward rate and the expected future spot rate, where the difference indicates the expected foreign-exchange profit per unit of the parent's reporting currency.[24]

For example, assume that the exchange rate has changed from $0.30/peso (Ps) to $0.15/Ps, and the forward-exchange rate is $0.20/Ps. Then, for an expected translation loss of $300,000 where the dollar is the reporting currency, the size of the forward contract is represented as

$$\text{Forward Contract Size} = \frac{\$300,000}{0.20 - 0.15} = \text{Ps } 6,000,000$$

Assuming that the subsidiary is correct about its expectations and that it sold Ps 6,000,000 forward, the transactions appear as follows:

1. At the time of sale: Sell pesos forward at $0.20/Ps, which amounts to Ps 6,000,000 × 0.20 = $1,200,000 to be received at maturity.

2. At maturity: Buy pesos at a spot rate of $0.15/Ps, which amounts to Ps 6,000,000 × 0.15 = $900,000 to pay out at maturity.

3. Profit: $1,200,000 − $900,000 = $300,000, which exactly offsets the translation loss of $300,000 before taxes.

## CONCLUSION

This chapter examines the issues and solutions surrounding the problem of accounting for foreign-currency translation. Foreign-currency translation methods include the current–noncurrent method, the monetary–nonmonetary method, the current-rate method, and the temporal method. In addition, the techniques used to manage translation exposure are examined.

However, various limitations of such hedging have been identified in the literature, including the uncertainty in determining the forward-contract size, the potential effect of an increased transaction exposure, and the added borrowing costs and the uncertainty of a subsidiary's forecasted earnings.

## NOTES

1. A. Belkaoui, *International Accounting: Issues and Solutions,* (Westport, CT: Greenwood Press, 1981), 16–37.

2. American Institute of Certified Public Accountants, Accounting Research Bulletin No. 43, *Professional Standards* (Chicago: Commerce Clearing House, 1975).

3. S. R. Hepworth, *Reporting Foreign Operations,* (Ann Arbor, MI: University of Michigan, 1966), 15–25.

4. National Association of Accountants, *Accounting Problems in Foreign Operations,* Research Report No. 36 (New York: NAA, 1960).

5. Accounting Principles Board, *Status of Accounting Research Bulletins*, APB Opinion No. 6 (New York: APB, 1965), par. 5.

6. Financial Accounting Standards Board, *Accounting for the Translation of Foreign Currency Transactions and Foreign Currency Financial Statements,* Statement of Financial Accounting Standard No. 8 (Stamford, CT: FASB, October 1975), par. 126.

7. Institute of Chartered Accountants in England and Wales, *Member's Handbook, Statement No. 25* (London: Institute of Chartered Accountants in England and Wales, 1968), par. 14.

8. M. R. Parkinson, *Translation of Foreign Currencies* (Toronto: CICA, 1972), 16–18.

9. Ibid., 26.

10. F. D. S. Choi and G. G. Mueller, *An Introduction to Multinational Accounting* (Englewood Cliffs, NJ: Prentice-Hall, 1978), 79.

11. L. Lorensen, *Reporting Foreign Operations of U.S. Companies in U.S. Dollars,* AICPA Accounting Research Study No. 12 (New York: AICPA, 1972), 25–26.

12. A more exhaustive example of translation methods is presented in a subsequent section of this chapter to illustrate the requirements of SFAS 52.

13. FASB, *Accounting for the Translation of Foreign Currency Transactions,* SFAS 8, par. 6.

14. Exxon. *Annual Report* (1978).

15. Financial Accounting Standards Board, *Foreign Currency Translation,* Statement of Financial Accounting Standard No. 52 (Stamford, CT: FASB, December 1981).

16. Ibid., 3.

17. Accounting Standards Committee, *Accounting Recommendations* (Toronto: CICA, 1983), 4, 5.

18. J. M. Kligman, "Foreign Currency Translation: From Exposure Draft to Standard," *Chartered Accountant Magazine* (June 1983): 57.

19. Such an exchange gain or loss is considered an element of the cost or benefit of holding a foreign-currency-denominated monetary item related to the period of time during which the item is unsettled.

20. In such circumstances, the reporting firm's exposure to exchange-rate changes is limited to its net investment in the foreign operation, and the exchange gain or loss arising on translation has no direct effect on the reporting firm's activities.

21. Statement of Standard Accounting Practice No. 20, April 1983.

22. Examples of situations in which the temporal method may be used include situations in which the foreign firm (1) acts as a selling agency receiving stocks of goods from the investing company and remitting the proceeds back to the company; (2) provides a raw material or manufactures parts or subassemblies that are then shipped to the investing company for inclusion in its own products; and (3) is located overseas for tax, exchange control, or similar reasons to act as a means of raising funds for other companies in the group.

23. International Accounting Standards Committee, *Accounting for the Effects of Changes of Foreign Exchange Rates,* International Accounting Standard No. 21 (IASC, London, 1985).

24. D. K. Eitman and A. I. Stonehill, *Multinational Business Finance* (Reading, MA: Addison-Wesley, 1989), 231–232.

## BIBLIOGRAPHY

Accounting Standards Committee. *Accounting Recommendations.* Toronto: CICA, 1983.

Accounting Principles Board. *Status of Accounting Research Bulletins,* APB Opinion No. 6. New York: AICPA, 1965.

Belkaoui, A. *International Accounting: Issues and Solutions.* Westport, CT: Greenwood Press, 1981.

Choi, F. D. S., and G. G. Mueller. *An Introduction to Multinational Accounting.* Englewood Cliffs, NJ: Prentice-Hall, 1978.

Eitman, D. K., and A. I. Stonehill. *Multinational Business Finance.* Reading, MA: Addison-Wesley, 1989.

Financial Accounting Standards Board. *Accounting for the Translation of Foreign Currency Transactions and Foreign Currency Financial Statements,* Statement of Financial Accounting Standard No. 8. Stamford, CT: October 1975.

Financial Accounting Standards Board. *Foreign Currency Translation,* Statement of Financial Accounting Standard No. 52. Stamford, CT: December 1981.

Hepmark, S. R. *Reporting Foreign Operations.* Ann Arbor, MI: University of Michigan, 1966.

Institute of Chartered Accountants in England and Wales. *Member's Handbook, Statement No. 25.* London: Institute of Chartered Accountants in England and Wales, 1968.

Kligman, J. M. "Foreign Currency Translation: From Exposure Draft to Standard." *Chartered Accountant Magazine* (June 1983): 25–32, 57.

Lorensen, L. *Reporting Foreign Operations of U.S. Companies in U.S. Dollars,* Accounting Research Study No. 12. New York: AICPA, 1972.

Parkinson, M. R. *Translation of Foreign Currencies.* Toronto: CICA, 1972.

# 4

## ACCOUNTING FOR INFLATION PROPOSALS

### INTRODUCTION

Internationally, inflation is here to stay. Accounting does not create bad news, but simply reports it. How to report the effects of inflation on the financial position, performance, and conduct of a firm is the issue. Various models have been advocated in the literature and in practice. This chapter explains the differences, advantages, and limitations of each of the proposals advocated in the literature.

### DEFINING INCOME

Why measure income? Arguments in favor of measuring income could be extended ad infinitum. Income is a basic and important item of financial statements. It has various uses in various contexts. Income is generally perceived as a basis for taxation, a determinant of dividend-payment policy, a guide for investment and decision making, and an element of prediction.

The most popular expression of income is as *accounting income*, which is defined operationally as the difference between the realized revenues arising from the transactions of the period and the corresponding historical costs. This definition suggests five characteristics of accounting income. First, accounting income is based on the actual transactions entered into by the firm, with revenues primarily arising from the sale of goods or services minus the costs necessary to achieve these sales. Second, accounting income is based on the period postulate, meaning that it refers to the financial performance of a firm for a given period. The third characteristic of accounting income is that, for the recognition of revenues, it is based on the revenue principle in general and the realization test in particular. Fourth, accounting income requires the measurement of expenses in terms of the historical cost to the enterprise, necessitating a strict adherence to the cost principle. Finally, it is based on the matching principle, which requires that the realized revenues of the period be related to appropriate or corresponding costs.

Accounting income has been the subject of praise and criticism. Among the advantages claimed for accounting income are the facts that it has survived the test of time, it is objective and verifiable, it meets the criterion of conservatism, and it is useful for control purposes and especially useful in reporting on stewardship. Among the criticisms of accounting income are that it fails to recognize unrealized increases in the value of assets held in a given period because of the application of the historical and realization principles, it makes comparability difficult given the different acceptable methods of computing "cost," it leads to misleading and irrelevant data given reliance on the realization, historical cost, and conservatism principles, and it may give the impression to the users that the balance sheet represents an approximation of value rather than merely a statement of unallocated cost balances.

Given the limitations of accounting income, especially its failure to account for the effects of inflation, various proposals have been considered in the literature and in practice. An understanding of all the proposals rests on an understanding of the economic concept of income that serves as a basis for all these proposals.

Hicks used concepts introduced by various economists, such as Irving Fisher and Lindahl, to develop a general theory of economic income. He defined a person's personal income as "the maximum amount he can consume during a week, and still expect to be as well-off at the end of the week as he was at the beginning."[1] This definition has become the basis of many discussions concerning the concept of income. One problem encountered in defining accounting income is the lack of consensus on the interpretation of "capital maintenance"; according to "Hicksian" income, capital maintenance is the maximum amount that may be consumed in a given period and still maintain the capital intact.

## CAPITAL MAINTENANCE

The concept of capital maintenance implies that income is recognized after capital has been maintained or costs have been recovered. *Return on capital* (income) is distinguished from *return of capital* (cost recovery). Two principal concepts of capital maintenance or cost recovery may be expressed in terms of units of money and units of the same general purchasing power:

financial capital and physical capital. We have, therefore, four concepts of capital maintenance.

**1.** Financial capital can be measured in terms of money (*money maintenance*), which implies that the financial capital invested or reinvested by the owners is maintained. Conventional accounting, because it relies on historical cost for the valuation of assets and liabilities, conforms to the money-maintenance concept.

**2.** Financial capital can also be measured in units of the same purchasing power (*general-purchasing-power money maintenance*), which implies that the purchasing power of the financial capital invested or reinvested by the owner is maintained. General price-level-adjusted historical-cost accounting conforms to the general-purchasing-power money-maintenance concept.

**3.** Physical capital can be measured in units of money (*productive-capacity maintenance*), which implies that the physical productive capacity of the firm is maintained. Alternative definitions of capacity are the following:

a. Productive capacity should be defined as the physical assets possessed by the company, so that profit would be the amount that could be distributed after making sufficient provision to replace the physical assets held by the company as they are consumed or wear out.

b. Productive capacity should be defined as the capacity to produce the same volume of goods and services in the following year as could be produced in the current year.

c. Productive capacity should be defined as the capacity to produce the same value of goods and services in the following year as could be produced in the current year.[2]

Productive-capacity maintenance is the concept of capital maintenance used in current-value accounting, in which assets and liabilities are disclosed in the financial statements at their current values.

**4.** Physical capital can also be measured in units of the same purchasing power (*general-purchasing-power productive-capacity maintenance*), which implies that the physical productive capacity of the firm measured in units of the same purchasing power is maintained.

The following example illustrates the impact on income statements of each of the four concepts of capital maintenance. Let us suppose that a given firm has $4,000 of net assets at the beginning and $6,000 of net assets at the end of a given period. Let us also assume that $5,000 of net assets is required to maintain the actual physical productive capacity of the firm and that the general price level increased by 10% during the period. Income under each of the concepts of capital maintenance would be calculated as follows:

*Money maintenance*
   $6,000 - \$4,000 = \$2,000$
*General-purchasing-power money maintenance*
   $6,000 - (\$4,000 + 0.10 \times \$4,000) = \$1,600$
*Productive-capacity maintenance*
   $6,000 - \$5,000 = \$1,000$
*General-purchasing-power productive-capacity maintenance*
   $6,000 - (\$5,000 + 0.10 \times \$5,000) = \$500$

The accounting income, therefore, is $2,000, the general-price-level-adjusted accounting income is $1,600, the current-value-based income is $1,000, and the general-price-level-adjusted current-value-based income is $500. Each of these income concepts is discussed below.

## ALTERNATIVE ASSET VALUATION AND INCOME DETERMINATION MODELS

To illustrate the different accounting models, let's consider the simplified case of the "Zribi Company," formed on January 1, 19X6, to distribute a new product called Hedi. Capital is composed of $33,000 equity and $3,000 liabilities, carrying a 10% interest. On January 1, the Zribi Company began operations by purchasing 600 units of Hedi at $10 per unit. On May 1, the company sold 500 units at $15 per unit. Changes in the general and specific price levels for the year 19X6 are as follows:

|                          | January 1 | May 1  | December 31 |
| ------------------------ | --------- | ------ | ----------- |
| Replacement cost         | $ 10      | $ 12   | $ 13        |
| Net realizable value     | —         | $ 15   | $ 17        |
| General-price-level index | $100     | $130   | $156        |

A brief description of each accounting model follows, accompanied by examples using the data given.

### Alternative Accounting Models Expressed in Units of Money

To illustrate and isolate timing differences only, the alternative accounting models that do not reflect changes in the general price level are presented first. These models are historical-cost accounting, replacement-cost accounting, and net-realizable-value accounting. Exhibits 4.1 and 4.2 provide the income statements and the balance sheets, respectively, for the Zribi Company for 19X6 under the three accounting models.

#### Historical-Cost Accounting

Historical-cost accounting, or conventional accounting, is characterized by the use of historical cost as the primary attribute of the elements of financial statements, the assumption of a stable monetary unit, the match-

**Exhibit 4.1**
**Income Statements, Zribi Company, December 31, 19X6**

| | Historical Cost | Replacement Cost | Net Realizable Value |
|---|---|---|---|
| Revenues | $7,500a | $7,500 | $9,200b |
| Cost Goods Sold | 5,000c | 6,000d | 7,300e |
| Gross Margin | $2,500 | $1,500 | $1,900 |
| Interest | 300 | 300 | 300 |
| Operating Profit | $2,200 | $1,200 | $1,600 |
| Realized Holding | | | |
| Gains and Losses | Included above | 1,000f | 1,000 |
| Unrealized Holding | | | |
| Gains and Losses | Not applicable | 300g | 300 |
| General Price-Level | | | |
| Gains and Losses | Not applicable | Not applicable | Not applicable |
| | | | |
| Net Profit | $2,200 | $2,500 | $2,900 |

a 500 * $15 = $7,500.
b 7,500 + $17 (100) = $9,200.
c 500 * $10 = $5,000.
d 500 * $12 = $6,000.
e 6,000 + $13 (100) = $7,300.
f 500 ($12 - $10) = $1,000.
g 100 ($13 - $10) = $300.

ing principle, and the realization principle. Accordingly, historical-cost income, or accounting income, is the difference between the realized revenues and the corresponding historical costs. In Exhibit 4.1, accounting income is equal to $2,200. What does this figure represent for the Zribi Company? Generally, it is perceived as a basis for the computation of taxes and dividends and for the evaluation of performance. Its possible use in various

**Exhibit 4.2**
**Balance Sheets, Zribi Company, December 31, 19X6**

|                    | Historical Cost | Replacement Cost | Net Realizable Value |
|--------------------|:---------------:|:----------------:|:--------------------:|
| **Assets**         |                 |                  |                      |
| Cash               | $7,200          | $7,200           | $7,200               |
| Inventory          | 1,000           | 1,300a           | 1,700b               |
| Total Assets       | $8,200          | $8,500           | $8,900               |
|                    |                 |                  |                      |
| **Equities**       |                 |                  |                      |
| Bonds (10%)        | $3,000          | $3,000           | $3,000               |
| Capital            | 3,000           | 3,000            | 3,000                |
|                    |                 |                  |                      |
| **Retained Earnings** |              |                  |                      |
| Realized           | 2,200           | 2,200c           | 2,200c               |
| Unrealized         | Not applicable  | 300              | 700d                 |
| Total Equities     | $8,200          | $8,500           | $8,900               |

a 100 * ($13) = $1,300.

b 100 * ($17) = $1,700.

c May be divided into current operating profit ($1,200) and
  realized holding gains and losses ($1,000).

d Unrealized operating gain of $400 ($1,700 - $1,300) + unrealized
  holding gain of $300.

decision models results from the unconditional and longstanding acceptance of this version of income by the accounting profession and the business world. This attachment to accounting income may be explained primarily by the fact that it is objective, verifiable, practical, and easy to
understand. Accountants and business people may prefer accounting income over other measures of income for its practical advantages, and they

may fear the confusion that could result from the adoption of another accounting model.

In spite of these practical advantages, the Zribi Company's $2,200 accounting income contains both timing- and measurement-unit errors. Timing errors occur because accounting income includes, in a single figure, operating income and holding gains and losses that occurred and are recognized in the current period, but which are recognizable in future periods. Measurement-unit errors are present because accounting income does not take into account changes in the general price level that would have resulted in amounts expressed in units of general purchasing power and, by relying on historical cost as the attribute of the elements of financial statements rather than either replacement cost or net realizable value, it does not take into account changes in the specific price level.

How, then, should historical-cost financial statements be evaluated? First, they are interpretable. They are based on the concept of money maintenance. The attribute being expressed is the number of dollars (NOD). The balance sheet reports NOD at December 31, 19X6, and the income statement reports the change in NOD during the year. Second, historical-cost financial statements are not relevant because the command of goods (COG) is not measured. A measure of COG permits reflection of the changes in both the specific and general price levels and, therefore, such a measure represents the ability to buy the amount of goods necessary for capital maintenance.

In summary, historical-cost financial statements contain timing and measurement errors, are interpretable, and are not relevant.

### Replacement-Cost Accounting

Replacement-cost accounting, as a particular case of current-entry-price accounting, is characterized by the use of replacement cost as the primary attribute of the elements of financial statements, the assumption of a stable monetary unit, the realization principle, the dichotomization of operating income and holding gains and losses, and the dichotomization of realized and unrealized holding gains and losses.

Accordingly, replacement-cost net income is equal to the sum of replacement-cost operating income and holding gains and losses. Replacement-cost operating income is equal to the difference between the realized revenues and the corresponding replacement costs. In Exhibit 4.1, the Zribi Company's replacement-cost net income of $2,500 is derived from replacement-cost operating income of $1,200, realized holding gains and losses of $1,000, and unrealized holding gains and losses of $300.

What do these figures represent for the Zribi Company? The replacement-cost operating income represents the "distributable" income, which is the maximum amount of dividends the company can pay and maintain its productive capacity intact. The realized holding gains and losses constitute an indicator of the efficiency of holding resources up to the time of sale. The realization holding gains and losses are indicators of the efficiency of holding performances. In addition to these practical advantages, replacement-cost net income contains timing errors only on operating profit. It does, however, also contain measurement-unit errors.

Replacement-cost net income contains timing errors because it omits the operating profit that occurred in the current period but which is realizable in future periods. It includes the operating profit recognized in the current period but which occurred in previous periods. It also includes holding gains and losses in the same period as they occur.

In addition, replacement-cost net income contains measurement-unit errors because it does not take into account changes in the general price level that would have resulted in amounts expressed in units of general purchasing power. Also, it does take into account changes in the specific price level, as it relies on replacement cost as the attribute of the elements of financial statements.

Evaluation of replacement-cost financial statements reveals the following information. First, they are interpretable. They are based on the concept of productive-capacity maintenance. The attribute being expressed in the income statement is the NOD. The asset figures, however, are interpretable as measures of COG; in Exhibit 4.2, asset figures are expressed in terms of the purchasing power of the dollar at the end of the year. They reflect changes in both the specific and the general price levels and, therefore, represent the COG necessary for capital maintenance. Second, because COG is the relevant attribute, the replacement net income is not relevant, even though the asset figures are relevant.

In summary, replacement-cost financial statements present these characteristics: they contain operating-profit timing errors and measurement-unit errors, are interpretable as NOD for income figures and COG for asset figures, and only the asset figures are relevant as measures of COG.

### Net-Realizable-Value Accounting

Net-realizable-value accounting, as a particular case of current-exit-price accounting, is characterized primarily by the use of net realizable value as the attribute of the elements of financial statements, the assumption of a stable monetary unit, the abandonment of the realization principle, and the dichotomization of operating income and holding gains and losses.

Accordingly, under net-realizable-value accounting, net income is equal to the sum of the net-realizable-value operating income and holding gains and losses. Net-realizable-value operating income is equal to the operating income arising from sales and the net operating income from inventory. Operating income from sales is equal to the difference between the realized revenues and the corresponding replacement cost of the items sold.

In Exhibit 4.1, the Zribi Company's net-realizable-value net income of

$2,900 is derived from a net-realizable-value operating income of $1,600, realized holding gains of $1,000, and unrealized holding gains and losses of $300.

Note that the net-realizable-value operating income is composed of operating income on sales of $1,200 and operating income on inventory of $400. Thus, unrealized retained earnings equal the sum of the unrealized holding gains and losses of $300 and the operating income on inventory of $400 (see Exhibit 4.2).

What do these figures represent for the Zribi Company? They are similar to the figures obtained with replacement-cost accounting, except for the operating income on inventory, which results from the abandonment of the realization principle and the recognition of revenues at the time of production and at the time of sale. Net-realizable-value net income indicates the firm's ability to liquidate and to adapt to new economic situations.

To these practical advantages may be added the fact that net-realizable net income does not contain timing errors; it does contain measurement-unit errors. It does not contain any timing errors because it reports all operating profit and holding gains and losses in the same period in which they occur and it excludes all operating profit and holding gains and losses occurring in previous periods.

Net-realizable-value net income contains measurement-unit errors because it does not take into account changes in the general price level (if it did, it would result in amounts expressed in units of purchasing power) and because it does take into account changes in the specific price level, since it relies on net realizable value as the attribute of the elements of financial statements.

Evaluation of net-realizable-value financial statements reveals, first, that they are interpretable. They are based on the concept of productive-capacity maintenance. The attribute being measured is expressed in NOD in the income statement and COG in the balance sheet. Unlike replacement-cost accounting, under net-realizable-value accounting, asset figures are expressed as measures of COG in the output market rather than the input market. Second, because COG is the relevant attribute, the net-realizable-value income is not relevant, while the asset figures are.

In summary, net-realizable-value financial statements do not contain timing errors (see Exhibit 4.3). They do contain measurement-unit errors. Also, they are interpretable as NOD for the net income and COG for the asset figures; only the asset figures are relevant as measures of COG.

### Alternative Accounting Models Expressed in Units of Purchasing Power

To illustrate both timing- and measurement-unit errors, this section presents accounting models that reflect changes in the general price level. These models are general-price-level-adjusted historical-cost accounting, replace-

**Exhibit 4.3**
**Timing-Error Analysis, Zribi Company, 19X6**

| TOTAL OPERATING AND HOLDING GAINS | HISTORICAL COST Reported Income | Error | REPLACEMENT COST Reported Income | Error | NET REALIZABLE VALUE Reported Income | Error |
|---|---|---|---|---|---|---|
| $2,900 | $2,000 | $700 | $2,500 | $400 | $2,900 | 0 |

ment-cost accounting, and net-realizable-value accounting. Continuing with the example of the Zribi Company, Exhibits 4.4 and 4.5 provide the income statements and the balance sheets, respectively, for 19X6 under the three accounting models expressed in units of purchasing power. The general-price-level gain or loss is shown in Exhibit 4.6.

*General-Price-Level-Adjusted*
*Historical-Cost Accounting*

General-price-level-adjusted historical-cost accounting is characterized primarily by the use of historical cost as the attribute of the elements of financial statements, the use of units of general purchasing power as the unit of measure, the matching principle, and the realization principle. Accordingly, general-price-level-adjusted historical-cost income is the difference between the realized revenues and the corresponding historical costs, both expressed in units of general purchasing power.

In Exhibit 4.4, the general-price-level-adjusted historical-cost income for the Zribi Company in 19X6 is equal to $1,080; included in this figure is a $180 general-price-level gain, computed as shown in Exhibit 4.6. To the Zribi Company, the $1,080 figure represents accounting income expressed in dollars that have the purchasing power of dollars at the end of 19X6. In addition to the practical advantages given for accounting income, general-price-level-adjusted historical-cost income is expressed in units of general purchasing power. For these reasons, the use of such an accounting model may constitute a less radical change for those accustomed to historical-cost income than any model based on current value.

In spite of these practical advantages, the general-price-level-adjusted historical-cost income of $1,080 contains the same timing errors as historical-cost income. It contains no measurement-unit errors because it does take into account changes in the general price level. It does not, however, take into account changes in the specific price level because it relies on

**Exhibit 4.4**
**General-Price-Level Income Statement, Zribi Company, December 31, 19X6**

| | Historical Cost | Replacement Cost | Net Realizable Value |
|---|---|---|---|
| Revenues | $9,000a | $9,000 | $10,700b |
| Costs | 7,800c | 7,200d | 8,500e |
| Gross Margin | $1,200 | $1,800 | $ 2,200 |
| Interst | 300 | 300 | 300 |
| Operating Profit | 900 | $1,500 | $ 1,900 |
| Real Realized Holding Gains and Losses | Included above | (600)f | (600) |
| Real Unrealized Holding Gains and Losses | Not applicable | (260)g | (260) |
| General Price-Level Gain or Loss | 180h | 180 | 180 |
| Net Profit | $1,080 | $ 820 | $ 1,220 |

a $7,500 * 156/130 = $9,000.

b $9,000 + ($17 * 100 units) = $10,700.

c $5,000 * 156/100 = $7,800.

d $6,000 * 156/130 = $7,200.

e $7,200 + ($13 * 100 units) = $8,500.

f [($12 * 156/130) - ($10 * 156/100)] * 500 = ($600).

g ($13 - $10 * 156/100) * 100 units = ($260).

h From Exhibit 4.6.

**Exhibit 4.5**
**General-Price-Level Balance Sheet, Zribi Company, December 31, 19X6**

| | Historical Cost | Replacement Cost | Net Realizable Value |
|---|---|---|---|
| Assets | | | |
| Cash | $7,200 | $7,200 | $7,200 |
| Inventory | 1,560a | 1,300 | 1,700 |
| Total Assets | $8,760 | $8,500 | $8,900 |
| | | | |
| Equities | | | |
| Bonds (10%) | $3,000 | $3,000 | $3,000 |
| Capital | 4,680b | 4,680 | 4,680 |
| | | | |
| Retained Earnings | | | |
| Realized | 900 | 900 | 900 |
| Unrealized | Not applicable | 260 | 140c |
| General Price-Level | | | |
| Gain or Loss | 180 | 180 | 180 |
| Total Equities | $8,760 | $8,500 | $8,900 |

a $1,000 * 156/100 = $1,560.

b $3,000 * 156/100 = $4,680.

c Unrealized operating gain of $400 ($1,700 - $1,300) + unrealized gain of ($260).

historical cost as the attribute of the elements of financial statements rather than on replacement cost or net realizable value.

In evaluating the general-price-level-adjusted historical-cost financial statements presented in Exhibits 4.4 and 4.5, first, we find they are interpretable. They are based on the concept of purchasing-power money maintenance. The attribute being measured is NOD, in some cases, and COG in

**Exhibit 4.6**
**General-Price-Level Gain or Loss, Zribi Company, December 31, 19X6**

| | Unadjusted | Conversion Factor | Adjusted |
|---|---|---|---|
| Net Monetary Assets on | | | |
| January 1, 19X5 | $ 3,000 | 156/100 | $ 4,680 |
| Add Monetary Receipts | | | |
| during 19X6 Sales | 7,500 | 156/130 | 9,000 |
| Net Monetary Items | $10,500 | | $13,680 |
| | | | |
| Less Monetary Payments | | | |
| Purchases | 6,000 | 156/100 | 9,360 |
| Interest | 300 | 156/156 | 300 |
| Total | $ 6,300 | | $ 9,660 |
| | | | |
| Computed Net Monetary | | | |
| Assets, December 31, 19X6 | | | 4,020 |
| Actual Net Monetary | | | |
| Assets, December 31, 19X6 | | | 4,200 |
| General Price-Level Gain | | | $ 180 |

others. Hence, general-price-level-adjusted historical-cost income and all balance-sheet figures (with the exception of cash and monetary assets and liabilities) may be interpreted as NOD measures. Only the cash figure and monetary assets and liabilities may be interpreted as COG measures. Second, only the cash figures and monetary assets and liabilities are relevant because they are expressed as COG measures.

In summary, general-price-level-adjusted historical-cost financial statements contain timing errors but no measurement-unit errors, are interpretable, and only the cash figures and monetary assets and liabilities are relevant as COG measures.

*General-Price-Level-Adjusted*
*Replacement-Cost Accounting*

General-price-level-adjusted replacement-cost accounting is characterized primarily by the use of replacement cost as the attribute of the elements of financial statements, by the use of units of general purchasing power as the unit of measure, by the realization principle, by the dichotomization of operating income and real realized holding gains and losses, and by the dichotomization of real realized and real unrealized holding gains and losses. Accordingly, general-price-level-adjusted replacement-cost income is equal to the difference between realized revenues and the corresponding replacement costs, with both expressed in units of general purchasing power. Similarly, general-price-level-adjusted replacement-cost financial statements eliminate the "fictitious" holding gains and losses to arrive at the "real" holding gains and losses. Fictitious holding gains and losses represent the general-price-level restatement necessary to maintain the general purchasing power of nonmonetary items.

In Exhibit 4.4, the general-price-level replacement-cost net income for the Zribi Company in 19X6 is equal to $820. Included in this figure is a $180 general-price-level gain, computed as shown in Exhibit 4.6. For the Zribi Company, the $820 represents the replacement-cost net income expressed in units of general purchasing power at the end of 19X6. This measure of income has the same advantages as replacement-cost accounting income, with the added advantage of being expressed in units of general purchasing power. For these reasons, general-price-level restated-replacement-cost accounting constitutes a net improvement over replacement-cost accounting. Not only does this accounting model use replacement cost as an attribute of the elements of financial statements, it also uses general purchasing power units as the unit of measure. In spite of these improvements, however, general-price-level-adjusted replacement-cost income contains the same timing errors as replacement-cost income, but it contains no measurement-unit errors because it takes into account changes in the general price level. In addition, it takes into account changes in the specific price level because it adopts replacement cost as the attribute of the elements of financial statements.

In evaluating the general-price-level-adjusted replacement-cost financial statements presented in Exhibits 4.4 and 4.5, we find that, first, they are interpretable. They are based on the concept of purchasing-power productive-capacity maintenance. The attribute expressed is COG in both the income statement and the balance sheet. Second, the general-price-level-adjusted replacement-cost financial statements are relevant because they are expressed as measures of COG; note, however, that it is COG in the input market rather than the output market.

In summary, general-price-level-adjusted replacement-cost financial

statements contain timing errors but no measurement-unit errors, are interpretable, and are relevant as COG measures in the input market.

### General-Price-Level-Adjusted
### Net-Realizable-Value Accounting

General-price-level-adjusted net-realizable-value accounting is characterized primarily by the use of net realizable value as the attribute of the
elements of financial statements, the use of units of general purchasing
power as the unit of measure, the abandonment of the realization principle,
the dichotomization of operating income and real holding gains and losses,
and the dichotomization of real realized and unrealized gains and losses.
Accordingly, general-price-level-adjusted net-realizable-value net income is
equal to the sum of the net-realizable-value operating income and holding
gains and losses, with both expressed in units of general purchasing power.
The general-price-level-adjusted net-realizable-value operating income is
equal to the sum of operating income arising from sales and operating
income from inventory, with both expressed in units of general purchasing
power.

In Exhibit 4.4, the general-price-level-adjusted net-realizable-value net
income for the Zribi Company in 19X6 of $1,220 is derived from a general-
price-level-adjusted net-realizable-value operating income of $1,900, real
realized holding losses of $600, real unrealized holding losses of $260, and
a general-price-level gain of $180 (see Exhibit 4.6 for computation of this
item).

Note also that the general-price-level-adjusted net-realizable-value operating income on sales of $1,900 is derived from the general-price-level-
adjusted net-realizable-value operating income on sales of $1,500 and
general-price-level-adjusted net-realizable-value operating income on inventory of $400.

In addition to the advantages of net-realizable-value net income, general-price-level-adjusted net-realizable-value net income has the advantage of
being expressed in units of general purchasing power. For these reasons,
general-price-level net-realizable-value accounting represents a net improvement over net-realizable-value accounting. Not only does it use net realizable value as an attribute of the elements of financial statements, but general purchasing power is the unit of measure.

Thus, general-price-level-adjusted net-realizable-value income contains
no timing errors and no measurement-unit errors.

In evaluating the general-price-level-adjusted net-realizable-value financial statements presented in Exhibits 4.4 and 4.5, we find that, first, they
are interpretable. They are based on the concept of purchasing-power productive-capacity maintenance. The attribute being measured is COG in
both the income statement and the balance sheet statement. Second, the

**Exhibit 4.7**

**Comparison of Alternative Accounting Models by Error Type**

| Accounting Model | Timing Error | | Measuring | Interpretation | | Relevance |
| --- | --- | --- | --- | --- | --- | --- |
| | Operating Profit | Holding Gains | Unit Error | NOD | COG | |
| 1. Historical Cost Accounting | Yes | Yes | Yes | Yes | No | No |
| 2. Replacement Cost Accounting | Yes | Eliminated | Yes | Yes (Income Statement) | Yes (Asset figures) | Yes (Asset figures only) |
| 3. Net Realizable Value Accounting | Eliminated | Eliminated | Yes | Yes (Income Statement) | Yes (Monetary assets & liabilities) | Yes (Monetary assets & liabilities) |
| 4. General Price-Level Adjusted Historical Cost Accounting | Yes | Yes | Eliminated | Yes | Yes | Yes |
| 5. General Price-Level Adjusted Replacement Cost Accounting | Yes | Eliminated | Eliminated | Eliminated | Yes | Yes |
| 6. General Price-Level Adjusted Net Realizable Value Accounting | Eliminated | Eliminated | Eliminated | Eliminated | Yes | Yes |

financial statements are relevant because they are expressed as measures of COG. Note that the COG is in the output market rather than the input market.

In summary, general-price-level-adjusted net-realizable-value financial statements contain no timing errors or measurement-unit errors, are interpretable, and are relevant as measures of COG in the output market. Such statements, therefore, meet all the criteria established for the comparison and evaluation of the alternative accounting models shown in Exhibit 4.7.

## CONCLUSIONS

Eight alternative asset-valuation and income-determination models are discussed in this chapter:

1. Historical-cost accounting
2. Replacement-cost accounting
3. Net-realizable-value accounting
4. Present-value accounting
5. General-price-level-adjusted historical-cost accounting
6. General-price-level-adjusted replacement-cost accounting
7. General-price-level-adjusted net-realizable-value accounting
8. General-price-level-adjusted present-value accounting

In this chapter, these models are compared and evaluated on the basis of four criteria: their interpretability, the avoidance of timing errors, the avoidance of measurement-unit errors, and their relevance as measures of COG.

Although conceptually preferable, the present-value models are not included in the comparison and evaluation because of the subjectivity and uncertainty surrounding their use, which makes their implementation impractical currently. The comparison of the remaining models shows the general-price-level-adjusted net-realizable-value accounting model to be the closest to a preferred-income-position concept because it meets each of the criteria set forth in the chapter.

## NOTES

1. J. R. Hicks, *Value and Capital,* 2d ed., (Oxford, England: Clarendon Press, 1946) 122.
2. *Inflation Accounting: Report of the Inflation Accounting Committee,* (London: Her Majesty's Stationery Service, 1975), 35.

## BIBLIOGRAPHY

Basu, S., and J. R. Hanna. *Inflation Accounting: Alternative, Implementation Issues and Some Empirical Evidence.* Hamilton, Ontario, Canada: Society of Management Accountants, 1977.

Chambers, R. J. *Accounting, Evaluation, and Economic Behavior.* Englewood Cliffs, NJ: Prentice-Hall, 1966.

_____. "NOD, CPG and PuPu: See How Inflation Teases!" *Journal of Accountancy* (September 1975): 56–62.

Edwards, E. O., and P. W. Bell. *The Theory and Measurement of Business Income.* Berkeley, CA: University of California Press, 1961.

Gunther, R. S. "Capital Maintenance, Price Changes, and Profit Determination." *Accounting Review* (October 1970): 712–730.

Hanna, J. R. *Accounting Income Models: An Application and Evaluation,* Special Study No. 8. Toronto: Society of Management Accountants of Canada, July 1974.

Kerr, J. St. G. "Three Concepts of Business Income." In *An Income Approach to Accounting Theory,* edited by S. Davidson, et al., 40–48. Englewood Cliffs, NJ: Prentice-Hall.

Louderback, J. G. "Projectability as a Criterion for Income Determination Methods" *Accounting Review* (April 1971): 289–305.

Parker, P. W., and P. M. D. Gibbs. "Accounting for Inflation — Recent Proposals and Their Effects" *Journal of the Institute of Actuaries* (December 1974): 1–10.

Revsine, L., and J. J. Weygandt. "Accounting for Inflation: The Controversy." *Journal of Accounting* (October 1974): 72–78.

Rosen, L. S. *Current Value Accounting and Price-Level Restatements.* Toronto: Canadian Institute of Chartered Accountants, 1972.

Rosenfield, P. "Accounting for Inflation: A Field Test." *Journal of Accountancy* (June 1969): 45–50.

_____. "CCP Accounting: Relevance and Interpretability." *Journal of Accountancy* (August 1975): 52–60.

_____. "The Confusion between General Price Level Restatement and Current Value Accounting." *Journal of Accountancy* (October 1972): 63–68.

"Statement of Standard Accounting Practice No. 16: Current Cost Accounting." *Accountancy* (April 1980): 99–100.

Sterling, R. R. "Relevant Financial Reporting in an Age of Price Changes." *Journal of Accountancy* (February 1975): 42–51.

_____. *Theory of Measurement of Enterprise Income.* Lawrence, KS: University Press of Kansas, 1970.

# 5

# ACCOUNTING FOR INFLATION INTERNATIONALLY

## INTRODUCTION

The solutions adopted for accounting for inflation differ from one nation to another, covering the spectrum of methods that account for specific price-level changes, general price-level changes, or both. In addition to discussion of the methods used routinely, this chapter elaborates on more controversial inflation issues and how they are treated internationally. This chapter, therefore, constitutes an application of comparative accounting theory to the problem of inflation accounting.

## U.S. SOLUTIONS TO ACCOUNTING FOR INFLATION

### Early Attempts

Long recognized as a problem in the accounting literature, the issue of accounting for changing prices has been studied extensively by the various accounting standards-setting bodies. The Committee on Accounting Procedure, in 1947, 1948, and 1953,[1] and, in 1965, the Accounting Principles Board[2] examined the problems relating to changes in the general price level without any success. These attempts were followed by the AICPA's publication of Accounting Research Study No. 6, *Reporting the Financial Effects of Price-Level Changes,* in 1963,[3] and by APB Statement No. 3, *Financial Statements Restated for General Price-Level Changes,* in June 1969.[4] Both recommended supplemental disclosure of general-price-level information, without any success. The FASB approached the price-level subject at a time when inflation was a major concern in the economy. After issuing a

Discussion Memorandum, *Reporting the Effects of General Price-Level Changes in Financial Statements* on February 15, 1974;[5] an Exposure Draft, *Financial Reporting in Units of General Purchasing Power,* on December 31, 1974;[6] a Research Report, *Field Tests of Financial Reporting in Units of General Purchasing Power,* in May 1977;[7] a second Exposure Draft, *Financial Reporting and Changing Prices,* on December 28, 1978;[8] and a further Exposure Draft as a supplement to the 1974 proposed Statement on general purchasing power adjustments, *Constant Dollar Accounting,* on March 2, 1979;[9] in September 1979, the FASB issued SFAS 33, *Financial Reporting and Changing Prices,*[10] which calls for information on the effects of both general inflation and specific price changes.

### FASB Statement of Financial Accounting Standard No. 33

SFAS 33 is truly the result of years of attempts by the diverse standards-setting bodies to develop methods of reporting the effects of inflation on earnings and assets. In its deliberations, the FASB considered a variety of accounting systems, which can be grouped under the following headings:[11]

1. Measurement of inventory and property, plant, and equipment
   a. Historical cost
   b. Current reproduction cost
   c. Current replacement cost
   d. Net realizable value
   e. Net present value of expected future cash flows (value in use)
   f. Recoverable amount
   g. Current cost
   h. Value to business (current cost or lower recoverable amount)
2. Concepts of capital maintenance
   a. Financial capital maintenance
   b. Physical capital maintenance (the maintenance of operating capacity)
3. Measurement units
   a. Measurement in nominal dollars
   b. Measurement in constant dollars

The list above suggests that the FASB examined all the alternative asset-evaluation and income-determination models presented in this chapter. The FASB concluded, however, that supplementary information should be presented according to historical-cost/constant-dollar accounting and current-cost accounting (CCA). More specifically, the FASB requires major companies to disclose the effects of both general inflation and specific price changes as supplementary information in their annual published reports. Major companies are those having assets of more than $1 billion (after deducting accumulated depreciation) or those whose inventories and property, plant, and equipment (before deducting accumulated depreciation) amount to more than $125 million. Specifically, major firms are required to report the items that follow.[12]

1. Constant-dollar disclosures (current year)
   a. Information on income from continuing operations for the current fiscal year on a historical-cost/constant-dollar basis
   b. The purchasing-power gain or loss on net monetary items for the current fiscal year

The purchasing-power gain or loss on net monetary items shall *not* be included in income from continuing operations.

2. Current-cost disclosures (current year)
   An enterprise is required to disclose:
   a. Information on income from continuing operations for the current fiscal year on a current-cost basis
   b. The current-cost amounts of inventory and property, plant, and equipment at the end of the current fiscal year
   c. Increases or decreases for the current fiscal year in the current-cost amounts of inventory and property, plant, and equipment, net of inflation

The increases or decreases in current-cost amounts shall *not* be included in income from continuing operations.

3. Five-year summary data
   a. Net sales and other operating revenues
   b. Historical-cost/constant-dollar information
      (1) Income from continuing operations
      (2) Income per common share from continuing operations
      (3) Net assets at fiscal-year end
   c. Current-cost information (except for individual years in which the information was excluded from the current-year disclosures)
      (1) Income from continuing operations
      (2) Income per common share from continuing operations
      (3) Net assets at fiscal-year end
      (4) Increases or decreases in the current-cost amounts of inventory and property, plant, and equipment, net of inflation
   d. Other information
      (1) Purchasing-power gain or loss on net monetary items
      (2) Cash dividends declared per common share
      (3) Market price per common share at fiscal-year end

4. Limitation

Whenever the recoverable amount of an asset is less than either the constant-dollar value or the current-cost value, the recoverable amount should be used to value the asset. "Recoverable amount" means the current value of the net cash flow expected to be realized from the use or sale of the asset.

5. Methodology

a. The constant-dollar method should use the Consumer Price Index for All Urban Consumers (CPI-U).

b. The current-cost method may use internally or externally developed specific price indexes or such evidence as vendors' invoice prices or price lists to determine the current cost of an asset. The method selected should be based on availability and cost and should be applied consistently.

c. The constant-dollar amounts should be based on average-for-the-year indexes.

d. The current costs should be based on average current costs of the period for the restatement of items required to compute operating income (cost of goods sold, depreciation, and depletion), and should be restated at end-of-period current costs net of general inflation for measuring the increases or decreases in inventory, plant, property, and equipment. This latter statement requires the use of year-end current costs restated in average-of-the-period constant dollars.

The FASB also provided additional information, given in the list that follows, to explain the minimum-disclosure requirements for constant-dollar and current-cost data.[13]

1. Income from continuing operations is income after applicable income taxes but excludes the results of discontinued operations, extraordinary items, and the cumulative effects of accounting changes. If none of the foregoing is present for a business enterprise, income from continuing operations is identical to net income.

2. The purchasing-power gain or loss on net monetary items and the increase or decrease in current-cost amounts are excluded from income from continuing operations.

3. Current-cost information need not be disclosed if it is not materially different from constant-dollar information. The reason for omitting current-cost information must be disclosed in notes to the supplementary information.

4. Information relating to income from continuing operations may be presented either in the format of a conventional income statement or in a reconciliation format that discloses adjustments to income from continuing operations in the historical-cost/nominal-dollar income statement.

5. The average CPI-U is used by business enterprises that present only the minimum constant-dollar data for a fiscal year. If an enterprise presents comprehensive financial statements on a constant-dollar basis, either the average or the end-of-year CPI-U may be used.

6. An enterprise that presents only the minimum data required by SFAS 33 need not restate any financial-statement amounts other than inventories, plant assets, cost of goods sold, and depreciation, depletion, and amortization expenses.

7. If the historical-cost/constant-dollar amounts or the current-cost amounts of inventories and plant assets exceed the recoverable amounts of those assets, all data required by SFAS 33 must be presented on the basis of the lower recoverable amounts. The recoverable amount for an asset expected to be sold is its net realizable value (expected sales proceeds less costs of completion and disposal). The recoverable amount for an asset continuing in use is its value in use (net present value of future cash inflows, including ultimate proceeds on disposal). Thus, *value in use* is synonymous with *direct valuation*.

8. Current cost of inventories, plant assets, cost of goods sold, and depreciation, depletion, and amortization expenses may be determined by one of the following methods: (a) indexation by using either externally or internally developed specific price indexes or (b) direct pricing by using current-invoice prices, vendors' price lists, quotations, or estimates, or standard manufacturing costs that reflect current costs.

Exhibits 5.1, 5.2, and 5.3 illustrate these requirements. Thus, SFAS 33 requires two supplementary income computations, one dealing with the effects of general inflation and the other dealing with specific price changes. Both types of information are intended to help users with their decisions regarding investments, lending, and other matters in specific ways:

1. Assessment of future cash flows. Present financial statements include measurements of expenses and assets at historical prices. When prices are changing, measurements that reflect current prices are likely to provide useful information for the assessment of future cash flows.

2. Assessment of enterprise performance. The worth of an enterprise can be increased as a result of prudent timing of asset purchases to times when prices are changing. The increase in worth is one aspect of performance, even though it may be distinguished from operating performance. Measurements that reflect current prices can provide a basis for assessing the extent to which past decisions on the acquisition of assets have created opportunities for earning cash flows.

3. Assessment of the erosion of operating capability. An enterprise typically must hold minimum quantities of inventory, property, plant, equipment, and other assets to maintain its ability to provide goods and services. When the prices of those assets are increasing, larger amounts of money investment are needed to maintain the previous levels of output. Information on the current prices of resources that are used to generate revenues can help users to assess the extent and the manner in which operating capability has been maintained.

## Exhibit 5.1

**Statement of Income from Continuing Operations Adjusted for Changing Prices, Year Ended December 31, 19X6 (in thousands of average 19X5 dollars)**

| | As Reported in the Primary Statements | Adjusted for General Inflation | Adjusted for Changes in Specific Prices (Current Costs) |
|---|---|---|---|
| Net sales and other operating revenues | $500,000 | $500,000 | $500,000 |
| Cost of goods sold | 400,000 | 450,000 | 455,000 |
| Depreciation and amortization expense | 20,000 | 25,000 | 26,000 |
| Other operating expense | 40,000 | 40,000 | 40,000 |
| Interest expense | 15,000 | 15,000 | 15,000 |
| Provision for income taxes | 20,000 | 20,000 | 20,000 |
| | 495,000 | 550,000 | 556,000 |
| Income (loss) from Continuing operations | $ 5,000 | $(50,000) | $(56,000) |
| Gain from decline in purchasing power of net amounts owed | | $ 5,000 | $ 5,000 |
| Increase in specific prices (current cost) of inventories and property, plant, and equipment held during the year(a) | | | $ 30,000 |

**Exhibit 5.1 (Continued)**

| | |
|---|---:|
| Effect of increase in general price level | 20,000 |
| Excess of increase in specific prices over increase in the general price level | $ 10,000 |

(a) At December 31, 19X5, current cost of inventory was $55,000 and current cost of property, plant, and equipment, net of accumulated depreciation was $80,000.

4. Assessment of the erosion of general purchasing power. When general price levels are increasing, larger amounts of money are required to maintain a fixed amount of purchasing power. Investors typically are concerned with assessing whether information that reflects changes in general purchasing power can help with that assessment.[14]

Because it requires the presentation of both general-price-level and specific-price-level information, SFAS 33 obviously is a step forward. However, it falls short of a total solution, which would require using general-price-level restated current-cost accounting, along with general-price-level restated replacement-cost accounting or general-price-level restated net-realizable-value accounting. Moreover, some of the specific requirements discussed in SFAS 33 do not pertain to most situations.[15] In 1986, the issuance of SFAS 89 by the FASB rescinded the requirement that qualifying firms disclose the information specified in amended SFAS 33.[16] It also encourages the continued and voluntary disclosure of information about the effects of changing prices. The voluntary disclosures are discussed in the remainder of this section.

According to SFAS 89, the selected disclosures for the current year are as follows:

1. Income from continuing operations under the current-cost basis, including disclosure of the current-cost amounts of cost of goods sold and depreciation, depletion, and amortization expense

2. Purchasing-power gain or loss on net monetary items (excluded from income from continuing operations)

3. Current-cost (or lower recoverable) amount of inventory and of property, plant, and equipment at the end of the current year

**Exhibit 5.2**

**Five-Year Comparison of Selected Supplementary Financial Data Adjusted for the Effects of Changing Prices (in thousands of average 19X5 dollars)**

| | Years Ended December 31 | | | | |
|---|---|---|---|---|---|
| | 19x1 | 19x2 | 19x3 | 19x4 | 19x5 |
| Net sales and other operating revenues | $350,000 | $400,000 | $420,000 | $450,000 | $500,000 |
| Historical cost information adjusted for general inflation | | | | | |
| Income (loss) from continuing operations | | | | (29,000 ) | (20,000) |
| Income (loss) from continuing operations per common share | | | | (2.0) | (2.0) |
| Net assets at year-end | | | | 100,000 | 120,000 |
| Current cost information | | | | | |
| Income (loss) from continuing operations | | | | (10,000) | (26,000) |
| Income (loss) from continuing operations per common share | | | | (1) | (2.6) |
| Excess of increase in specific prices over increase in the general price level | | | | 5,000 | 10,000 |
| Net assets at year-end | | | | 120,000 | 130,000 |
| Gain from decline in purchasing power of net amounts owed | | | | 4,500 | 5,000 |
| Cash dividends declared per share | 2.00 | 2.05 | 2.1 | 2.15 | 2.2 |
| Market price per common share at year-end | 40 | 30 | 45 | 40 | 39 |
| Average consumer price | 170.5 | 181.5 | 195.4 | 205.00 | 220.9 |

**Exhibit 5.3**
**Statement of Income from Continuing Operations Adjusted for Changing Prices for the Year Ended December 31, 19X6 (in thousands of average 19X5 dollars)**

| | | |
|---|---:|---:|
| Income from continuing operations, as reported in the income statement | | $   5,000 |
| Adjustments to restate costs for the effect of general inflation | | |
| Cost of goods sold | $(50,000) | |
| Depreciation and amortization expense | (5,000) | (55,000) |
| | | |
| Loss from continuing operations adjusted for general inflation | | (50,000) |
| Adjustments to reflect the difference between general inflation and changes in specific prices (current costs) | | |
| Cost of goods sold | (5,000) | |
| | (1,000) | (6,000) |
| | | |
| Loss from continuing operations adjusted for changes in specific prices | | $(56,000) |
| | | |
| Gain from decline in purchasing power of net amounts owed | 5,000 | |
| Increase in specific prices | 30,000 | |
| Effect of increase in general price level | 20,000 | |
| Excess of increase in specific prices over increase in general price level | 10,000 | |

4. Increase or decrease in the current-cost (or lower recoverable) amount of inventory and of property, plant, and equipment, before and after eliminating the effects of inflation (excluded from income from continuing operations)

5. Aggregate foreign-currency-translation adjustment on a current-cost basis, if applicable[17]

Under SFAS 89, the selected disclosures included in a 5-year summary, adjusted to average-for-the-year, end-of-year, or base-period constant purchasing power are the following:

1. Net sales and other operating revenues

2. Income from continuing operations (and related earnings per share) under the current-cost basis

3. Purchasing-power gain or loss on net monetary items

4. Increase or decrease in the current-cost (or lower recoverable) amount of inventory and of property, plant, and equipment, net of inflation

5. Aggregate foreign-currency-translation adjustment on a current-cost basis, if applicable

6. Net assets at year-end or on a current-cost basis

7. Cash dividends declared per common share

8. Market price per common share at year-end[18]

The 5-year summary may be also presented either in current purchasing price (year-end or average-for-the-year) or in the purchasing power of the base period of the Consumer Price Index (CPI).

## UNITED KINGDOM SOLUTIONS TO ACCOUNTING FOR INFLATION

### Statement of Standard Accounting Practice No. 7

In November 1972, the Institute of Chartered Accountants in England and Wales (ICAEW) supported the publication of Exposure Draft No. 8, *Accounting for Changes in the Purchasing Power of Money*.[19] However, shortly before the exposure period expired, the government intervened and appointed a committee (known as the Sandilands Committee after its chairman, Sir Francis Sandilands) to work on this topic. Rather than proceed with a standard and risk alienating those responsible for the government's efforts, the Accounting Standards Committee of the ICAEW issued a provisional rather than a full standard, known as Statement of Standard Accounting Practice No. 7 (SSAP 7), *Accounting for Changes in the Purchasing Power of Money,* which was substantially the same as the Exposure Draft.[20] Basically, SSAP 7 recommended the adoption of general-price-level-adjusted historical-cost accounting.

### The Sandilands Report

The Sandilands Committee rejected the general-price-level-adjusted historical-cost accounting advocated by SSAP 7 and recommended what it labeled current-cost accounting (CCA). Essentially, it concluded that the

following developments are necessary for changes in the law of corporations: (1) the same unit of measure should be used by all; (2) the operating
profit should be disclosed separately from the holding gains and losses;
and (3) the financial statements should include relevant information for
assessing the liquidity of the company. The most important recommendation of the Sandilands report, however, was the use of the

value at an amount which represents the opportunity costs to the firm, that is, the
maximum loss which might be incurred if the firm is deprived of these assets. Thus,
the value to the firm in most cases will be measured by the replacement cost,
given that replacement cost represents the amount of cash necessary to obtain the
equivalent or identical asset. If the replacement cost is greater than the net realizable
value and the discounted cash flow value, the value to the firm will be (1) the
discounted cash-flow if it is greater than net realizable value, given that it is preferable to use the asset rather than to sell it, and (2) the net realizable value if it is
greater than the discounted cash flow, given that it is preferable to sell the asset
rather than to use it.[21]

The Sandilands report also recommended that all holding gains and
losses be excluded from current-cost profit, which leads to the following
accounting actions:

1. All realized gains arising from the reevaluation of fixed assets (and stock, where
   applicable) should be shown in reevaluation reserves in the balance sheet.
2. Realized holding gains arising from fixed assets similarly should be included in
   movements in balance-sheet reserves.
3. The cost-of-sales adjustment (where applicable) should be moved to a balance-
   sheet "stock-adjustment reserve" whether it is positive or negative.
4. Extraordinary gains should be classed as "extraordinary items," which implies
   that they may be included in profit for the year, provided they are shown separately and distinguished from current-cost profit.
5. Operating gains should be shown "above the line" in the profit-and-loss account
   (earnings statement) as current-cost profit for the year.[22]

The report recommends also that a "summary statement of total gains
and losses for the year" appear immediately after the income statement.[23]
Such a summary statement may appear in the following manner:

| | |
|---|---|
| Current-cost profit after tax (as shown in profit-and-loss account) | £XXX |
| Extraordinary items less tax | XXX |
| Net profit after tax and extraordinary items | £XXX |

| | | |
|---|---|---|
| Movements in reevaluation reserve net of tax | | |
| Stock-adjustment reserve | £XXX | |
| Reevaluation reserves | | |
| Gain or loss due to change in bases or valuation of assets | | XXX |
| Other gains or losses | XXX | XXX |
| Total gain (loss) for the year after tax | | £XXX |

## Exposure Draft No. 18

In January 1976, following the publication of the Sandilands report, the accounting profession in the United Kingdom set up the Inflation Accounting Steering Group (IASG); their task was to produce an Exposure Draft based on the Sandilands report concerning CCA. The IASG published Exposure Draft No. 18 (ED 18), *Current Cost Accounting,* in November 1976.[24] Under ED 18, financial statements would include a profit-and-loss account, an appropriation account, a balance sheet, a statement of the change in net equity interest after allowing for the change in the value of money, and a statement of source and application of funds. The basic principles of ED 18 were the following:

1. The nonmonetary assets of the business should be shown in the balance sheet at their value to the business at the balance-sheet date.

2. Revenue should be charged with the depreciation of fixed assets calculated on their value to the business, and with the cost of stock consumed valued at its replacement cost at the date of sale.

3. Reevaluation surpluses, which arise mainly from the reevaluation of fixed assets and from the difference between the replacement cost and historical cost of stock consumed, should be credited in the first instance to the appropriate account.

4. Directors should appropriate out of reevaluation surpluses and, if necessary, out of current-cost profit, an amount based on their assessment of the needs of the business, including provisions for the effect of inflation on monetary items, gearing, and backlog depreciation.[25]

## The Hyde Guidelines

The response to ED 18 was critical. It was judged as too complex, too subjective, and too rapidly introduced. The Accounting Standards Committee decided to prepare simple guidelines to supplement the use of historical-cost results. The Hyde Guidelines were published on November 4, 1977, and recommended that financial results be amended by the following adjustments:

1. Depreciation was to be the difference between depreciation based on the current cost of fixed assets and the depreciation charged in computing the historical-cost result.

2. Cost of sales was to be an adjustment for the difference between the current cost of stock at the date of sale and the amount charged in computing the historical-cost result.

3. Gearing was to be treated in two ways: (a) if the total liabilities of a business exceeded its total monetary assets, so that part of its operating capacity effectively was financed by the net monetary liabilities, an adjustment should be made to reflect the extent to which the depreciation and cost-of-sales adjustment did not need to be provided in full from the current revenues of the business in showing the profit attributable to the shareholders; or (b) if the total monetary assets of a business exceeded its total liabilities, an adjustment should be made to reflect the increase in net monetary assets needed to maintain its scale of operation.[26]

### Exposure Draft No. 24

The Hyde Guidelines were found to be more acceptable to industry than the previous proposals. However, the IASG continued its work on a revised Exposure Draft concerning CCA that would be more acceptable to all interested parties. The result was the April 1979 publication of Exposure Draft No. 24 (ED 24), *Current Cost Accounting*.[27] Unlike ED 18 and the Sandilands report, ED 24 required only supplementary CCA statements. It also recommended the provision of a CCA profit-and-loss account and balance sheet.

### Statement of Standard Accounting Practice No. 16

Statement of Standard Accounting Practice No. 16 (SSAP 16) was published on March 31, 1980.[28] It does not differ materially from ED 24. Its objective was to guide users on such matters as the financial viability of a business; return on investment; pricing policy, cost control, and distribution decisions; and gearing. It provides for current-cost information, in addition to historical-cost information, to be included in annual financial statements. Current-cost information includes the following data:

1. Current-cost operating profit derived after adjustments for depreciation, cost of sales, and monetary working capital. The depreciation adjustment is the differ-

ence between the value to the business of the part of fixed assets consumed during the accounting period and the amount of depreciation charged on a historical basis. The cost-of-sales adjustment is the difference between the value to the business of stock consumed and the cost of stock charged on a historical basis. The monetary-working-capital adjustment represents the amount of additional (or reduced) finance needed for monetary working capital as a result of changes in the input prices of goods and services used and financed by the business.

2. A current-cost profit (after operations) attributable to shareholders derived after making a gearing adjustment. The gearing adjustment is calculated by first expressing net borrowing as a proportion of the net operating assets using average figures for the year from the current-cost balance sheets, and then multiplying the total charges or credits made to allow for the impact of price changes on the net operating assets of the business by the proportion determined at the first step.

3. A current-cost balance sheet with fixed assets and inventory at net current-replacement cost and a capital maintenance reserve to reflect reevaluation surpluses or deficits and adjustments made to allow for the impact of price changes in arriving at current-cost profit attributable to shareholders. The notes should describe the bases and methods adopted in preparing the accounts, particularly in relation to (a) the value to the business of fixed assets and the depreciation thereon, (b) the value to the business of stock and work in progress and the cost of sales adjustment, (c) the gearing adjustment, (d) the basis for translating foreign currencies and dealing with translation differences that arise, (e) other material adjustments to the historical-cost information, and (f) the corresponding amounts of the preceding items.

4. Current-cost earnings per share based on the current-cost profit attributable to equity shareholders before extraordinary items.[29]

Exhibits 5.4, 5.5, and 5.6 are examples of the presentation of current-cost accounts.

Under SSAP 16, the gearing adjustment basically measures the benefit accruing to common stockholders when the firm finances some of its assets through debt during an inflationary period. Paragraph 50 of the Standard computes the gearing adjustments in the following manner:

$$\frac{\text{(Net Borrowing) (Current-Cost Adjustment)}}{\text{(Net Operating Assets on a Current-Cost Basis)}}$$

Paragraph 45 of SSAP 16 defines *net borrowing* as the difference between the aggregate of all liabilities and provisions fixed in monetary terms (including convertibles) other than those included within monetary working capital and other than those that are, in substance, equity capital, and the aggregate of all current assets other than those subject to a cost-of-sales adjustment and those included within monetary working capital.

**Exhibit 5.4**
**Group Current-Cost Profit-and-Loss Account, ABC Limited and Subsidiaries, Year Ended December 31, 19X3 (in thousands)**

| | |
|---|---:|
| Turnover......................................... | 29,000 |
| | |
| Profit before interest and taxation on | |
| the historical cost basis..................... | 5,800 |
| Less: Current cost operating adjustment (Note 2)(a) | 3,020 |
| | |
| Current cost operating profit.................... | 2,780 |
| Gearing adjustment....................(332) | |
| Interest payable less receivable......_400_ | |
| | |
| .................................................... | 68 |
| | |
| Current cost profit before taxation.............. | 2,712 |
| Taxation......................................... | 1,460 |
| | |
| Current cost profit attributable to shareholders.. | 1,252 |
| Dividends........................................ | 860 |
| | |
| Retained current cost profit of the year.......... | 392 |
| | |
| Current cost earnings per share.................. | 20.80 |

Statement of retained profits/reserves

| | |
|---|---:|
| Retained current cost profit of the year.......... | 392 |
| Movements on current cost reserve (Note 4)(a)..... | 4,108 |
| Movements on other reserves...................... | NIL |

**Exhibit 5.4   (Continued)**

| | |
|---|---:|
| ..................................................... | 4,500 |
| Retained profits/reserves at the beginning | |
| of the year..................................... | <u>32,160</u> |
| | |
| Retained profits/reserves at the end of the year.. | 36,660 |

(a)   Notes are included as Exhibit 5.6.

From the information above, the gearing adjustment also can be computed as

$$GA = [NB/(INV + M + FA)][DP + C + W]$$

where
  $GA$ = gearing adjustment
  $NB$ = net borrowing
  $INV$ = inventory
  $M$ = monetary working capital
  $FA$ = fixed assets
  $DP$ = depreciation
  $C$ = cost-of-sales adjustment
  $W$ = monetary-working-capital adjustment

In effect, to be consistent with the physical capital maintenance concept and to facilitate the measurement of current-cost-accounting profit, SSAP 16 requires a monetary-working-capital adjustment. It consists of (a) trade debtors, prepayments, and trade bills receivable plus (b) stocks not subject to a cost-of-sales adjustment minus (c) trade creditors, accruals, and trade bills payable, and is computed as

$$W = M \times \text{Changes in } S$$

where
  $W$ = monetary-working-capital adjustment
  $M$ = monetary working capital
  $S$ = changes in specific prices relevant to the computation

The following rationale is offered in SSAP 16 for the inclusion of a monetary-working-capital adjustment:

**Exhibit 5.5**
**Summarized Group Current-Cost Balance Sheet, ABC Limited and Subsidiaries, December 31, 19X3 (in thousands)**

|  | £000 | £000 |
|---|---|---|
| Assets employed: ..................................... |  |  |
| Fixed assets (Note 3)(a).......................... |  | 39,060 |
| Net current assets: |  |  |
| Stock............................ | 8,000 |  |
| Monetary working capital.......... | 1,600 |  |
| Total working capital ............ | 9,600 |  |
| Proposed dividends ............... | (860) |  |
| Other current liabilities (Net).. | (1,140) |  |
| ................................... |  | 7,600 |
|  |  | 46,660 |
| Financed by: |  |  |
| Share capital and reserves: |  |  |
| Share capital .................... | 6,000 |  |
| Current cost reserve (Note 4)(a).. | 28,808 |  |
| Other reserves and retained profit | 7,852 |  |
| ................................... |  | 42,660 |
| Loan capital...................... |  | 4,000 |
| ................................... |  | 46,660 |

(a)   Notes are included as Exhibit 5.6.

Most businesses have other working capital besides stock (inventory) involved in their day-to-day operating activities. For example, when sales are made on credit the business has funds tied up in debtors. Conversely, if the suppliers of goods and services allow a period of credit, the amount of funds needed to support working capital is reduced. This monetary working capital is an integral part of the net operating assets of the business. Thus, the Standard provides for an adjustment in

**Exhibit 5.6**

**Notes to the Current-Cost Accounts, ABC Limited and Subsidiaries, Year Ended December 31, 19X3 (in thousands)**

1.  Explanatory notes:

    (see paragraph 58 of Statement of Standard Accounting Practice No. 16 and the example in the Guidance Notes to the Standard [see text Note 28])

2.  Adjustments made in deriving current cost operating profit:

| | 1983 |
|---|---|
| | £000 |
| Cost of sales | 920 |
| Monetary working capital | 200 |
| | |
| Working capital | 1,120 |
| Depreciation | 1,920 |
| | |
| Current cost operating adjustments | 3,020 |

3.  Fixed assets:

| | Gross | 31 Dec. 1983 Depreciation | Net | 1982 Net |
|---|---|---|---|---|
| | £000 | £000 | £000 | £000 |
| Land and buildings | 7,560 | 1,360 | 6,200 | 6,140 |
| Plant and machinery | 50,560 | 18,700 | 32,860 | 30,120 |
| | 58,120 | 20,060 | 39,060 | 36,260 |

4.  Current cost reserve

| | £000 | £000 | £000 |
|---|---|---|---|
| Balance at 1 January 1983 | | | 24,700 |

**Exhibit 5.6    (Continued)**

```
    Revaluation surpluses reflecting
     price changes:


         Land and buildings              400
         Plant and machinery           2,860
         Stocks and work in progress    980      4,240


    Monetary working capital adjustment          200
    Gearing adjustment                          (332)      4,108
                                                          28,808


                unrealized                                23,820
                                                          28,808
```

respect to monetary working capital when determining current cost operating profit. This adjustment should represent the amount of additional (or reduced) finance needed for monetary working capital as a result of changes in the input prices of goods and services used and financed by the business.[30]

SSAP 16 fails, however, to consider the requirement of the disclosure of purchasing-power gains or losses on holding monetary items and the measurement-unit problems in financial reporting. This last limitation is criticized by Bloom and Debessay:

Investors and other users of financial reports presumably make comparative trend analysis. Such time-series analysis can be facilitated by financial reports that are restated in a common unit of measurement, such as the constant dollars required by SFAS No. 33. Although the need for a constant unit of measure is acknowledged in SSAP No. 16, this standard did not call for such a measurement unit to reduce the complexity of implementing the new CCA standard (par. 37). The fact that SSAP No. 16 did not gain general acceptability has been attributed to its neglect of the measurement unit problem and to its failure to account properly for purchasing power gains on debt in an inflationary period.[31]

To add to its problems, SSAP 16 was downgraded in 1985 to a nonmandatory status preparatory to being replaced by a better standard.

## CANADIAN SOLUTION TO
## ACCOUNTING FOR INFLATION

The Canadian experiences with accounting for inflation are similar to the U.S. and British experiences, namely, a consideration of general-price-level accounting before an adoption of some form of current-value accounting. The general-price-level accounting phase in Canada is characterized by two developments. First, in December 1974, the Accounting Research Committee of the Canadian Institute of Chartered Accountants (CICA) published an accounting guideline, *Accounting for the Effects of Changes* in *the General Purchasing Power of Money*, suggesting that general-price-level accounting statements be presented on a supplementary basis.[32] The guideline was followed in July 1975 by the issuance of an Exposure Draft, *Accounting for Changes in the General Purchasing Power of Money,* which presented a detailed description of the procedures for producing general-price-level accounting statements.[33]

The current-value-accounting phase is characterized by the issuance of a discussion paper in 1976, an Exposure Draft in 1979, a Reexposure Draft in 1981, and, finally, a pronouncement in Section 4510 of the *CICA Handbook* titled "Reporting the Effects of Inflation," to be effective in 1983. Section 4510 of the *CICA Handbook* places primary emphasis on CCA.[34] In paragraph 4510A.9, it calls for the adoption of two capital-maintenance concepts:

Consideration was given to recommending that enterprises disclose supplementary data in a format that explicitly discloses income under different concepts of capital, but constraints of simplicity and understandability led the Committee to reject this approach. Instead, it concluded that sufficient information should be presented to enable users to make an assessment of income on a current-cost basis under both the operating concept of capital and under the financial concept of capital. Also, the Recommendations include specific requirements where management decides to report income attributable to common shareholders on a current cost basis under either of the two capital maintenance concepts.[35]

Like SFAS 33, Section 4510 of the *CICA Handbook* requires large, publicly traded companies to provide additional information with respect to the effects of inflation on the financial statements.

The basic supplementary information to be disclosed is as follows:

Supplementary information about the effects of changing prices should be included in the annual report that contains an enterprise's historical-cost financial statements.

Supplementary information about the effects of changing prices should disclose the following items:

1. The current-cost amounts of cost of goods sold and of depreciation, depletion, and amortization of property, plant, and equipment, or the amounts of the current-cost adjustments for those items

2. Current and deferred amounts of income-tax expense

3. Income before extraordinary items, after reflecting the above items

Supplementary information about the effects of changing prices should also disclose the following items:

1. The amount of the changes during the reporting period in the current-cost amounts of inventory and property, plant, and equipment, identifying the reduction from current cost to lower recoverable amount

2. The carrying value of inventory and property, plant, and equipment, on a current-cost basis at the end of the reporting period, identifying the reduction from current cost to lower recoverable amount

3. Net assets after restating inventory and property, plant, and equipment on a current-cost basis at the end of the reporting period[36]

An additional disclosure requirement from the *CICA Handbook* is that supplementary information about the effects of changing prices should disclose the amount of the financing adjustment, separately identifying the amount that would result if the financing adjustment were based on current-cost adjustments made to income for the period.[37]

When income attributable to common shareholders on a current-cost basis under an operating-capability concept of capital is disclosed, income on a current-cost basis should be adjusted by dividends on nonparticipating preferred shares and the financing adjustment. If an enterprise decides to exclude unrealized changes in current cost from income attributable to common shareholders, the amount of the financing adjustment would be based on the current-cost adjustments made to income for the period.[38]

According to the *CICA Handbook*, supplementary information about the effects of changing prices should disclose the following items:

1. The amount of the changes during the reporting period in the current-cost amounts of inventory and property, plant, and equipment that is attributable to the effects of general inflation

2. The amount of the gain or loss in general purchasing power that results from holding net monetary items during the reporting period[39]

Paragraphs B.33 and B.34 compute the Canadian financing or gearing adjustment as

$$\frac{\text{(Average net monetary liability for the year)}}{\text{(Current-cost adjustments)}}$$
$$\text{(Average net monetary liability and average common-shareholders'}$$
$$\text{equity on a current-cost basis)}$$

The net monetary liability is based on all liabilities, including current liabilities but not deferred taxes, as in the British gearing adjustment. The current-cost adjustments reflect cost of sales, depreciation, and depletion.

## THE NETHERLANDS' RESPONSE TO ACCOUNTING FOR INFLATION

The Dutch have been aware of current-value accounting for a long time. Accounting and business economics are considered to be closely related, which leads to a concern with the important notions of value and cost. The replacement value theory, known as the Limberg Theory, originates in the Netherlands. It integrates balance sheet valuation and income determination and views income as that portion of the increase in net assets of an enterprise that could be consumed without impairing the source of income of an entity in a continuous or going concern operation. Also, following the adoption of the Act Annual Account in 1971, a joint committee from the Federation of Enterprises, the trade unions and the Netherlands Institut Van Registraccountants (NIVRA), known as the Tripartite Study Group, recommended, among other things, the use of current value accounting.[40] No specific professional recommendation requiring the use of current value accounting was issued.[41] However, a large Dutch multinational called N.V. Philips has been experimenting with current value accounting for both financial and managerial accounting.[42] Basically, the application of the replacement value theory is integrated into the accounting system of all sections of the concern at every stage. All information for management is compiled in accordance with this principle, and thus the replacement value automatically enters into all management considerations and decisions. Basically, Philips uses a current value system with some general price level adjustment for monetary items. All accounts are adjusted every year on the basis of indexes developed by the purchasing department for fixed assets, the engineering department for internally produced machines, and the building design and plant engineering department for buildings; and increases (or decreases) in their values are credited to a revaluation account in equity. The major objective is to maintain intact the purchasing power of the company's net worth. Two actions are deemed necessary to reach that objective.

1. If a change in the price of internally manufactured products is caused by an internal technological price fall exceeding the general technological price fall, the difference — initially charged to the revaluation account as part of the total price difference — is transferred to a debit in the profit-and-loss statement.

2. In the case where monetary assets exceed monetary liabilities, the annual profit is charged with an amount equal to the percentage decrease in purchasing power applied to the difference. This is of great importance for profit determination in the inflationary countries.

## FRENCH RESPONSE TO ACCOUNTING FOR INFLATION

The French accounting system is governed by the Accounting Plan, which codifies generally accepted accounting standards and requires compliance by all firms. The plan is based, however, on historical-cost accounting.

In May 1976, the Delmas-Marsalet Report presented the recommendations of a working group to be integrated into the Seventh National Plan. The report suggested adopting a form of general-price-level-adjusted historical-cost accounting. This proposition was ignored in favor of a better notion of "value." This situation led to the French Finance Acts of 1977 and 1978, which decreed that balance-sheet items should be reevaluated as of December 31, 1976 by a coefficient of 1.4. Therefore, since 1977, depreciation is based on the reevaluated assets. This was a one-time reevaluation of fixed assets that was intended to reflect a *valeur d'utilité* (value in use) and has not yet been repeated. The value in use is basically the replacement cost of an identical asset.

Given that the revised accounting plan that came into effect in 1983 does not include any proposals for accounting for inflation, one may assume that the French government either does not have any intention of dealing with the issue or intends to deal with it in the future on an ad hoc basis.[43] The issue is far from forgotten, however. The executive committee of the *Orde des Experts Compatables* published a memorandum in February 1981 that suggested that French firms publish supplementary information on the effects of inflation and of changes in specific prices. This is basically in line with the provisions of the Fourth Directive of the European Economic Community that gives member states the option to permit or require forms of inflation accounting. An item of current cost reevaluation reserve in owners' equity is disclosed to indicate the aggregation of any differences between historical valuations and replacement-cost or current-market valuations.

## INTERNATIONAL RESPONSE TO
## ACCOUNTING FOR INFLATION

Various international organizations have taken positions regarding accounting for inflation and this section briefly deals with some of these actions as discussed in an article by Macharzina and Coenenberg.[44]

**1.** One instance is mentioned above, that the European Economic Community, through its Fourth Directive, gave the option to member states to experiment with forms of accounting for inflation.

**2.** In November 1981, the International Accounting Standards Committee (IASC) issued International Accounting Standard No. 15 (IAS 15), *Information Reflecting the Effects of Changing Prices.* IAS 15 requires disclosing, on a supplementary basis for economically significant entities, adjustments for the effects of changing prices on depreciation of fixed assets, cost of sales, and monetary items, and also disclosing the overall effect of the adjustments on the results for the period.

**3.** The U.N. Working Group of Experts on International Standards of Accounting and Reporting, in a 1977 report, *International Standards of Accounting and Reporting for Transnational Corporations,* calls for disclosure of accounting policies, including any asset-valuation bases. A similar motion was adopted by the Organization for Economic Cooperation and Development (OECD).

**4.** Supplementary general-price-level-adjusted accounting figures were mandated in Argentina in a 1972 pronouncement of the Argentine Technical Institute of Public Accountants and also in a 1980 regulation of the Argentine Professional Council of Economic Sciences of the Federal District.

**5.** In Belgium in 1976, a footnote disclosure of the current cost of inventories, fixed assets, cost of goods sold, and depreciation, as well as a revaluation account showing valuation differences was suggested by the *Royal Decree on Financial Statements of Enterprises.*

**6.** To deal with galloping domestic inflation, Brazilian accounting principles have always required some form of inflation adjustments for both tax and book purposes. General-price-level adjustments are required for both permanent assets and equity accounts on the basis of ORTN, a Brazilian government treasury-bond index. The tax code allows the deduction of the price-level-adjusted depreciation.

**7.** "Capital-maintenance statements" may be added to the basic financial statements in Germany as a result of a 1975 proposal, *Accounting for Capital Maintenance in the Measurement of Capital Profits* by the main technical committee (HFA) of the Institut der Wirtschaftsprüfer (IDW). The supplementary statement suggested is based in the following formula:

Additional Depreciation of Fixed Assets (Wasting Assets) — Amount Necessary to Maintain Inventory = Total of Necessary Adjustments (Inflationary Profits)

The inflationary profits are defined as the difference between the depreciation of fixed assets and cost of sales using the historical-cost and replacement-cost bases, less an adjustment for that part of the fixed assets and inventories that are not financed by equity capital.

## AN AUSTRALIAN SOLUTION

The Australian position relating to accounting for inflation is contained in the Australian Society of Accountants and the Institute of Chartered Accountants in Australia's Statement of Accounting Practice No. 1, *Current Cost Accounting*.[45] A physical-capital-maintenance concept is adopted and its stated objective is to ensure that, in regard to changes in specific prices, the results and resources of an entity are realistically measured so as to be of maximum value to users and assist management in optimizing its use of resources in cost control, in the determination of pricing policies, and in capital-raising decisions.

Under the Australian method, the assets and liabilities are assured to be measured on a current-cost or lower-recovery basis. The *lower-recovery basis* is defined as:

"Recoverable amount," in relation to an asset, means the net amount that is expected to be recovered:

(i) from the total cash inflows less the relevant cash outflows arising from its continued use; and/or

(ii) through its sales.[46]

A gearing adjustment is added to the CCA profit. Called *loan capital*, it is equal to the amount borrowed for financing the operating capability of an entity; the current portion of long-term debt is included while other current monetary liabilities are excluded.

## CONTROVERSIAL INFLATION ISSUES

### Treatment of Backlog Depreciation

Under CCA, depreciation expenses must be computed as the basis of replacement cost. Most proponents of replacement cost agree on the need to include added amounts in current expenses as a "catch-up," "make-up," or "backlog" depreciation if the replacement costs continue to increase over the useful life of the asset. To illustrate the argument for backlog depreciation, assume a firm purchases an asset with a 4-year useful life for $2,000 and its replacement cost increases $1,000. Determination of the "backlog" depreciation is shown in the following schedule:

| YEAR | 1 | 2 | 3 | 4 |
|---|---|---|---|---|
| Year-end replacement cost | $3,000 | $4,000 | $5,000 | $6,000 |
| Depreciation expense based on replacement cost | 750 | 1,000 | 1,250 | 1,500 |
| Backlog Depreciation | -- | 250 | 500 | 750 |
| Opening accumulated depreciation | -- | 750 | 2,000 | 3,750 |
| Adjusted accumulated depreciation | $ 750 | $2,000 | $3,750 | $6,000 |

Thus, the accounting entries in each year would be:

Year 1:

| Asset (replacement cost) | $1,000 | |
| Depreciation | 750 | |
| Holding Gain | | $1,000 |
| Accumulated Depreciation | | 750 |

Year 2:

| Asset (replacement cost) | 1,000 | |
| Depreciation | 1,000 | |
| Backlog Depreciation | 250 | |
| Holding Gain | | 1,000 |
| Accumulated Depreciation | | 1,250 |

Year 3:

|  | | |
|---|---|---|
| Asset (replacement cost) | 1,000 | |
| Depreciation | 1,250 | |
| Backlog Depreciation | 500 | |
| Holding Gain | | 1,000 |
| Accumulated Depreciation | | 1,750 |

Year 4:

|  | | |
|---|---|---|
| Asset (replacement cost) | 1,000 | |
| Depreciation | 1,500 | |
| Backlog Depreciation | 750 | |
| Holding Gain | | 1,000 |
| Accumulated Depreciation | | 2,250 |

If, however, we assume that the value of the asset increases uniformly over the year, then the depreciation expense should be computed on the basis of the average current entry price for the year. The entries for the first year result from the fact that depreciation expense is $625 (25% of the average asset value of $2,500) and that the holding gain will be $875 ($1,000 less one-half year depreciation on the $1,000 increase). Accordingly, the entries for each year would appear as follows:

Year 1:

|  | | |
|---|---|---|
| Asset (replacement cost) | $1,000 | |
| Depreciation | 625 | |
| Holding Gain | | $ 875 |
| Accumulated Depreciation | | 750 |

Year 2:

|  | | |
|---|---|---|
| Asset (replacement cost) | 1,000 | |
| Depreciation (0.25 * $3,500) | 875 | |
| Holding Gain | | 625 |
| Accumulated Depreciation | | 1,250 |

Year 3:

|  | | |
|---|---|---|
| Asset (replacement cost) | 1,000 | |
| Depreciation (0.25 * $5,500) | 1,125 | |

```
        Holding Gain                              375

        Accumulated Depreciation               1,750


Year 4:

     Asset (replacement cost)          1,000

     Depreciation (0.25 * $5,500)      1,375

          Holding Gain                              725

          Accumulated Depreciation             2,250
```

Three methods have been suggested to account for backlog depreciation: (1) charge or credit to retained earnings, (2) charge or credit to current income, and (3) adjust holding gains and losses by the amount of backlog depreciation.

The first method, in which backlog depreciation is charged or credited to retained earnings, treats backlog depreciation as a prior-period adjustment because it represents the amount that should have been charged in previous periods for the replacement of the asset.

The second method treats backlog depreciation as an expense of the current period in that income should be charged with all of the estimated costs of replacing assets. In support of this method, Bloom and Debessay make the following argument:

By segregating the backlog from the current period depreciation expense, the income statement can be readily modified by the user to reflect a more suitable matching of current costs against current revenues. Backlog is not a current period expense. Additionally, inclusion of backlog in the income statement should put users on notice that cash flows from operations ought to be reduced by backlog funding.[47]

The third method argues that the true holding gain or loss should reflect the age of the asset.

Backlog depreciation has not been accepted universally. One argument against backlog provisions is that they are unnecessary if the firm has a regular asset-replacement pattern and bases depreciation on the current cost of the asset at the end of the period. One example of this argument was made in 1976:

Catch-up additions to current expenses are unnecessary as long as an enterprise regularly replaces assets. Thus if the enterprise . . . has five assets instead of one and replaces on the average one each period, current depreciation expense for each period equals the replacement cost of the asset being replaced, and that is all that is required to maintain productive capacity in a going concern.[48]

A second argument, made by Cynther, is that backlog depreciation is unnecessary if the firm uses a comprehensive current-cost model that includes current-cost adjustments both for monetary working capital and nonmonetary items. Basically, if the firm reinvests the funds from accumulated depreciation in nonmonetary assets, this will result in a higher depreciation expense that reduces distributable income. Similarly, if the firm reinvests the funds from accumulated depreciation in monetary assets, a holding loss is recognized in the monetary-working-capital adjustment that will reduce the distributable income.[49] Bell emphasizes the same point:

The argument is that if accumulated depreciation allowances are put into goods, the value of the assets they go into will, of course, keep up with [price changes for the goods] but if they are put into monetary assets the "holding loss" (as measured by the value of physical assets of the firm) debit against revenues must be credited to the capital maintenance reserve account and in this way backlog depreciation gets into the system by the back door since monetary assets equal to backlog depreciation are retained initially in the firm with the corresponding credit being to the capital maintenance reserve.[50]

## Accounting for Holding Gains and Losses

The valuation of assets and liabilities at entry prices gives rise to holding gains and losses as entry prices change during the period of time they are held or owed by a firm. Holding gains and losses may be divided into two elements: (1) the realized holding gains and losses that correspond to the items sold or to the liabilities discharged, and (2) the nonrealized holding gains and losses that correspond to the items still held or to the liabilities owed at the end of the reporting period. These holding gains and losses may be classified as capital adjustments, because they measure the additional elements of income that must be retained to maintain the existing productive capacity. They also may be classified as income when capital maintenance is viewed solely in monetary terms. Thus, justification for the holding gains and losses on capital adjustment may be related to a particular definition of income.

Proponents of the capital-adjustment alternative favor a definition of income based on the preservation of physical capital. Such an approach would define the profit of an entity for a given period as the maximum amount that could be distributed and still maintain the operating capability at the level that existed at the beginning of the period. Because the changes in replacement cost cannot be distributed without impairing the operating capability of the entity, this approach dictates that replacement-cost changes be classified as capital adjustment.

Proponents of the other alternative favor a definition of income based on the preservation of financial capital (the money-maintenance concept). Such an approach would define profit as the maximum amount that could be distributed and still maintain the financial capital invested at the level that existed at the beginning of the period. Such an approach dictates that replacement-cost changes be classified as holding gains and losses. The academic literature provides two alternative arguments in support of the holding-gains treatment. The first argument is that holding gains represent a "realizable cost savings" in the sense that the entity is better off because it would now cost more to acquire the asset. The second argument is that replacement-cost changes may be viewed as "surrogates" for changes in net realizable value or capitalized value. Thus, the holding gains represent increases in the expected net receipts from using or selling the asset in the future.

## Currency Translation in Inflationary Environments

### Official Pronouncements

A problem arises when a firm consolidates the financial statements of foreign affiliates from inflationary environments. The problem is how to treat the effects of changes in the exchange rate and the effects of changes in the specific and general price levels on the financial statements of foreign affiliates simultaneously. The first option advocated is just to restate the foreign-account balances to reflect the changes in the general price level of the foreign country, then translate the adjusted amounts to their domestic-currency equivalent. This option is known as the *restate-translate* option. Choi and Mueller report on the advantages of the restate-translate option in the following manner:

1. It enables statement readers to assess ordinary operating results in terms of the local currency as well as the separate effects of inflation on these results.

2. It enables management to gauge better the performance of a subsidiary after providing for the "maintenance" of the subsidiary's financial assets.

3. It enables management to evaluate the performance of a subsidiary in terms of the environment in which the subsidiary's assets are domiciled.

4. It enables management to ascertain the full effect of any currency devaluation on a subsidiary's operating results if devaluation occurs.[51]

The limitations of this method include the facts that the end results reflect units measured in terms of different purchasing power and the end results count the effects of inflation twice, given that exchange rates reflect the effects of inflation.

The second option advocated is first to translate the foreign-account balances to the domestic currency of the parent arrays, then adjust for the general-price-level changes equivalents. Advantages of this method include the ease of computation, and the use of a single standard of measurement, which is dollars of domestic purchasing power.[52]

The use of one method versus the other results in significant differences in the consolidated results. In any case, the currency-translation problem related to inflation was not solved by either SFAS 33 or SFAS 52. In 1982, appropriate modifications were introduced by SFAS 70.[53]

The requirements of SFAS 70 are illustrated in Exhibit 5.7. There are basically two requirements of SFAS 70. In the first, if the U.S. dollar is the functional currency, the requirements of SFAS 33 apply and no other

**Exhibit 5.7**
**Restatement Methodology for Foreign Operations as Given by SFAS 70**

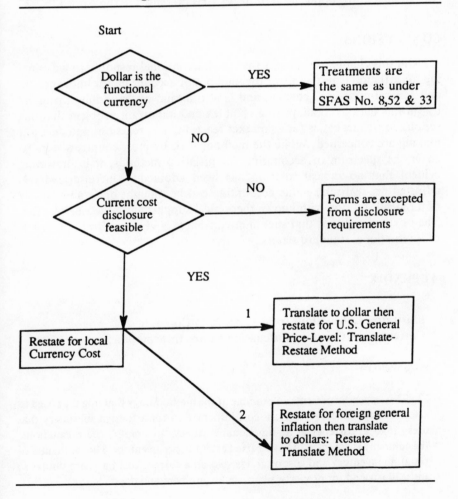

disclosures are required. In the second, if the U.S. dollar is not the functional currency, two situations arise:

*Situation 1.* If the firms measuring their operations in functional currencies other than the dollar have historical-cost/constant-dollar disclosure, they are exempted from disclosures.

*Situation 2.* If current-cost disclosures are feasible, then the financial statements are first restated to current cost before either a translate-restate or a restate-translate option is chosen. Under the translate-restate option, the current costs are translated to dollars, then restated to the U.S. general price level. Under the restate-translate option, the current costs are restated for foreign general inflation, then translated to dollars.

An example of the application of SFAS 70 is presented in the Appendix.

## CONCLUSIONS

From this chapter, it appears that the international response to accounting for inflation is just a mix of the methods of accounting for both specific and general-price-level changes and is also a kind of "muddling through" by various nations to adapt to a complex and important problem that has serious consequences as far as market reaction, user reaction, and decision making are concerned. While the methods used by most countries seem to cover the spectrum of accounting for inflation methods, it is, however, evident that no radical solution has been adopted. General-price-level-adjusted net-realizable-value accounting can be thought of as an example of a radical solution with known theoretical support and practical benefits. The obvious reality is that such innovativeness is very far from the minds of international standard setters.

## APPENDIX

### Illustrative Calculations from SFAS 70 to Compute Current-Cost/Constant-Purchasing-Power Information

#### Introduction

22. This appendix presents an example of the methodology that might be used to calculate supplementary current cost information for a foreign subsidiary that uses the local currency as its functional currency. To simplify the calculations, the company is assumed to have a fixed asset but no inventory. The mechanics of restating inventory and cost of goods sold on a current cost basis are similar to those illustrated for property, plant, and equipment and depreciation.

23. The methodology used in this example is essentially the same as that illustrated in Appendix E of Statement 33. The major adaptation needed to accommodate the functional currency concept is first to measure not only current cost amounts but also increases or decreases therein for the foreign subsidiary in its local currency and then to translate those amounts into U.S. dollar equivalents in accordance with Statement 52. The effect of general inflation may be measured either (a) after translation and based on the U.S. CPI(U) or (b) before translation and based on the local price index. To prepare consolidated supplementary information, dollar equivalent amounts determined in accordance with either (a) or (b) would be aggregated with dollar equivalent amounts computed in a similar fashion for other subsidiaries with foreign functional currencies and dollar amounts for operations for which the U.S. dollar is the functional currency. Statement 33 (paragraph 27) encourages presentation of information by segments of business enterprises, and it may be helpful to present foreign operations separately.

24. Throughout this illustration, CFC indicates constant functional currency amounts, and CFC$ indicates the translated dollar equivalents of CFC amounts. Nominal functional currency is indicated by FC, and C$E indicates dollar equivalents of FC amounts restated by the U.S. index.

**Assumptions**

25. The functional currency financial statements of Sub Company appear below:

**Sub Company**
**Historical Cost FC Balance Sheets**

|  | December 31 | |
|---|---|---|
|  | 1982 | 1981 |
| Cash | FC2,550 | FC1,250 |
| Equipment | 2,500 | 2,500 |
| Accumulated depreciation | 750 | 500 |
| Net equipment | 1,750 | 2,000 |
| Total assets | FC4,300 | FC3,250 |
| Current liabilities | FC 600 | FC 500 |
| Long-term debt | 2,000 | 1,500 |
| Total liabilities | 2,600 | 2,000 |
| Capital stock | 500 | 500 |
| Retained earnings | 1,200 | 750 |
| Total equity | 1,700 | 1,250 |
| Total liabilities and equity | FC4,300 | FC3,250 |

**Sub Company**
**Historical Cost FC Statement of Income and Retained Earnings**
**Year Ending December 31, 1982**

| | |
|---|---:|
| Revenue | FC5,000 |
| | |
| Salaries | 2,500 |
| General and administrative expenses | 1,000 |
| Depreciation | 250 |
| Interest | 350 |
| | 4,100 |
| | |
| Income before taxes | 900 |
| Income taxes | 450 |
| | |
| Net income | 450 |
| Retained earnings—beginning of year | 750 |
| | |
| Retained earnings—end of year | FC1,200 |

26. The fixed asset was acquired on December 31, 1979. It is depreciated on a straight-line basis over 10 years and is expected to have no salvage value. There were no acquisitions or disposals of assets during the year.

27. Exchange rates between the functional currency and the dollar are:

| | |
|---|---|
| December 31, 1981 | FC1 = $1.20 |
| Average 1982 | FC1 = $1.10 |
| December 31, 1982 | FC1 = $1.00 |

28. Management has measured the current cost of equipment at December 31, 1981 and 1982 as follows:

| | 1982 | 1981 |
|---|---|---|
| Current cost | FC5,500 | FC4,000 |
| Accumulated depreciation | (1,650) | (800) |
| Net current cost | FC3,850 | FC3,200 |

The "net recoverable amount" has been determined to be in excess of net current cost at both dates.

29. Current cost equity in nominal FC at the beginning and end of the year may be computed by adding net monetary items and net property, plant, and equipment at current cost. To determine current cost equity in nominal dollars, those FC amounts are translated at the appropriate exchange rate:

| | December 31 | | | | | |
| | 1982 | | | 1981 | | |
| | | Exchange | | | Exchange | |
| | FC | Rate | $ | FC | Rate | $ |
|---|---|---|---|---|---|---|
| Monetary items (par. 25): | | | | | | |
| Cash | FC2,550 | $1 | $2,550 | FC1,250 | $1.20 | $1,500 |
| Current liabilities | (600) | $1 | (600) | (500) | $1.20 | (600) |
| Long-term debt | (2,000) | $1 | (2,000) | (1,500) | $1.20 | (1,800) |
| Net monetary liabilities | FC (50) | | $ (50) | FC (750) | | $ (900) |
| | | | | | | |
| Equipment—net (par. 28) | FC3,850 | $1 | $3,850 | FC3,200 | $1.20 | $3,840 |
| | | | | | | |
| Equity at current cost | FC3,800 | | $3,800 | FC2,450 | | $2,940 |

30. The U.S. and local general price level indexes are:

| | Local | U.S. |
|---|---|---|
| December 1981 | 144 | 281.5 |
| Average 1982 | 158 | 292.5* |
| December 1982 | 173 | 303.5* |

---

*Assumed for illustrative purposes.

## The Translate-Restate Method

31. To apply the translate-restate method, amounts measured in nominal FC are first translated into their dollar equivalents. Changes in those dollar equivalent amounts are then restated to reflect the effects of U.S. inflation.

### Current Cost Depreciation and Income from Continuing Operations

32. The first step is to determine current cost depreciation for the year as follows:

| | |
|---|---|
| Current cost—beginning of year | FC4,000 |
| Current cost—end of year | 5,500 |
| | 9,500 |
| ÷ | 2 |
| Average current cost, gross | FC4,750 |

Current cost depreciation expense for the year measured in average 1982 CFC is CFC475 (FC4,750 × 10%). Computation of current cost depreciation and income from continuing operations does not involve use of a general price level index if measurements are made in average-for-the-year currency units. Accordingly, reported current cost depreciation under the translate-restate method is $523 (FC475 × $1.10).

33. Income from continuing operations on a current cost basis measured in average 1982 CFC is computed by simply replacing historical cost depreciation in income from continuing operations in the primary financial statements with the current cost amount. Accordingly, current cost income from continuing operations measured in average 1982 CFC is:

Net income + historical cost depreciation − current cost depreciation
= income from continuing operations

FC450 (par. 25) + FC250 (par. 25) − FC475 (par. 32) = $\underline{\underline{CFC225}}$

Reported current cost income from continuing operations under the translate-restate method is C$E248 (CFC225 × $1.10).

### Excess of Increase in Specific Prices over Increase in General Price Level

34. The second step is to compute the change in the current cost of equipment and the effect of the increase in the general price level. To measure the increase in current cost of equipment in nominal FC dollar equivalents, the effect of the exchange rate change must be excluded (paragraphs 60-62). One way to accomplish that is to translate the 12/31/81 and 12/31/82 FC current cost amounts to dollar equivalents at the average exchange rate and then restate those dollar amounts to average 1982 constant dollar equivalents:

| | Current Cost/FC | Exchange Rate | Current Cost/$ | Conversion Factor | Current Cost/C$E |
|---|---|---|---|---|---|
| Current cost, net— 12/31/81 (par. 28) | FC3,200 | $1.10 | $3,520 | $\frac{292.5(\text{Avg.1982})}{281.5(\text{Dec.1981})}$ | C$E3,658 |
| Depreciation | (475) | $1.10 | (523) | • | (523) |
| Current cost, net— 12/31/82 (par. 28) | 3,850 | $1.10 | 4,235 | $\frac{292.5(\text{Avg.1982})}{303.5(\text{Dec.1982})}$ | 4,081 |
| Increase in current cost | FC1,125 | | ,$1,238 | | C$E 946 |

*Assumed to be in average 1982 C$E.

The inflation component of the increase in current cost amount is the difference between the nominal dollar and the constant dollar equivalent amounts:

| | |
|---|---|
| Increase in current cost ($) | $1,238 |
| Increase in current cost (C$E) | C$E 946 |
| Inflation component | 292 |

## Purchasing Power Gain or Loss on Net Monetary Items

35. The third step is to compute the purchasing power gain or loss on net monetary items. Under the translate-restate method, the translated beginning and ending net monetary liabilities are restated to average 1982 dollars. The U.S. purchasing power gain is then the balancing amount:

| | FC | Exchange Rate | $ |
|---|---|---|---|
| Net monetary liabilities— 12/31/81 (par. 29) | FC750 | $1.20 | $900 |
| Net monetary liabilities— 12/31/82 (par. 29) | 50 | $1.00 | 50 |
| Decrease during the year | FC700 | | $850 |

| | $ | Conversion Factor | C$E |
|---|---|---|---|
| Net monetary liabilities 12/31/81 | $900 | $\dfrac{292.5(\text{Avg. }1982)}{281.5(\text{Dec. }1981)}$ | C$E935 |
| Decrease during the year | (850) | * | (850) |
| Net monetary liabilities 12/31/82 | $ 50 | $\dfrac{292.5(\text{Avg. }1982)}{303.5(\text{Dec. }1982)}$ | 48 |
| Purchasing power gain | | | C$E 37 |

*Assumed to be in average 1982 C$E.

The above computation is the same as that used to compute the purchasing power gain or loss on net monetary items under the original translate-restate provisions of Statement 33. In some circumstances, that procedure will include a part of the effect of exchange rate changes on net monetary items in the purchasing power gain or loss. A more theoretically correct computation that would completely exclude the effect of exchange rate changes would be to compute a separate purchasing power gain or loss for each functional currency operation in a manner similar to that illustrated in paragraph 34 for the increase in specific prices. For the example, that alternative method produces a purchasing power gain of $34:

| | FC | Average Exchange Rate | $ | Conversion Factor | C$E |
|---|---|---|---|---|---|
| Net monetary liabilities— 12/31/81 (par. 29) | FC750 | $1.10 | $825 | 292.5 (Avg. 1982) / 281.5 (Dec. 1981) | C$E857 |
| Decrease during the year | (700) | $1.10 | 770 | * | (770) |
| Net monetary liabilities— 12/31/82 (par. 29) | FC50 | $1.10 | $ 55 | 292.5 (Avg. 1982) / 303.5 (Dec. 1982) | 53 |
| Purchasing power gain | | | | | C$E34 |

*Assumed to be in average 1982 C$E.

However, the first procedure illustrated is less costly because it can be applied on a consolidated basis, and it generally provides a reasonable approximation. Accordingly, that method is acceptable.

**Reconciliation of Equity**

36. Although neither Statement 33 nor this Statement requires disclosure of a reconciliation of equity, such a reconciliation serves as a check of the calculations and is a convenient way to compute the translation adjustment:

Equity at 12/31/81 in average 1982 C$
  $2,940 (par. 29) x 292.5/281.5                                C$3,055

Income from continuing operations
  (par. 33)                                  C$E248
Purchasing power gain (par. 35)                 37
Excess of increase in specific prices over
  increase in general price level (par. 34)    946
Translation adjustment (par. 37)              (624)
Increase in equity in terms of U.S.
  purchasing power                                               607

                                                              C$3,662

Equity at 12/31/82 in average 1982 C$
  $3,800 (par. 29) x 292.5/303.5                                C$3,662

*Translation Adjustment*

37. The translation adjustment is the amount needed to balance the reconciliation of equity. The translation adjustment determined under the translate-restate method may be checked by translating the beginning- and end-of-year equity on a C$ basis into FC amounts and using those FC amounts in a calculation similar to that illustrated in **paragraph 61 of Appendix B**:

| | CS | Exchange Rate | FC |
|---|---|---|---|
| Equity at 12/31/81 in average 1982 C$ (par. 36) | C$3,055 | $0.833* | FC2,545 |
| Equity at 12/31/82 in average 1982 C$ (par. 36) | 3,662 | $1.00 | 3,662 |
| Increase in equity | C$ 607 | | FC1,117 |

| | | |
|---|---|---|
| Restated opening equity | | FC2,545 |
| Exchange rate change during 1982 ($1.20 − $1.00) | × | (.20) |
| | | $ (509) |
| Plus increase in equity | | FC1,117 |
| Difference between ending exchange rate and average rate for 1982 ($1.10 − $1.00) | × | (.10) |
| | | $ (112) |
| Translation adjustment | | $ (621) |

*IFC ÷ $1.20 = $0.833.

The difference of $3 ($624 − $621) between the translation adjustment computed above and the translation adjustment that appears in paragraph 36 reflects the $3 difference ($37 − $34) between the short-cut and theoretically correct procedures illustrated in paragraph 35.

**The Restate-Translate Method**

38. To apply the restate-translate method, the steps illustrated in paragraphs 31-35 are followed except that all restatements to reflect the effects of general inflation are made before translation to dollar equivalents and using the local general price level index.

**Current Cost Depreciation and Income from Continuing Operations**

39. Current cost depreciation and income from continuing operations are CFC475 and CFC225, respectively, as determined in paragraphs 32 and 33.

**Purchasing Power Gain or Loss on Net Monetary Items**

40. To apply the restate-translate method, the FC amount of net monetary items at the beginning of the year, changes in the net monetary items, and the amount at the end of the year are restated into average 1982 CFC. The purchasing power gain or loss on net monetary items is then the balancing item:

| | FC | Conversion Factor | CFC |
|---|---|---|---|
| Net monetary liabilities 12/31/81 (par. 29) | FC750 | 158 (Avg.1982) / 144 (Dec.1981) | CFC823 |
| Decrease during the year | (700) | * | (700) |
| Net monetary liabilities 12/31/82 (par. 29) | FC 50 | 158 (Avg.1982) / 173 (Dec.1982) | 46 |
| Purchasing power gain | | | CFC 77 |

*Assumed to be in average 1982 CFC.

**Excess of Increase in Specific Prices over Increase in General Price Level**

41. Under the restate-translate method, the local index is used to restate the beginning and ending current cost/FC amounts into average 1982 CFC:

| | Current Cost/FC | Conversion Factor | Current/ Cost/CFC |
|---|---|---|---|
| Current cost, net—12/31/81 | FC3,200 | 158 (Avg.1982) / 144 (Dec.1981) | CFC3,511 |
| Depreciation | (475) | * | (475) |
| Current cost, net—12/31/82 | (3,850) | 158 (Avg.1982) / 173 (Dec.1982) | (3,516) |
| Increase in current cost | FC1,125 | | CFC 480 |

*Assumed to be in average 1982 CFC.

The inflation component of the increase in current cost amount is the difference between the nominal functional currency and constant functional currency amounts:

|                                    |              |
|------------------------------------|-------------:|
| Increase in current cost (FC)      |     FC1,125  |
| Increase in current cost (CFC)     |     CFC 480  |
| Inflation component                |         645  |

## Reconciliation of Equity

42. As with the translate-restate method, a reconciliation of equity acts as a check of the calculations. A reconciliation of equity also is a convenient point at which to translate the functional currency amounts determined in the preceding paragraphs into dollar equivalents and is a convenient way to compute the translation and parity adjustments.

43. If opening and closing equity are restated to average 1982 CFC using the local index, the reconciliation of equity under the restate-translate method would be:

|  | CFC | Exchange Rate | CFC$ |
|---|---:|---:|---:|
| Equity at 12/31/81 in average 1982 CFC FC2,450 (par. 29) × 158/144 | CFC2,688 | 1.20 | CFC$3,225 |
| Income from continuing operations (par. 39) | 225 | 1.10 | 248 |
| Purchasing power gain (par. 40) | 77 | 1.10 | 85 |
| Excess of increase in specific prices over increase in general price level (par. 41) | 480 | 1.10 | 528 |
| Translation adjustment (par. 44) | | | (616) |
| | CFC3,470 | | CFC$3,470 |
| Equity at 12/31/82 in average 1982 CFC FC3,800 (par. 29) × 158/173 | CFC3,470 | 1.00 | CFC$3,470 |

### *Translation Adjustment*

44. The translation adjustment is the amount needed to balance the CFC$ reconciliation of equity. The adjustment may be computed as (a) the change in exchange rates during the period multiplied by the restated amount of net assets at the beginning of the period plus (b) the difference between the average exchange rate for the period and the end-of-period exchange rate multiplied by

the increase or decrease in restated net assets for the period. Accordingly, the translation adjustment under the restate-translate method is:

| | |
|---|---:|
| Restated opening equity (par. 43) | CFC2,688 |
| Exchange rate change during 1982 ($1.20 − $1.00) | ×_____(.20) |
| | $ (538) |
| Plus (equity at 12/31/82 minus equity at | |
| 12/31/81 = 3,470 − 2,688) | CFC  782 |
| Difference between ending exchange | |
| rate and average rate for 1982 ($1.10 − $1.00) | ×_____(.10) |
| | (78) |
| Translation adjustment | $ (616) |

### Parity Adjustment

45. The reconciliation of equity in paragraph 43, in which beginning-of-year and end-of-year equity are stated in average 1982 CFC, is needed to calculate the translation adjustment in CFC$. However, beginning-of-year and end-of-year equity and the increase in equity must be stated in average 1982 constant dollars in the supplementary current cost information. Beginning-of-year and end-of-year equity in average 1982 constant dollars are C$3,055 and C$3,662, respectively, as computed in paragraph 36. The overall increase in U.S. purchasing power for the year thus is C$3,662 − C$3,055 = C$607. The difference between that amount and the increase of CFC$245 (CFC$3,470 − CFC$3,225) that appears in the reconciliation of equity in paragraph 43 is the parity adjustment needed to adjust the ending net investment and the increase in the net investment to measures in average 1982 constant dollars (paragraph 74). Accordingly, the parity adjustment is C$607 − CFC$245 = C$362. That amount represents (a) the effect of the difference between local and U.S. inflation from 12/31/81 to average for 1982 on the restatement of opening equity to average units plus (b) the effect of the difference between local and U.S. inflation from average for 1982 to 12/31/82 on the restatement of ending nominal dollar equity to average units:

| | |
|---|---:|
| Equity at 12/31/81 (par. 29) | $ 2,940 |
| Difference between local and | |
| U.S. inflation from 12/31/81 | |
| to average 1982 (158/144 − 292.5/281.5) | × 0.0581 |
| | $   171 |
| Plus equity at 12/31/82 (par. 29) | $ 3,800 |
| Difference between U.S. and | |
| local inflation from average 1982 to | |
| 12/31/82 (292.5/303.5 − 158/173) | × 0.0504 |
| | $   191 |
| Parity adjustment | $   362 |

For display purposes, the parity adjustment is combined with the $(616) translation adjustment (paragraph 43). Accordingly, the net translation adjustment disclosed in the supplementary current cost information prepared using the restate-translate method would be $(616) + $362 = $(254). The components of current cost information based on the restate-translate method thus would be:

| | | |
|---|---|---|
| Beginning-of-year equity | | C$3,055 |
| | | |
| Income from continuing operations | CFC$248 | |
| Purchasing power gain | 85 | |
| Excess of increase in specific prices over increase in general price level | 528 | |
| Translation and parity adjustments | (254) | |
| Increase in equity in terms of U.S. purchasing power | | 607 |
| | | |
| End-of-year equity | | C$3,662 |

*Source:* Financial Accounting Standards Board, *Financial Reporting and Changing Prices: Foreign Currency Translation, An Amendment of FASB Statement No. 33,* Statement of Financial Accounting Standard No. 70 (Norwalk, CT: FASB, 1982), par. 9. Copyright by Financial Accounting Standards Board, 401 Merritt 7, P.O. Box 5116, Norwalk, CT, 06856-5116, U.S.A. Reprinted with permission. Copies of the complete document are available from the FASB.

## NOTES

1. Committee on Accounting Procedure, *Depreciation and High Costs*, Accounting Research Bulletin No. 33 (New York: AICPA, December 1947); Committee on Accounting Procedure, letter to AICPA members affirming the recommendations of Accounting Research Bulletin No. 33, October 1948; and Committee on Accounting Procedure, *Restatement and Revision of Accounting Research Bulletins,* Accounting Research Bulletin No. 43 (New York: AICPA, June 1953), chap. 9, sect. A, "Depreciation and High Costs."

2. Accounting Principles Board, *Status of Accounting Research Bulletins,* APB Opinion No. 6 (New York: AICPA, 1965).

3. American Institute of Certified Public Accountants, *Reporting the Financial Effects of Price-Level Changes*, Accounting Research Study No. 6 (New York: AICPA, 1963).

4. Accounting Principles Board, *Financial Statements Restated for General Price-Level Changes,* APB Statement No. 3 (New York: AICPA, June 1969).

5. Financial Accounting Standards Board, *Reporting the Effects of General Price-Level Changes in Financial Statements*, Discussion Memorandum (Stamford, CT: FASB, February 15, 1974).

6. Financial Accounting Standards Board, *Financial Reporting in Units of General Purchasing Power,* Exposure Draft (Stamford, CT: FASB, December 31, 1974).

7. Financial Accounting Standards Board, *Field Tests of Financial Reporting in*

*Units of General Purchasing Power,* Research Report (Stamford, CT: FASB, May 1977).

8. Financial Accounting Standards Board, *Financial Reporting and Changing Prices,* Exposure Draft (Stamford, CT: FASB, December 28, 1978).

9. Financial Accounting Standards Board, *Constant Dollar Accounting,* Exposure Draft (Stamford, CT: FASB, March 2, 1979).

10. Financial Accounting Standards Board, *Financial Reporting and Changing Prices,* Statement of Financial Accounting Standard No. 33 (Stamford, CT: FASB, September 1979).

11. Ibid., pars. 47–48.

12. Ibid., pars. 29, 30, 35, 51, and 52.

13. Ibid., pars. 9, 11, 12, 14, 17, 20, and 22.

14. Ibid., pars. 1–2.

15. Several Financial Accounting Standards Board pronouncements dealing with specific situations have been issued by the FASB subsequent to SFAS 33. These include SFAS 39, *Financial Reporting and Changing Prices: Specialized Assets—Mining and Oil and Gas,* October 1980; SFAS 40, *Financial Reporting and Changing Prices: Specialized Assets—Timberlands and Growing Timber,* November 1980; SFAS 41, *Real Estate,* November 1980; and SFAS 46, *Financial Reporting and Changing Prices: Motion Picture Films,* March 1981.

16. Financial Accounting Standards Board, *Financial Reporting and Changing Prices,* Statement of Financial Accounting Standard No. 89 (Stamford, CT: FASB, 1986).

17. Ibid.. par. 10.

18. Ibid., par. 15.

19. Institute of Chartered Accountants in England and Wales, *Accounting for Changes in the Purchasing Power of Money,* Exposure Draft No. 8 (November 1972).

20. Accounting Standards Committee, *Accounting for Changes in the Purchasing Power of Money,* Statement of Standard Accounting Practice No. 7 (1972).

21. C. A. Westwick, "The Lessons to Be Learned from the Development of Inflation Accounting in the U.K.," *Accounting and Business Research* (Autumn 1980): 354–373.

22. F. E. P. Sandilands, *Reporting of the Inflation Accounting Committee,* No. 6225 (London: Her Majesty's Stationery Office, Reg. 6225, September 1975), par. 621.

23. Ibid., par. 10.

24. Inflation Account Steering Group, *Current Cost Accounting,* Exposure Draft No. 18 (London: IASG 1976).

25. Westwick, "The Lessons to Be Learned," 363.

26. Ibid., 366–367.

27. Inflation Account Steering Group, *Current Cost Accounting,* Exposure Draft No. 24 (London: IASG 1979).

28. Accounting Standards Committee, *Current Cost Accounting,* Statement of Standard Accounting Practice No. 16 (London: IASG, 1980).

29. For a complete discussion of SSAP 16, see "Statement of Standard Accounting Practice No. 16: Current Cost Accounting," *Accountancy* (April 1980): 99–100.

30. Accounting Standards Committee, *Current Cost Accounting,* SSAP 16, par. 11.

31. R. Bloom and A. Debessay, "A Comparative Analysis of Recent Pronouncements as Accounting for Changing Prices," *International Journal of Accounting* (Spring 1985): 127.

32. Accounting Research Committee, *Accounting for the Effects of Changes in the General Purchasing Power of Money,* Accounting Guideline (Toronto: CICA, December 1974).

33. Accounting Research Committee, *Accounting for Changes in the General Purchasing Power of Money,* Exposure Draft (Toronto: CICA, July 1975).

34. *CICA Handbook,* sec. 4510 (Toronto: CICA, 1985).

35. Ibid., par. 4510A.9.

36. Ibid., pars. 4510.6–4510.18.

37. Ibid., par. 4510.21.

38. Ibid., par. 4510.25.

39. Ibid., par. 4510.24.

40. H. Volten, "A Response from the Netherlands," *Journal of Accountancy* (March 1978): 44–45.

41. E. Stamp and A. K. Mason, "Current Cost Accounting: British Panacea or Quagmire?" *Journal of Accountancy* (April 1977): 66.

42. AAA Committee on International Accounting, "The 1973 Annual Report of N.V. Philips — The Netherlands," *Accounting Review* (Supplement, 1976): 111.

43. D. Boussard, *Compatibilitèet Inflation* (Paris: Nasson, 1983), 125–126.

44. K. Macharzina and A. F. Coenenberg, "Current-Cost or Current Purchasing-Power Accounting? An Internationally Based Assessment of FASB Statement No. 33 on Financial Reporting and Changing Prices," *International Journal of Accounting* (Spring 1981): 157.

45. Australian Society of Accountants and the Institute of Chartered Accountants in Australia, *Statement of Accounting Practice No. 1* (Sydney, Australia: Australian Society of Accountants, 1982).

46. Ibid., par. 11.

47. R. Bloom and A. Debessay, "An Appraisal of the Conceptual Issues on Backlog Depreciation and a Comparative Analysis of International Accounting Practice," *Journal of International Accounting* (Fall 1983): 110.

48. Financial Accounting Standards Board, *Discussion Memorandum on the Conceptual Framework* (Stamford, CT: FASB, 1976), 128.

49. R. S. Cynther, *Accounting for Price Level Changes: Theory and Procedures* (Pergamon Press, Ltd., 1966).

50. P. W. Bell, *American and Australian Approaches to Current Value Accounting: How Fundamental are the Differences?* (Sydney: Australian Accounting Research Foundation, 1982), 37.

51. F. D. S. Choi and G. G. Mueller, *International Accounting* (Englewood Cliffs, NJ: Prentice-Hall, 1984), 194.

52. Ibid., 195.

53. Financial Accounting Standards Board, *Financial Reporting and Changing Prices: Foreign Currency Translation, An Amendment of FASB Statement No. 33,* Statement of Financial Accounting Standard No. 70 (Stamford, CT: FASB, December 1982), par. 10.

# BIBLIOGRAPHY

Agrawal, S. P. "Current Cost Accounting in the United Kingdom and the United States: A Comparative Analysis." *International Journal of Accountancy* (Spring 1983): 95–109.

Bloom, R., and A. Debessay. "An Appraisal of the Conceptual Issues on Backlog Depreciation and a Comparative Analysis of International Accounting Practice." *International Journal of Accounting* (Fall 1983): 107–122.

Buckmaster, D. "Inflation Gains and Losses from Holding Monetary Assets and Liabilities, 1918 to 1936: A Study of the Development of Accounting Thought in the United States." *International Journal of Accounting* (Spring 1982): 1–22.

Leech, S., D. J. Pratt, and W. G. W. Magill. "Asset Revaluations and Inflation in Australia, 1950 to 1975: An Industry Study." *International Journal of Accounting* (Spring 1982): 23–34.

Macharzina, K., and A. G. Coenenberg. "Current-Cost or Current Purchasing-Power Accounting? An Internationally Based Assessment of FASB Statement No. 33 on Financial Reporting and Changing Prices." *International Journal of Accounting* (Spring 1981): 149–162.

# 6

# SEGMENTAL REPORTING

## INTRODUCTION

The growth of conglomerate multinational corporations, international accounting, and international trade has led to a need for segmental reporting. Rather than being limited to reporting financial position, performance, and conduct of the whole firm, segmental reporting adds specific information concerning the activities of identifiable and reportable segments of the firm. In addition, there was an international call for such reporting as firms expanded beyond their domestic activities to generate revenues and perform operations outside the borders of their parent countries. Diversification, added to internationalization of firms, presented an opportunity for a change in the framework of accountability and disclosure toward a combination form of aggregate and segmental reporting. Also, users of accounting information in general, and shareholders in particular, are interested in segmental information as it may affect a firm's cash flows. As stated by Roberts and Gray:

They are therefore interested in the performance of the company as a whole rather than the performance of any specific part of a company. However, this does not mean that only consolidated information is of value to them. Both the size and uncertainty of future cash flows are likely to be affected by many factors including those that are related to the industries and countries that a company operates in. Different industries and different countries have various profit potentials, degrees and types of risk, and growth opportunities. Different rates of return on investment and different capital needs are also likely to occur across the various segments of a business.[1]

There is, then, a definite international need for segmental reporting. Like all reporting issues, segmental reporting generated a debate about its implementation affecting the nature of accounting standards, its impact on users and the market, and its potential predictive ability. This chapter elaborates on the various aspects of this debate and international ramifications of the issue.

## NATURE OF SEGMENTAL REPORTING

Firms have been reacting to their environment by adopting new organizational structures based on decentralization and the development or acquisition of domestic or foreign segments, resulting in companies that are more diversified. Mautz defines a *diversified company* as a company which is either so managerially decentralized, so lacks operational integration, or has such diversified markets that it may experience rates of profitability, degrees of risk, and opportunities for growth which vary within the company to such extent that an investor requires information about these variations in order to make informed decisions.[2]

What appears from this definition is that, first, the phenomenon of diversification emanates from management decentralization, a lack of operational integration, or activity in diversified markets and, second, that the differences in the financial profits of the segments call for segmental reporting that is deemed useful to investors.

Segmental reporting consists, therefore, of providing relevant information about segments. It can be rationalized within the "Fineness Theorem" of the information-economics literature. It implies that the information system $\eta_1$ is said to be "as fine as" the information system $\eta_0$ if $\eta_1$ is a "subpartition" of $\eta_0$, that is, if each data set of $\eta_1$ provides a partitioning of the states of nature that is at least as detailed (or as "fine") as that present in the data sets of $\eta_0$. Applied to segmental reporting, the theorem implies that the information system obtained by segmental reporting and consolidated data together is "finer" than the disclosure of consolidated data alone. The fineness argument does not, however, consider the incremental costs required by the additional disclosure. Mohr elaborates on these costs as follows:

It must be noted, however, that the costs of the "finer" disclosures could impair the theoretical result. Although the gathering and reporting costs associated with segmental disclosure may be small (due to the use of similar data in managerial decision contexts), externalities and practical data limitations would still impose greater cost. For example, competitive reactions or managerial reluctance to adopt "risky" projects may affect the expected payoff to the decision maker. Furthermore, uncertainty about data reliability and comparability would inhibit the use of the more detailed disclosure. This latter assertion is particularly applicable to the incremental disclosure of segment earnings data, wherein differences in cost determination methods and in common cost allocation schemes can influence the reported amounts.[3]

## ISSUES IN SEGMENTAL REPORTING

### Use of Segmental Reporting

The use of segmental reporting was on the increase even before the international standard setters made requests for its implementation. Attitudinal studies of preparers and users in the United States showed an expressed interest in the dissemination of segmental reporting. These studies include one by Backer and McFarland involving financial analysts and commercial bankers[4] and a study of financial analysts and corporate executives by Mautz.[5] An attitudinal study by Cramer reported some of the perceived problems of segmental reporting experienced by corporate controllers, namely, the restrictions on data comparability that might result from the use of different cost allocation and transfer-pricing techniques to define the segments, and, additionally, the externality costs associated with the development of auditing standards, the increased legal exposure of managers and auditors, and the reactions of competitors.[6]

Gray and Radebaugh examined the extent of geographical information provided in practice in the United States and the United Kingdom and the significant differences in the nature and content of disclosures between countries, both in terms of voluntary disclosures and those required by accounting standards.[7] Given the greater flexibility in the application of regulations governing segmental disclosures in the United States, as well as the reduced scope in terms of the amount of information to be disclosed, it is not surprising that their findings indicate that U.S. firms disclose more segmental information, especially with respect to intraenterprise sales, profits, and assets. In the case of employees, however, the increased emphasis on employee reporting in the United Kingdom may explain the greater disclosure of employee information in that country. An interesting result of the study was that U.S. firms disclosed fewer geographic segments and a higher level of aggregation than did U.K. firms. The explanation that follows is provided by Gray and Radebaugh:

One final note relates to the demand of investors for information. U.K. segment disclosure practices are determined by the London Stock Exchange and, therefore, its investors. This has resulted in more segments than for U.S. firms . . . but certainly not in more information per segment. Large MNEs [multinational enterprises], such as those in this study, actively use the international markets to raise debt as well as equity capital, so they effectively compete with each other for capital.

In spite of this, the more extensive information required of U.S. MNEs has not resulted in U.K. firms trying to match U.S. firms in terms of disclosure. It is evident that the capital market has not insisted on this information from U.K. firms, leading one to question the necessity of the fuller range of U.S. disclosure.[8]

Gray also examined the European experience with segmental reporting and found that U.K.-based companies exhibited greater disclosure of business analyses of profits and geographical analyses of sales and profits.[9] Factors explaining the differences include managerial (corporate strategy, organizational structure, and cost and competitive aspects), legal and political, professional, and stock-market and investment environments. Two variables were singled out as more important: the structure of the company with respect to the extent of its economic integration and managerial coordination, and the differential stimulus to disclosure provided by the regulatory environment of legal, professional, and stock-market requirements. According to Gray:

The impact of the former variable is difficult to assess from company reports, and further research into this aspect would seem useful to determine the feasibility of disclosure. With regards to the impact of the latter variable, there is little doubt about the unsatisfactory nature of existing disclosure requirements, such as they are. The critical problem is that of defining appropriate criteria for the identification of reporting segments. This is a difficulty which is currently thwarting the developing of segment reporting in the EEC, given that a case for providing such information is perceived to exist by some of the rule-making bodies concerned.[10]

## Evaluation of Segmental Reporting

Various arguments have been made in favor of segmental reporting since business concerns began to grow and acquire multisegmental characteristics.

The usefulness of segmental reporting has been linked generally to (1) the informational content of the information in terms of the profitability, risk, and growth of the different segments of a firm, and (2) the relevance to users in their assessment of the earnings potential and the risk of the company as a whole, to governments in their development of public policy positions concerning multinational and/or large companies, and to management encouraging a corporate strategy. This last point is elaborated on as follows:

Managerial efficiency may be promoted by the attention to corporate strategy that the publication of segmented reporting will encourage. Management may also be concerned to evaluate their internal management control system. The provision of segmental reports will necessitate managerial evaluation of cost allocation procedures and the bases on which transfer prices between segments are calculated. Perhaps the most important spur to efficiency could be the increased competition that may result from segmental disclosures with consequent benefits to the economy as a whole. The effect of this may be exaggerated, however, as all companies will be similarly placed. But it may at least redress to some extent the competitive disadvantage experienced by the unitary company, with no business or geographical diversification, as compared to the multi-business-multinational company whose operations have become progressively complex and whose financial statements have become correspondingly opaque.[11]

Various other reasons are given in favor of segmental reporting, including the following:

1. Segmental information is needed by the investor to make an intelligent investment decision regarding a diversified company.

   (a) Sales and earnings of individual segments are needed to forecast consolidated profits because of the differences between segments in growth rate, risk, and profitability.

   (b) Segmental reports disclose the nature of a company's businesses and the relative size of the components as an aid in evaluating the company's investment work.

2. The absence of segmented reporting by a diversified company may put its unsegmented, single product-line competitors at a competitive disadvantage because the conglomerate may obscure information that its competitors must disclose.[12]

Naturally, as in all accounting issues, not all arguments are in favor of segmental reporting. Not only is the usefulness of segmental reporting questioned when compared to the role of consolidated data, but also the costs of disclosure are raised as a subject of concern. The question is whether the costs of segmental disclosure could serve to offset the theoretical benefits of "finer" information systems. Undoubtedly, there is limited evidence with regard to the cost aspects of segmental disclosure, in addition to the lack of evidence on information-processing issues, data-reliability considerations, and externality costs. There is also the problem of the lack of comparability when apparently similar segments in different firms can be identified differently, there is a difference in the treatment of intersegment transfers, and the common costs are allocated over different bases.[13]

Various other reasons against segmental reporting are advocated, including these provided by Kieso et al.:

1. Without a thorough knowledge of the business and an understanding of such important factors as the competitive environment and capital investment requirements, the investor may find the segmented information meaningless or even draw improper conclusions about the reported earnings of the segments.

2. Additional disclosure may harm reporting firms because it may be helpful to competitors, labor unions, suppliers, and certain government regulatory agencies.

3. Additional disclosure may discourage management from taking intelligent business risks because segments reporting losses or unsatisfactory earnings may cause shareholder dissatisfaction with management.

4. The wide variation among firms in the choice of segments, cost allocation, and other accounting problems limits the usefulness of segmented information.

5. The investor is investing in the company as a whole and not in the particular segments, and it should not matter how any single segment is performing if the overall performance is satisfactory.

6. Certain technical problems, such as classification of segments and allocation of segment revenues and cost (especially "common costs"), are formidable.[14]

Needless to say, the advocates of segmental reporting are winning their case given that segmental reporting is mandated internationally.

## THE U.S. POSITION

The U.S. position on reporting financial information by segment is mainly expressed in FASB Statement of Financial Accounting Standard No. 14 (SFAS 14), *Financial Reporting for Segments of a Business Enterprise.*[15] Other applicable authoritative statements include Statements 18, 21, 24, 30, and 69,[16–20] and technical bulletins 79-4, 79-5, and 79-8.[21–23] SFAS 14 requires public companies whose securities are publicly traded or that are required to file financial statements with the Securities and Exchange Commission (SEC) to include disaggregated information about operations in various industries, foreign operations, export sales, and sales to major customers. SFAS 21, *Suspension of the Reporting of Earnings Per Share and Segment Information by Nonpublic Enterprises,* exempts nonpublic firms from the provisions of SFAS 14. Similarly, SFAS 24, *Reporting Segment Information in Financial Statements that are Presented in Another Enterprise's Financial Report,* exempts the reporting entity with consolidated financial statements containing separable financial statements in the following circumstances:

1. The separable financial statements are also consolidated or combined in a complete set of financial statements and both sets of financial statements are included in the same financial reports;

2. The separable financial statements are those of a foreign investee (not a subsidiary) of the primary reporting unit, and the separable financial statements do not follow the provisions of SFAS No. 14; or,

3. The separable financial statements are those of an investee accounted for using the cost or equity method.[24]

Therefore, SFAS 21 and SFAS 24 affect the applicability of SFAS 14 by putting forth limitations. Because SFAS 14 differentiates between domestic and foreign operations, the following section delineates this differentiation.

## Domestic Operations

In SFAS 14, an *industry segment* is defined as a component of an enterprise engaged in providing a product or service, or a group of related products and services, primarily to unaffiliated customers for a profit. The first requirement of SFAS 14 is the determination by a three-step procedure of the industry segments that need to be reported separately.

In the first step, the company should identify sources of revenue (by product or service rendered) on a worldwide basis for the entity. In the second step, the company should group related products and services into industry segments. Three factors are to be considered in determining industry segment:

1. *The nature of the product.* Related products have similar purposes or end uses. Thus, they may be expected to have similar rates of profitability, similar degrees of risk, and similar opportunities for growth.

2. *The nature of the production process.* Sharing of common or interchangeable production or sales facilities, equipment, labor force, or device group or use of the same or similar basic raw materials, may suggest that products or services are related. Likewise, similar degrees of labor or capital intensiveness may indicate a relationship among products or services.

3. *Markets and marketing methods.* Similarity of geographic marketing areas, types of customers, or marketing methods may indicate a relationship among products or services. The sensitivity of the market to price changes and to changes in general economic conditions may indicate whether products and services are related or unrelated.[25]

In the third step, the company should determine the reporting segments. Six tests are suggested to facilitate the decision, namely, the revenue, profitability, asset, comparability, dominance, and explanation tests. Application of these tests is discussed in the paragraphs that follow.

The *revenue test* requires that the segment revenue be 10% or more of the combined revenue of all the enterprise's industry segments (this includes sales to unaffiliated customers and intersegment sales or transfers). Segment revenue is calculated as follows:

$$SR = S + IS + INTO + INTR$$

where
$SR$ = segment revenue
$S$ = sales to unaffiliated customers
$IS$ = intersegment sales and transfers

*INTO* = interest income from sources outside the firm
*INTR* = interest income from intersegment notes receivable

The *profitability test* requires that the absolute of the segment's operating profit or loss be 10% or more, in absolute amount, of the greater of either the combined operating profits of all industry segments that did not incur an operating loss or the combined operating losses of all industry segments that did incur an operating loss. The operating profit or loss is equal to segment revenue less operating expenses except for the following items:

1. Any revenues earned at the corporate level and not related to any segment
2. General corporate expenses
3. Interest expense, except if segment operations are primarily financial in nature
4. Domestic and foreign income taxes
5. Equity in earnings of unconsolidated subsidiaries or investees
6. Extraordinary items
7. Gains and losses on discontinued operations
8. Minority interest
9. Cumulative effect of changes in accounting principles

If the segment fails both the revenue and profitability tests, the *asset test* requires that the identifiable assets of the segments be 10% or more of the combined segment identifiable assets. Identifiable assets include tangible and intangible assets, net of valuation allowances used by the industry segment, and the allocated portions of the assets used by two or more segments. Assets that are intended for general corporate purposes are excluded.

The *comparability test* requires that the segment be reported separately if management feels such a treatment is needed to achieve interperiod comparability.

The *test of dominance* requires that the segment not be reported separately if it can be classified as dominant. A dominant segment should represent 90% or more of the combined revenues, operating profits or losses, and identifiable assets; in addition, no other segment can meet any of the 10% tests.

The *explanation test* determines whether a substantial portion of an enterprise's operations is explained by its segment information. The combined total of the revenue from reportable segments must be 75% or more of all revenue from sales to unaffiliated customers. If combined revenues do not meet this test, additional segments must be added until the test is met.

Exhibit 6.1 illustrates the application of operational tests.

Following the choice of the reportable segments, SFAS 14 suggests spe-

**Exhibit 6.1**
**Determination of Reporting Segments by Use of Operational Tests**

| Segment | Unaffiliated Revenue | Intersegment Revenue | Total Revenue | Operating Profit(Loss) | Identifiable Assets |
|---------|------|------|------|------|------|
| U | 50 | 50 | 100 | 10 | 50 |
| V | 100 | | 100 | 10 | 40 |
| W | 150 | 100 | 250 | (20) | 100 |
| X | 200 | | 200 | 10 | 150 |
| Y | 250 | 50 | 300 | (100) | 100 |
| Z | 300 | | 300 | 100 | 80 |
| | $1,050 | | $1,250 | $ 10 | $520 |

Revenue Test: (10%)($1,250) = $125

    Reportable segments: W, X, Y, Z

Operating Profit or Loss Test: (10%)($130) = $13

    Reportable segments: W, Y, Z

    Because total operation profit ($130) is greater than the operating loss ($120), total operating profit is used as the base.

Identifiable Assets Test: (10%)($520) = $52

    Reportable segments: W, X, Y, Z

Explanation Test: (75%)($1,050) = $787.50

    Segments W, X, Y, and Z have total unaffiliated revenues of $900, which is greater than $787.50. Therefore, the explanation test is met and no additional segments need to be reported.

cific disclosure requirements for segmental reporting that appear in one of
three places:

1. In the financial statements, with reference to related footnote disclosures
2. In the footnotes to the financial statements
3. In a supplementary schedule that is not part of the four financial statements

The information to be reported in the reportable segments includes the
following items:

1. Revenue information, including sales to unaffiliated customers, intersegment
   sales or transfers (along with the basis of accounting for such sales or transfers),
   and a reconciliation of sales to unaffiliated customers and intersegment sales or
   transfers on the consolidated income statement
2. Profitability information
3. Identifiable assets information
4. Other disclosures, including the aggregate amount of depreciation, depletion,
   and amortization; the amount of capital expenditures; equity in unconsolidated
   but vertically integrated subsidiaries and their geographic location; the effect of
   a change in accounting principle on segment income; the type of products and
   services produced by each segment; specific accounting policies; the basis used
   to price intersegment transfers; the method used to allocate common costs; and
   the nature and amount of any unusual or infrequent items added to or deducted
   from segment profit

### Foreign Operations

SFAS 14 requires separate disclosure of domestic and foreign activities.
*Foreign operations* are those revenue-generating activities that are located
outside the enterprise's home country and are generating revenue either
from sales to unaffiliated customers or from intraenterprise sales or transfers between geographic areas.

Two tests may be used to determine if foreign operation activities are to
be reported separately: (1) revenue from sales to unaffiliated customers is
10% or more of consolidated revenue as reported in the firm's income
statement and (2) identifiable assets of the firm's foreign operations are
10% or more of consolidated total assets as reported in the firm's balance
sheet. After an individual foreign operation has been determined to be
reportable, its activities must be added to activities from foreign operations
in the same geographic area. *Geographic areas* are defined as individual
countries or groups of countries as determined appropriate according to a
firm's circumstances. The following factors are to be considered in group-
ing foreign operations: proximity, economic affinity, similarities in busi-

ness environment, and nature, scale, and degree of interrelationship of the firm's operations in the various countries.

The disclosure requirements for foreign operations are similar to those for domestic operations.

### Export Sales and Sales to Major Customers

*Export sales* are those sales made by a domestic segment to unaffiliated customers in foreign countries. If export sales amount to 10% or more of the total sales to unaffiliated customers, they should be separately disclosed in the aggregate statements by such geographic areas considered appropriate.

Similarly, if 10% or more of the revenue of a firm is derived from a single customer, a separate disclosure is required along with indications of the segments making the sale. SFAS 30, *Disclosure of Information about Major Customers,* identifies either a group of entities under common control, the federal government, a state government, a local government, or a foreign government as a single customer for purposes of compliance with the 10% test.

## INTERNATIONAL POSITIONS

In the United Kingdom, the 1981 Companies Act requires segmental reporting in the financial statements, stating specifically:

If in the course of the financial year, the company has carried out a business of two or more classes that, in the opinion of the directors, differ substantially from each other, there shall be stated in respect of each class [describing it]:

(a) the amount of the turnover attributable to that class, &

(b) the amount of the profit or loss of the company before taxation which is in the opinion of the directors attributable to that class.

In addition, the act calls for a disclosure of turnover by geographic areas when the firm has been supplying different markets. The disclosure is generally made in the directors' reports.

The Canadian position is more comprehensive, and is expressed in Section 1700 of the Canadian Institute of Chartered Accountants (CICA) handbook. The requirements of the section are, in general, similar to the provision of SFAS 14. The only exception relates to the required disclosure of information about major customers of the firm. While the Exposure Draft that preceded Section 1700 called for this information, it was later deleted from the final version.[26]

The international position on segmental reporting was reported in August 1981 by the release of International Accounting Standard No. 14 (IAS 14), *Reporting Financial Information by Segments,* by the International Accounting Standards Committee. IAS 14 basically suggests the following disclosures for each reported industry and geographic segment: (1) sales or other operating revenues, distinguishing between revenue derived from customers outside the firm and revenue derived from other segments; (2) segment results; (3) segment assets employed, expressed either in monetary amounts or as percentages of the consolidated totals; and (4) the basis of intersegment pricing. The reportable segments are referred to as economically significant entities, and defined as those subsidiaries whose levels of revenues, profits, assets, or employment are significant in the countries in which their major operations are conducted.[27]

With regard to the European Economic Community, one of the provisions of the Fourth Directive requires turnover only to be analyzed by activity and geographic segment.[28]

In Australia, there is no requirement to disclose segment information except disclosure of the extent to which each corporation in a group contributes to consolidated profit or loss.

Segmental reporting is also recommended by international organizations. The Organization for Economic Cooperation and Development (OECD) guidelines for multinational corporations call for the disclosure of the geographical areas where operations are carried out and the principal activities in each area, plus geographical disclosures of turnover, operating results, significant new capital investment, and the average number of employees.[29]

The United Nations proposals for accounting and reporting by multinational corporations also call for the disclosure of geographical and line of business information on external sales, internal transfers, operating results, and, to the extent identifiable, either total assets and net assets or total assets and total liabilities, with at least separate identification of gross property, plant, and equipment, accumulated depreciation, and long-term assets, as well as disclosure of investments, the principal activities, the basis of accounting for transfers, the total number of employees, and, for geographical areas, a description of any exposures to exceptional risks.[30]

## PREDICTIVE ABILITY OF SEGMENTAL REPORTING

The predictive ability of segmental reporting has been examined in several studies. In the first study, Kinney tested the relative predictive power of subentity data for a sample of firms that voluntarily reported sales and earnings data by subentity.[31] Kinney used the following form models:

*Model 1:* Consolidated earnings adjusted for changes in GNP

*Model 2:* Linear trend of earnings by double exponential smoothing with a smoothing constant of 0.4

*Model 3:* Expected segment sales × 3-year average consolidated-profits ratio, where expected segment sales = current year's sales × expected increase in industry sales

*Model 4:* Expected segment sales × 3-year average segment-profit ratio. Segment sales are defined as in Model 3.

The results of the study showed that Model 4 was significantly better than Models 1 and 2 and better (but not significantly) than Model 3. Basically, the predictions based on segmented sales and earnings data and industry predictions were on the average more accurate than predictions based on models using consolidated performance data. However, this study suffers from two serious limitations, namely, the small representative sample of 24 companies and the ad hoc choice of consolidated models that were not based on research into the time-series properties of earnings.

In the second study, Collins extended and updated the preliminary work of Kinney using data disclosed under the line-of-business reporting requirements initiated by the SEC.[32] The SEC required, beginning December 31, 1970, that all registrants engaged in various segments report, by product line, sales and profits before taxes and extraordinary items in their annual 10K report. The models used were either consolidated models, such as (1) linear regression, (2) strict martingale or random walk, (3) submartingale or random walk with a drift, (4) pure mean reversion, (5) moving average of pure mean reversion, (6) Kinney's double-exponential smoothing model, and (7) Kinney's GNP model, or segment models, where sales are based on expected industry sales of each segment and earnings are equal to either expected segment sales × prior-year consolidated profit margin or expected segment sales × prior-year segment profit margin. Collins's findings corroborated Kinney's earlier findings, suggesting that

SEC product line revenue and profit disclosures together with industry sales projections published in various government sources provide significantly more accurate estimates of future total-entity sales and earnings than the procedures that rely totally on consolidated data.[33]

A third study focused on the predictive ability of U.K. segment reports. Emmanuel and Pick confirmed, in a U.K. setting, the earlier findings that segmental disclosure of sales and profit data is useful in providing more accurate predictions of corporate earnings.[34] The authors also suggested more research with the predictive-ability paradigm.

Future studies may prove rewarding not only in determining whether disclosure is worthwhile, but also what form it should take if the predictions are to become more accurate. Two contenders in respect to accuracy are segment reports presented in terms of an industrial/geographical-segment matrix and the measurement of segment earnings by industrial growth fore-casts to be accommodated in the segment-based models, while the use of contribution would avoid the possibly significant distorting effects of trans-fer pricing and common cost allocations. Given the availability of data, the predictive-ability criterion may prove more useful in gauging the most appropriate form that segmental disclosure should follow.[35]

Finally, Silhan did not find evidence that consistently supported the pre-dictive superiority of either the "consolidated" or the "segmental" earnings data.[36] His study differed from the earlier research in two important as-pects, that his earnings-forecast models were based on the use of Box Jen-kins time-series analysis and his use of a simulation approach, permitting an examination of the effect of the number of segments on predictive accu-racy.

Related studies have examined the accuracy of published earnings fore-casts in conjunction with segmental reporting. Barefield and Comiskey[37] and Baldwin[38] were able to show a relationship between the forecast accu-racy and the presence of segmental reporting, indicating that the availability of segmental data could improve the accuracy of the earnings projections of analysts.

A positive evaluation of these results was stated by Mohr:

In summary, the studies addressing the accuracy of analysts' forecasts have utilized a variety of research techniques and have provided evidence that improved earnings predictions can accompany the disclosure of segmental data. Within the context of segmental reporting, improved accuracy of forecasts may be viewed as one of the "benefits" implicit in the theoretical "fitness" result. But the earnings forecast studies have also provided some evidence with regard to another "fineness" comparison. Specifically, no predictive improvements beyond those associated with the availabil-ity of segmental sales were obtained when segmental earnings amounts were added to the data set. Such a finding directs attention toward the desirability of testing for the decision effects of segmental earnings data in other contexts and assessing the costs of this added disclosure.[39]

## USERS' PERCEPTIONS OF
## SEGMENTAL REPORTING

The early research investigated the "real world" perceptions of segment reporting and provided evidence showing users' and preparers' interest in the production and dissemination of segment sales and data. Studies relying mostly on survey data include those by Backer and McFarland,[40] Mautz,[41] and Cramer.[42] Other studies used controlled experiments to evaluate the impact of segmental disclosure on individual decision making. The first study was by J. C. Stallman.[43]

The second study was done by Ortman.[44] He asked financial analysts to assign a per-share offering price to two diversified firms, one that provided segmental data and one that did not. The firms were expected to go public in the immediate future. The results of the study showed that, with segmental data, the value of each firm's stock was in accordance with the present value of its expected return as reflected by industry average price/earnings (P/E) ratios; without segmental data, the reverse was experienced. He concluded that:

The decrease in the variance with regard to the distributions of the per-share values of the diversified firms' stocks in this study may mean that segmental disclosure by all such firms could result in greater stability in the movement of the prices of these firms' stocks. The results of this study strongly suggest that diversified firms should include segmental data in their financial reports.[45]

These results could not, however, be taken as conclusive evidence of the impact of segmental reporting on users. As stated by Mohr:

Ortman's selected industries (auto parts and office/computer equipment), and the radical changes in industry involvement that were revealed only in the segmental data, could have driven the observed results.[46]

## MARKET PERCEPTIONS OF SEGMENTAL REPORTING

Various market-based studies examined the relationship between segmental reporting and mean returns on stocks. Twombly found no evidence of statistically significant differences between the mean-return vector of the experimental portfolios (partitioned by segmental-disclosure level and industry concentration) and the mean-return vector of the control portfolios (partitioned by industry concentration only).[47] He concluded that "the event of a firm's disclosure of both segment revenues and profits provided no unanticipated information to the capital market, whether the disclosures were conditional upon the market concentration or not."[48]

Because Twombly's study was limited to an examination of mean returns on stock of firms engaged in voluntary segmental reporting, Ajinkya decided to conduct a comprehensive empirical evaluation of the proposition that "the SEC's LOB [line-of-business] earnings disclosure requirements . . . enabled market participants to reassess the risk-return characteristics of conglomerate firms."[49] His results were, however, consistent with those reported by Twombly. A similar attempt by Horwitz and Kolodony provided similar evidence.[50] This evidence was, however, based on a portfolio, and the individual effects may be largely neutralized at the portfolio level.

Other strategies were also tried. For example, Foster examined the relationship between residual returns and the good and bad "news" aspects of segmental disclosure in the insurance industry.[51] His findings indicated that return-assessment effects could be associated with the disclosure of a segmental data set. Similarly, Kochanek examined whether the predictive aspects of good quality versus poor quality segmental disclosure could influence the timing of market return assessments.[52] Kochanek's evidence supported a relationship between return assessment, earnings prediction, and the disclosure of a segmental data set incorporating (at a minimum) segmental-sales amounts.

Prodhan examined the impact of segmental geographical disclosure on the systematic-risk profile of British multinational firms, showing an association between the two variables and finding that the onset of a geographical segmental disclosure is more likely to be abrupt than gradual.[53] Prodhan argued that his findings would provide some more evidential input to the debate on segmentation of the international capital market, known as the Grubel-Agmon controversy.[54] He makes the point as follows: "Since geographical information is associated with beta changes it can be said that the international capital markets are likely to be segmented, since an integrated international capital market share is unlikely to be a benefit from diversification across countries."[55]

Collins, however, tested the efficiency of the securities market and provided somewhat mixed evidence with respect to the assessment of segmental data on security returns.[56]

A different approach was to test the relationship of beta to the specific segmental disclosure. First, Kinney found beta and accounting risk to be correlated significantly for geographical disclosure but not for other disclosures.[57] Using a more refined methodology and examining the same research question, Mohr found a highly significant positive relationship between the two measures, especially in the case where industry involvement was measured on the basis of asset data.[58]

## CONCLUSIONS

Segmental reporting has now been mandated internationally. The resulting disclosures are going to be very useful to capital markets, investors, and users of accounting information. The informational context of segmental disclosure still needs to be tested empirically in the areas of prediction of such economic events as bankruptcy, takeover, bond ratings, and the like. Also, problems remain in the areas of segment identification as well as in the need for adequate regulation. As stated by Roberts and Gray:

While regulation is growing, and in the USA it is by far the most extensive, there remains the major problem of segment identification. The scope for managerial discretion provides substantial potential for the provision of misleading information. At the same time, it is noteworthy that the introduction of detailed rules may have had the effect of actually reducing the amount of information disclosed. There would seem to be scope, therefore, for guidelines which encourage disclosures and yet control their quality so that they are truly informative. In particular, the potential for more matrix presentations is clear, in that they seem likely to facilitate a more accurate assessment of company prospects.[59]

# NOTES

1. C. B. Roberts and S. Gray, "Segmental Reporting," in *Issues in International Accounting,* ed. C. Nobes and R. Parker (Oxford, England: Philip Allan, 1988), 106.

2. R. K. Mautz, *Financial Reporting by Diversified Companies* (New York: Financial Executives Research Foundation, 1968), 12–13.

3. R. M. Mohr, "The Segmental Reporting Issue: A Review of Empirical Research," *Journal of Accounting Literature* (Spring 1983): 41–42.

4. M. Backer and W. B. McFarland, *External Reporting for Segments of a Business* (New York: National Association of Accountants, 1968), 25.

5. Mautz, *Financial Reporting by Diversified Companies,* 16.

6. J. Cramer, "Income Reporting by Conglomerates," *Abacus* (August 1968): 17–26.

7. S. J. Gray and L. H. Radebaugh, "International Segment Disclosures by U.S. and U.K. Multinational Enterprises: A Descriptive Study," *Journal of Accounting Research* (Spring 1984): 351–360.

8. Ibid., 359–360.

9. S. J. Gray, "Segment Reporting and the EEC Multinationals," *Journal of Accounting Research* (Autumn 1978): 242–253.

10. Ibid., 252–253.

11. S. J. Gray, "Segmental or Disaggregated Financial Statements," in *Developments in Financial Reporting,* ed. T. A. Lee (London: Philip Allan, 1981), 31–32.

12. D. E. Kieso, D. E. Weygandt, J. J. Irvine, V. B. Silvester, and W. H. Silvester, *Intermediate Accounting,* 2d ed. (Toronto: John Wiley and Sons Canada, 1986), 1296.

13. Gray, "Segmental or Disaggregated Financial Statements," 33.

14. Kieso et al., *Intermediate Accounting,* 1296.

15. Financial Accounting Standards Board, *Financial Reporting for Segments of a Business Enterprise,* Statement of Financial Accounting Standard No. 14 (Stamford, CT: FASB, 1976), par. 10.

16. Financial Accounting Standards Board, *Financial Reporting for Segments of a Business Enterprise—Interim Financial Statements,* Statement of Financial Accounting Standard No. 18 (Stamford, CT: FASB, November 1977).

17. Financial Accounting Standards Board, *Suspension of the Reporting of Earnings Per Share and Segment Information by Nonpublic Enterprises,* Statement of Financial Accounting Standard No. 21 (Stamford, CT: FASB, April 1978), par. 10.

18. Financial Accounting Standards Board, *Reporting Segment Information in Financial Statements that are Presented in Another Enterprise's Financial Report,*

Statement of Financial Accounting Standard No. 24 (Stamford, CT: FASB, December 1978), par. 9.

19. Financial Accounting Standards Board, *Disclosure of Information about Major Customers,* Statement of Financial Accounting Standard No. 30 (Stamford, CT: FASB, August 1979), par. 20.

20. Financial Accounting Standards Board, *Disclosures About Oil-and-Gas Activities,* Statement of Financial Accounting Standard No. 69 (Stamford, CT: FASB, November 1982), par. 11.

21. Financial Accounting Standards Board, Technical Bulletin 79-4 (Stamford, CT: FASB).

22. Financial Accounting Standards Board, Technical Bulletin 79-5 (Stamford, CT: FASB).

23. Financial Accounting Standards Board, Technical Bulletin 79-8 (Stamford, CT: FASB).

24. FASB, *Reporting Segment Information in Financial Statements,* SFAS 24, par. 22.

25. FASB, *Financial Reporting for Segments of a Business Enterprise,* SFAS 14, par. 100.

26. Canadian Institute of Chartered Accountants (Toronto, Ontario: CICA, 1990), par. 21.

27. International Accounting Standards Committee, *Reporting Financial Information by Segments,* International Accounting Standard No. 14 (London: IASC, August 1981), par. 22.

28. Commission of the European Communities, *Fourth Council Directive for Co-ordination of National Legislation Regarding the Annual Accounts of Limited Liability Companies* (CEC, 1978).

29. Organization for Economic Cooperation and Development, *International Investment and Multinational Enterprises* (Paris: OECD, 1979), 15-26.

30. United Nations, *International Standards of Accounting and Reporting for Transitional Corporations* (New York: United Nations, 1977), 35-36.

31. W. R. Kinney, Jr., "Predicting Earnings: Entity vs. Subentity Data," *Journal of Accounting Research* 9 (Spring 1971): 127-136.

32. D. W. Collins, "Predicting Earnings with Sub-Entity Data: Some Further Evidence," *Journal of Accounting Research* (Spring 1976): 163-177.

33. Ibid., 175.

34. C. R. Emmanuel and R. H. Pick, "The Predictive Ability of U.K. Segment Reports," *Journal of Business Finance and Accounting* (Summer 1980): 201-218.

35. Ibid., 216.

36. P. Silhan, "Simulated Mergers of Existent Autonomous Firms: A New Approach to Segmentation Research," *Journal of Accounting Research* 20 (Spring 1982): 255-262.

37. R. M. Barefield and E. Comiskey, "Segmental Financial Disclosure by Diversified Firms and Security Prices: A Comment," *Accounting Review* 50 (October 1975): 818-821.

38. B. Baldwin, "Line-of-Business Disclosure Requirements and Security Analyst Forecast Accuracy," (D.B.A. diss., Arizona State University, 1979).

39. Mohr, "The Segmental Reporting Issue," 33.

40. Backer and McFarland, *External Reporting for Segments of a Business,* 15.

41. Mautz, *Financial Reporting by Diversified Companies,* 44.

42. Cramer, "Income Reporting by Conglomerates," 17–26.

43. J. C. Stallman, "Toward Experimental Criteria for Judging Disclosure Improvement," *Empirical Research in Accounting: Selected Studies, 1969, Journal of Accounting Research* 7 (Supplement, 1969): 29–43.

44. R. F. Ortman, "The Effects on Investment Analysis of Alternative Reporting Procedures for Diversified Firms," *Accounting Review* 50 (April 1975): 298–304.

45. Ibid., 304.

46. Mohr, "The Segmental Reporting Issue," 115.

47. J. Twombly, "An Empirical Analysis of the Information Content of Segment Data in Annual Reports from an FTC Perspective," in *Disclosure Criteria and Segment Reporting,* ed. R. Barefield and G. Holstrum (Gainesville, FL: University Press of Florida, 1979), 56–96.

48. Ibid., 77.

49. B. Ajinkya, "An Empirical Evaluation of Line-of-Business Reporting," *Journal of Accounting Research* 18 (Autumn 1975):, 283–292.

50. B. Horwitz and R. Kolodony, "Line-of-Business Reporting and Security Prices: An Analysis of an SEC Disclosure Rule," *Bell Journal of Economics* 8 (Spring 1977): 234–249.

51. G. Foster, "Security Price Revaluation Implications of Sub-Earnings Disclosure," *Journal of Accounting Research* 13 (Autumn 1975): 283–292.

52. R. F. Kochanek, "Segmental Financial Disclosure by Diversified Firms and Security Prices," *Accounting Review* 49 (April 1974): 245–258.

53. B. K. Prodhan, "Geographical Segment Disclosure and Multinational Risk Profile," *Journal of Business Finance and Accounting* (Spring 1986): 15–37.

54. J. Grubel, "Internationally Diversified Portfolios: Welfare Gains and Capital Flows," *American Economic Review* 12 (1968): 1299–1314; T. Agmon, "The Relationship among Equity Markets," *Journal of Finance* (May 1972): 839–855.

55. Prodhan, "Geographical Segment Disclosure," 31.

56. D. Collins, "SEC Product-Line Reporting and Market Efficiency," *Journal of Financial Economics* (June 1975): 125–164.

57. W. R. Kinney, "Covariability of Segment Earning and Multi-Segment Company Returns," *Accounting Review* (April 1972): 82.

58. R. M. Mohr, "The Operating Beta of a U.S. Multi-Activity Firm: An Empirical Investigation," *Journal of Business Finance and Accounting* (Winter 1985): 62.

59. Roberts and Gray, "Segmental Reporting," 107.

## BIBLIOGRAPHY

American Institute of Certified Public Accountants. Segment information, *Statement on Auditing Standards* 21. AICPA, 1977.

Backer, M., and W. B. McFarland. *External Reporting for Segments of a Business.* New York: National Association of Accountants, 1968.

Barefield, R. M., and E. E. Comiskey. "Segmental Financial Disclosures by Diversified Firms and Security Prices: A Comment." *Accounting Review* (October 1975): 818–821.

Canadian Institute of Chartered Accountants. Segmented information, *Section 1700.* CICA, 1979.

Collins, D. W. "Predicting Earnings with Sub-Entity Data: Some Further Evidence." *Journal of Accounting Research* (Spring 1976): 163–177.

Collins, D. W., and R. R. Simonds. "SEC Line-of-Business Disclosure and Market Risk Adjustments." *Journal of Accounting Research* (Autumn 1979): 352–383.

Commission of the European Communities. *Fourth Council Directive for Co-Ordination of National Legislation Regarding the Annual Accounts of Limited Liability Companies.* CEC, 1978.

Commission of the European Communities. *Proposal for a Seventh Directive Concerning Group Account.* CEC, 1976.

Dhaliwal, D. S., B. H. Spicer, and D. Vickrey. "The Quality of Disclosure and the Cost of Capital." *Journal of Business Finance and Accounting* (Summer 1979): 245–266.

Emmanuel, C. R., and N. Garrod. "Information Content in Segmental Reports" *Journal of Business Finance and Accounting* (forthcoming).

Emmanuel, C. R., and S. J. Gray. "Corporate Diversification and Segmental Disclosure Requirements in the U.S.A." *Journal of Business Finance and Accounting* (Winter 1977): 407–418.

———. "Segmental Disclosures and the Segment Identification Problem." *Accounting and Business Research* (Winter 1977): 37–50.

———. "The Segment Reporting Issue." *Management Accounting* (July–August 1977): 296–297.

———. "The Presentation of Segment Reports." *Accountancy* (June 1978): 91–92.

———. "Segmental Disclosure by Multi-Business Multinational Companies: A Proposal." *Accounting and Business Research* (Summer 1978): 169–177.

Emmanuel, C. R., and R. H. Pick. "The Predictive Ability of U.K. Segment Reports." *Journal of Business Finance and Accounting* (Summer 1980): 201–218.

European Federation of Financial Analysts Societies. *Corporate Reporting in Europe.* EFFAS, 1970.

Financial Accounting Standards Board. An Analysis of Issues Related to Financial Reporting for Segments of a Business Enterprise, *FASB Discussion Memorandum.* FASB, 1974.

Financial Accounting Standards Board. Financial Reporting for Segments of a Business Enterprise, *Statement of Financial Accounting Standards 14,* FASB, 1976.

Gray, S. J. "Segment Reporting and the EEC Multinationals." *Journal of Accounting Research* (Autumn 1978): 242–253.

Horwitz, B., and R. Kolodony. "Line-of-Business Reporting and Security Prices: An Analysis of an SEC Disclosure Rule." *Bell Journal of Economics* (Spring 1977): 234–249.

International Accounting Standards Committee. Reporting Financial Information by Segment, *Exposure Draft 15,* IASC, 1980.

Keane, S. M. *The Efficient Market Hypothesis.* Glascow: Gee & Co. for The Institute of Chartered Accountants of Scotland (IACAS), 1980.

Kinney, W., Jr. "Predicting Earnings: Entity versus Sub-Entity Data." *Journal of Accounting Research* (Spring 1971): 127–136.

Kochanek, R. F. "Segmental Financial Disclosure by Diversified Firms and Security Prices." *Accounting Review* (April 1974): 245–258.

London Stock Exchange. *Admission of Securities to Listing.* London Stock Exchange, 1979.

Mautz, R. K. *Financial Reporting by Diversified Companies.* New York: Financial Executives Research Foundation, 1968.

Miller, M. C., and M. R. Scott. *Financial Reporting by Segments.* Discussion Paper 4. Sydney: Australian Accounting Research Foundation (AARF), 1980.

Organisation for Economic Cooperation and Development. *International Investment and Multinational Enterprises.* OECD, 1976 (revised 1979).

Rappaport, A., and E. M. Lerner. *Segment Reporting for Managers and Investors.* New York: National Association of Accountants, 1972.

Solomons, D. "Accounting Problems and Some Proposed Solutions." In *Public Reporting by Conglomerates,* edited by A. Rappaport, P. A. Firmin, and S. A. Zeff, 91–104. Englewood Cliffs, NJ: Prentice-Hall.

United Nations. *International Standards of Accounting and Reporting for Transnational Corporations.* UN, 1977.

Walker, R. G. "Disclosure by Diversified Companies." *Abacus* (August 1968): 27–38.

# 7

# VALUE-ADDED REPORTING

## INTRODUCTION

Conventional accounting reporting, as it exists in most countries of the world, includes measurement and disclosure of the financial position of a firm through the balance sheet, the financial performance of a firm through the income statement, and the financial conduct of a firm through the statement of changes in the financial position. While the usefulness of the statements has been established by their sheer use over time, they fail to give important information on the total productivity of the firm and the involvement of the team of members (shareholders, bondholders, workers, and the government) involved in the management of resources. The value-added statement is assumed to fill this crucial role. Therefore, the objective of this chapter is to introduce the reader to the notion, measurement, and evaluation of this new mode of reporting.

## HISTORICAL DEVELOPMENT

The value-added statement can be traced back to the U.S. treasury in eighteenth century.[1] It has remained a debated subject with, at various times, attempts and/or suggestions made for having it included in financial accounting practice.[2] The emergence and introduction of value-added taxation in the European countries gave impetus to value-added reporting, although the new type of tax did not require the computation of a value-added statement.

The value-added concept was given serious attention during the late 1970s in various European countries. It reached greater popularity in the United

Kingdom with the publication of *The Corporate Report,* a discussion paper prepared by a working party drawn from the accounting bodies that was published by the Accounting Standards Steering Committee (now the Accounting Standards Committee) in August 1975.[3] It recommended, among other things, a statement of value added, showing how the benefits of the efforts of an enterprise are shared among employees, providers of capital, the state, and reinvestment. The rationale for the value-added statement appears to be contained in paragraphs 6.7 and 6.10:

6.7   The simplest and most immediate way of putting profit into proper perspective vis-à-vis the whole enterprise as a collective effort by capital, management and employees is by presentation of a statement of value added (that is, sales income less materials and services purchased). Value added (that is, sales income less materials and services purchased) is the wealth the reporting entity has been able to create by its own and its employees' efforts. This statement would show how value added has been used to pay those contributing to its creation. It usefully elaborates on the profit and loss account and in time may come to be regarded as a preferable way of describing performance.[4]

6.10  The statement of value added provides a useful measure to help in gauging performance and activity. The figure of value added can be a pointer to the net output of the firm; and by relating other key figures (for example, capital employed and employee costs) significant indicators of performance may be obtained.[5]

It was obvious that the recommendation was accepted when one of the legislative proposals contained in the U.K. government report, *The Future of Company Reports,* included a legislative proposal for a statement of value added.[6] What followed was an increasing number of companies each year producing value-added statements. One survey reported that even more than one-fifth of the largest U.K. companies disclosed value-added statements.[7] The growth of value-added reporting was helped by the trade-union support of the concept. For example, a document produced by one of the trade unions stated that "the Federation therefor aims to encourage the use of the added value as a discipline, so that all managers, with or without experience of accounting practices, will appreciate the financial environment within which decisions affecting manpower are taken."[8]

For the labor movement, the value-added report was deemed a good vehicle for information disclosure and a basis for determining wages and rewards, namely, by what is termed a value-added incentive-payment scheme (VAIPS).[9] In addition to these uses, several authors mention its occasional use in the context of the performance of British industry, in reforming companywide profit-sharing schemes, and in facilitating financial-performance analysis.[10-13] Aware of these developments, the various U.K. accounting bodies, namely, the Institute of Chartered Accountants in England and Wales (ICAEW),[14] the Institute of Chartered Accountants of Scotland,[15] the Institute of Cost and Management Accountants,[16] and the Association of Certified Accountants,[17] produced research reports on the value-added concept.

## VALUE ADDED: NOTION AND RATIONALE

*Value added* refers to the increase in wealth generated by the productive use of a firm's resources before they are allocated among shareholders, bondholders, workers, and the government. Thus, while profit is the final return earned by the shareholders, the value added refers to the total return earned by the team of workers, capital providers, and the government. The value added may be obtained by adding pretax profit to payroll costs and interest charges. Another way of computing value added is to deduct bought-in costs from sales revenues, where bought-in costs represent all costs and expenses incurred in buying goods and services from other firms.

As an example of value added, let us assume that Manufacturer 1 has determined to sell a product at $100. The $100 does not constitute the value added if the manufacturer had bought goods and services from Manufacturer 2 for $40. In such a case, Manufacturer 1 should show a value added of $60 ($100 − $40) as a measure of wealth creation in his or her going concern. All things being equal, an aggregation of all the value added of the going concerns would constitute the total wealth created in a given economy.

Various rationales have been provided for the use of the value-added concept. The first rationale has been provided by the economist's use of the value-added concept in the measurement of national income. Ruggles and Ruggles describe the rationale for the economist's model of value added in the following manner:

The value added by a firm, i.e., the value created by the activities of the firm and its employees above, can be measured by the difference between the market value of the goods that have been turned out by the firm and the cost of those goods and materials purchased from other producers. This measure will exclude the contributions made by other producers of the total value of this firm's production, so that it is essentially equal to the market value created by this firm. The value added measure assesses the net contribution made by each firm to the total value of production; by adding up all of those contributions, therefore, it is possible to arrive at a total for the whole economy that will represent the market value of production.[18]

The economist's rationale is deemed applicable to financial accounting, providing the beginning of an integration of financial accounting to macroeconomic accounting. Naturally, this assumes that, other things being equal, the value-added model is additive in the sense that individual measures for the firm may be summed to equal aggregate value added.

A second rationale for value added stems from the need to minimize the importance of the dominant objective, which is the maximization of shareholders' profit. The general atmosphere surrounding the business environment puts the focus on all the partners rather than only on the shareholders. Therefore, the value added provides a measure of the return due to all the partners, namely, the shareholders, the bondholders, the workers, and the government. The exact rationale, stemming from the change of attitudes, is that the accounting indicator of performance to be provided should be the total return to the team of workers and capital providers rather than merely to the shareholders. The firm then has an obligation to the welfare of the whole team rather than merely the shareholders. Like the shareholders, the other members of the team have a right to the total return, that is, the value added, as well as a right to information about the total return. This widens the responsibility of the economic entities to report the total return to the cooperating team of workers, investors, and government.

A final rationale for value added stems from the phenomena of adjustments in financial reporting resulting from social change. With government, as representative of society and labor, taking a more powerful role in its demands for special rights, the importance of the shareholders has diminished slightly, leading to a reduction in the importance of profit; the social change then dictates a production and disclosure of value added to meet the needs of government and labor. The importance of social change in the production of value-added information is stated by Morley:

Accountants have reported on profit for many centuries. Why do we now need to report on Value Added as well? One answer is that the Value Added Statement reflects a social change: shareholders have become less powerful and central government and organized labour have become more powerful.[19]

A question, however, arises over whether value added is a determining factor in the process of social change, a harbinger of social change, or a consequence of social change. Morley distinguished three different views on this:

(i) One might report Value Added in order to hurry the change along and to give impetus to the movement of power from capital owners towards labour and central government.

(ii) One might report Value Added in order to alert the business community to this change, hoping that it may thereby be reversed.

(iii) One might report Value Added in the hope that it would help one's new masters to make sensible decisions.

These three attitudes may perhaps explain why Value-Added enthusiasts are to be found at both ends of the political spectrum. One encounters both left and right wingers who support this new Statement though their expectations from it differ greatly.

Witness the following quote: "The enthousiasm for Value Added is partly a reaction to the fact that 'profit' is a dirty word to many workers. Amongst the ranks of the Value Added enthusiasts one finds those who sincerely believe that a better educated workforce deserves the dignity of explicit recognition as responsible participators in the process of Adding Value. One also finds those who cynically use Value Added in order to deemphasize the emotive word 'profit', although no change in the attitude or behaviour of management towards the workforce is intended."[20]

## STRUCTURE OF THE VALUE-ADDED STATEMENT

### Value-Added Equations and Format

The value-added statement may be viewed as a modified version of the income statement. Consequently, it can be derived from the income statement by a two-step process.

*Step 1.* The income statement computes retained earnings as the difference between sales revenues and costs, taxes, and dividends. Thus,

$$R = S - B - DP - W - I - DD - T \qquad (7.1)$$

where

$R$ = retained earnings
$S$ = sales revenue
$B$ = bought-in materials and services
$DP$ = depreciation
$W$ = wages
$I$ = interest
$DD$ = dividends
$T$ = taxes

*Step 2.* The value-added equation can be obtained by rearranging the profit equation as

$$S - B = W + I + DP + DD + T + R \qquad (7.2)$$

or

$$S - B - DP = W + I + DD + T + R \qquad (7.3)$$

Equation 7.2 expresses the gross value-added method. Equation 7.3 expresses the net value-added method. Note that, in either case, the left part of the equation shows the value added (gross or net) and the right part of the equation shows the allocation of the value added among the groups involved in the managerial production team, namely, the workers, the shareholders, the bondholders, and the government. The right-hand side is also known as the additive method and the left-hand side the subtractive method.

Exhibit 7.1 shows how the value-added statement can be derived from a regular income statement. It shows how a company deducted bought-in materials, services, and depreciation from sales to arrive at a value added of $1,120,000. It also shows how the $1,120,000 was divided among the team of workers ($400,000), shareholders ($100,000 as interest), bondholders and creditors ($120,000 as interest), and the government ($300,000), leaving $200,000 for retained earnings.

## Gross Value Added versus Net Value Added

Because of the options available to present the value-added statement in either the gross or net format, the relative merits of each need to be appraised.

**Exhibit 7.1**
**Deriving the Value-Added Statement**

A. The conventional income statement of a company for 19x8 was:

| Sales | | | $2,000,000 |
|---|---|---|---|
| Less: | Materials Used | $200,000 | |
| | Wages | 400,000 | |
| | Services Purchased | 600,000 | |
| | Interest Paid | 120,000 | |
| | Depreciation | 80,000 | |
| Profit Before Tax | | | 600,000 |
| Income Tax (Assume a 50% tax rate) | | | 300,000 |
| Profit After Tax | | | $ 300,000 |
| Less Dividend Payable | | | 100,000 |
| Retained Earnings for the Year | | | 200,000 |

B. A value-added statement for the same year would be:

| Sales | | | $2,000,000 |
|---|---|---|---|
| Less: Bought-in Materials and Services and Depreciation | | | 880,000 |
| Value-added available for distribution or retention | | | 1,120,000 |
| Applied as follows: | | | |
| To Employees | | | $ 400,000 |
| To Providers of Capital | | | |
| Interest | $120,000 | | |
| Dividends | 100,000 | | 220,000 |
| To Government | | | 300,000 |
| Retained Earnings | | | 200,000 |
| Value Added | | | $1,120,000 |

The gross value-added format was the only one suggested by *The Corporate Report,* which may explain its popularity.[21] In addition, various other reasons may be advanced in its favor. Morley suggests the following reasons:

1. The value added would be more objective given the flexibility and subjectivity involved in the computation of depreciation. The objectivity may also serve as a way of reassuring the workers of the validity of the base used to determine their productivity bonuses, given that the gross value added may be interpreted by the workers to be less amenable to manipulation or normalization.

2. The gross value-added statement allows the total amount available in a given year for reinvestment, namely, depreciation and retained earnings, to be shown. The gross value-added statement has features of more full disclosure.

3. The gross value-added statement is congruent with the economists' views and preferences for gross measures of national income.[22]

The net value-added format, as expressed in Eq. 7.3, also has some merits worth considering, including the following:

1. The net value added has a better connotation for wealth creation ready for distribution than the gross value-added method. The gross value-added method is overstated by depreciation as a measure of wealth creation and its total distribution may lead to asset depletion. The net value added is distributable, while the gross value added is not.

2. The net value-added method is a fairer base for the determination of productivity of bonuses for workers than the gross value-added method, given the allowance it makes for capital changes.

3. The net value-added method presents the advantage of being able to conform to the accounting principles of consistency and matching.

4. The net value-added method eliminates some double counting by deducting depreciation when the asset exchange between two firms is a depreciable fixed asset.[23]

5. Net value added would appear more congruent with the notion of a return to the team of workers, capital providers, and the government. This will cause an improvement in "team spirit" within the company.[24]

### Treatment of Some Items in the Value-Added Statement

While the treatment of some items is obviously defined by the value-added equation cited above, some other items have been the subject of various treatments. These include *nontrading credits* (defined as those revenues not arising out of a firm's own manufacturing or trading activities) and extraordinary gains and losses.

While revenues (operating revenues) and bought-in materials and services are subjected to a unique treatment, the nonoperating revenues (also labeled nontrading credits) have been treated in the following manner:

1. Understatement of input costs. If it is accepted that nontrading credits do not represent the organization's own value added, this treatment effectively overstates value added.

2. Presentation as a separately disclosed addition to value added calculated by the subtractive method

3. Netting against an application of value added. If it is accepted that nontrading credits do not represent the organization's own value added, this measure yields a proper measure of the organization's value added, but understates the total value added available for application by understating the application in question.

4. Presentation as a separately disclosed deduction from value added calculated by the additive method

5. Elimination from the statement entirely. This treatment poses the problem of determining what application is to be matched with the credit as the Statement of Value Added (SVA), so that the amount of the applications included in the SVA is reduced; the solution is invariably retained profit.[25]

The extraordinary gains and losses also pose a problem because each item has a different impact on value added. Morley concludes that the best treatment of an extraordinary credit depends on the nature of the income or gain or whether value can be said to be added by it. The same applies to extraordinary losses.[26] Needless to say, this potentially can lead to a diversity of treatments and lack of comparability. *The Corporate Report* did not make things easier by recognizing that "the presentation of value added statements involves overcoming many of the problems associated with the presentation of profit and loss accounts, for example, the treatment of extraordinary profits and losses."[27]

There is definitely a need for more experimentation before final accounting policy is enacted on all the issues subject to diverse treatments. However, the optimistic view for a large trial of experimental innovations is not shared by all.[28] There are also some possible misconceptions. One misconception about value added is that it could not be prepared in the service industry because of the absence of creation of tangible wealth.[29] Services are considered as valuable today as any tangible product, and a value-added statement can be prepared easily for a company in a service industry.

Another misconception concerns the relationship between the value-added statement and value-added taxation. Although both are based on the concept of deducting input costs from sales, they can and do exist separately.

## EVALUATION OF VALUE-ADDED REPORTING

Although the concept has not yet reached the level of expansion experienced by more conventional modes of reporting, various authors have already examined some of the benefits and limitations associated with value-added reporting.

## Advantages of Value-Added Reporting

The advantages of value-added reporting stem basically from the multidimensional scope of the technique when compared to the conventional mode of reporting the financial affairs of a going concern. The most-cited advantages of value-added reporting are discussed in the paragraphs that follow.

**1.** Value-added reporting generates a good organizational climate for workers by highlighting their importance to the final results of the firm. What is expected from the disclosure of the value-added statement is an increased favorable and positive attitude of employees toward their employing companies. Considering the employees as major participants in the making of the firm may act as a good motive for better work, more cooperation, and a closer identification with the company.

**2.** Value-added reporting may provide a more practical way of introducing productivity bonus increases and link rewards to changes in the value-added amounts.[30]

**3.** A claim is made that value-added–based ratios may act as good diagnostic and predictive cues. In other words, they may be useful in detecting or predicting economic events of importance to the firm. An example of a useful ratio suggested is the value-added/payroll ratio, which is assumed to draw attention to trends in labor costs and may be useful in wage bargaining as a means of informing labor representatives.[31] Another example of a useful ratio is the taxation/value-added ratio, which is used as an indicator of the government share in the activities of the firm. An additional popular ratio is value added/sales, used as a measure of the degree of vertical integration of a group of companies and, possibly, as an index of vulnerability to disruptive action affecting supplies of material and services.[32]

Cox mentions the potential use of

1. value added/capital employed as a measure of the productivity of the capital used in the business

2. value added/operating assets as a measure of the productivity of operating assets

3. value added/capital expenditure

4. value added/cost of capital consumed (depreciation) as a noble measure of the productivity of physical assets

5. operating profit/value added as a measure of the profit contribution to value added

6. value added/sales as a measure of the impact of sales

7. value added/number of employees as a measure of the value added per person

8. value added/direct labor hour

9. value added/payroll costs as a measure of the labor contribution to value added.[33]

Sinha mentions the potential use of (1) net value added/total capital employed as an index of managerial efficiency, (2) net value added/sales as a measure of productive efficiency, (3) wages/net value added as a measure of how much of net value added is shared by wages, and (4) net value added/wages as an index of labor productivity.[34]

**4.** Value-added reporting is more congruent with the concepts used to measure national income and may create a useful link to the macroeconomic databases and techniques used by economists. It is useful to government in measurements of national income, which involves aggregating (among other things) the value added (net output) of firms. According to Maunders:

The reason why value added rather than sales or the sales value of production (both measures of gross output) is used is to avoid "double counting" in the aggregation process, since the cost of materials and services which would be included in the gross output measures of one firm will probably already have been included in the gross output measures of its supplier. Hence national income, if it involved aggregating gross outputs, would be a function of the degree of vertical integration in the economy. Thus, value added information from firms forms a useful function in macro-economic measurement and forecasting, from government's point of view. In line with this, therefore, it will presumably be useful to individual economists in constructing and testing explanatory models of the economy.[35]

There are, however, qualifications to the general rules equating the sum of the value added by all companies to national income. Morley lists them as follows:

1. National income includes Value Added by government and by other public bodies. For example, the Value Added by defense expenditures is assumed to be equal to its costs.

2. The VA of a company may rise partly in foreign territories. Similarly, Value may be Added in the domestic country by a foreign concern.

3. Economic measures of national income concentrate on production rather than on sales. Differences arise, therefore, in the valuation of increases/decreases in inventories.

4. National income conventions involve several major simplifying assumptions which are not used by financial accountants. For example, the output of durable consumer goods is assumed to have been consumed in the year of manufacture. In effect, the economist depreciates a car by 100 percent in the first year while the accountant would write off his company's fleet of vehicles at, say, 25 percent of cost in each year.[36]

**5.** Value-added reporting may act as a good measure of the size and importance of companies. It is a better measure of the net creation of wealth a company has achieved. Both sales and capital, generally used as surrogate for size, may be misleading. This case is argued by Morley as follows:

When an accountant is asked "Is BP bigger than ICI?", his first reaction is to decide which is the best measure of size for the purpose in question. For some purposes sales might be appropriate, but that figure can give a false impression if a large proportion of a company's turnover is merely representing the passing on to customers of costs incurred in buying-in from other companies. For some purposes, net capital employed may be appropriate, but this can overstate the company's importance if the industry is a very capital intensive one.[37]

    **6.** Value-added reporting may be useful to the employee group because it could affect their aspirations and those of their negotiating representatives. Value-added reporting may be used as a measure of "relative equity" in relation to other stockholder groups. This argument is made by Maunders:

> This is because such a statement reveals (or should reveal) the comparative shares of each of the stockholder groups in the firm's net output for a given period. For this purpose compared with, say the profit and loss account, it has the advantage that it shows explicitly what relative share each group takes. It should be noted, however, that its usefulness in this respect will be dependent on both its coverage and classification of group rewards.[38]

The rules may also be used as a measure of "ability to pay" and a measure of total productivity in the bargaining process.

    **7.** Value-added reporting may be useful to the equity investor group in that the value-added information could be related to the prediction of either the systematic risk of a firm's securities or the expected return and total risk of those securities, depending upon which view of the efficiency of the market is considered relevant. The link can be made by the possible indirect impact of value added on the earnings of a firm. Maunders offers the following rationale:

> Value added information can affect the conduct of collective bargaining and hence the company's future labor costs. Unless such changes in labor costs are exactly canceled by increases in the values of output (an unlikely coincidence), company earnings will also change. So, on the presumption that we are able to show . . . that value added information may affect collective bargaining, we can also deduce that it is potentially useful to investors for forecasting a company's earnings and, hence, the expected returns and total risk associated with securities.[39]

    **8.** Value added appears to offer a useful tool for a prediction of earnings.[40] This notion follows from the evidence that indicates a relationship between earnings measures and security prices.[41] More specifically, the empirical evidence on the relationship between accounting-based measures and market-based measures suggests that the information provided by some accounting measures is consistent with the underlying information set used by investors to assess the riskiness of securities. If the benefits of value added, outlined above, indicate a better measure of the total return of the firm, the value-added series will provide a risk measure that is a better proxy of market risk than the corresponding cash-flow and/or earnings series. The evidence, at least in the United States, is that value-added accounting information can supply considerable explanatory power of market risk beyond that provided by earnings or cash-flow measures, especially at the individual firm level.[42] Given this evidence, there is a definite case for the mandating of value-added reporting in the United States. As stated by Karpik and Belkaoui:

Thus an important accounting policy issue is whether firms should be required to disclose the underlying data needed to calculate value added variables. The current disclosure system does not mandate the disclosure of some of the information needed to compute the value added. At present, less than 10 percent of firms listed on COMPUSTAT consistently disclose labor expenses, a key variable. The cost of reporting this data should be relatively immaterial given the general availability of such information; firms already process this information for payroll purposes and report such information to various governmental agencies. Given the low cost relative to the potentially much greater benefit shown in this study, releasing value added reports or disclosing the underlying data needed to calculate the value added appears to be an improvement over the present U.S. reporting system. Whether such disclosures should be mandated by standard setting establishments is an issue worth considering.[43]

### Disadvantages of Value-Added Reporting

There are several disadvantages to value-added reporting. First, value-added reporting relies on the erroneous assumption that a company is a team of cooperating groups. The facts may show that, in general, the groups implied have a basically conflicting relationship as to the allocation of the firm's resources, the firm's increase in wealth, and the best way of managing the firm. Besides, some may question the legitimacy of including the government as a cooperating or even invited member. Another point raised is that some legitimate member of the cooperating team may be excluded. The case in point is the specialist supplier to a sole customer, who would be excluded from the team even though the supplier had no other outlet for his production.[44]

Second, the value-added statement can lead to confusion, especially in those cases in which the value added is increasing while earnings are decreasing. If the shareholders understand that the value-added statement is not a report to shareholders, the problem is resolved. Some would then argue that there is still a need to use the earnings statement as a special report to shareholders and the value-added statement as a special report on the welfare of a more broadly defined team. Needless to say, this argument

would certainly lead to cries of information overload and information re-
dundancy.

Third, the inclusion of the value-added statement may lead management
wrongly to seek to maximize the firm's value added. Unfortunately, this
unwise objective has already been advocated in some publications.[45] The
impact of such unsound objectives has been demonstrated in the following
manner:

Suppose a company is buying a component for £5 and the question is asked, "Should
we make it ourselves?" An investigation reveals that the cost of a self-made component would be £4 for direct materials plus £10 for direct labour (we shall ignore
overhead for simplicity). Assume that the labour costs are all variable and therefore
the company's management does not need to incur losses as the price of keeping
together the workforce. In these circumstances any sensible manager would be
grateful for the outside supplier and forget about the idea of in-house manufacture
of the component. But not so for the value-added maximizers. They would cancel
the order to buy at £5 from outside and manufacture the component themselves for
£14. They would make this inefficient and wasteful decision because it would raise
their value added by £9. The amount to be shared out among the company team
(value added) would have risen by £1 per component, but the workers would require
£10 extra per component for the additional hours worked and the £9 difference
represents the loss to the shareholders. Here, the attempt to maximize value added
resulted in a disastrous decision.[46]

## DIVERSITY OF APPLICATIONS IN
## THE UNITED KINGDOM

The application of the value-added statement in the United Kingdom
suffers from lack of uniformity and standardization. Writers view this lack
of uniformity as detrimental to the potential success of value-added reporting:

Published statements of value added have, to date, been characterized by ambiguous
terminology and by the treatment of items in ways inconsistent with the model
of value added, and inconsistent within and between individual statements. The
impression received by lay users of SVAs must be one of confusion—though possibly, with a conviction that value added, like profit, can be made to mean whatever
the accountant wishes it to mean.[47]

The advantages offered by Value Added Statement are, however, currently jeopard-
ized by a great diversity of practice.[48]

Most of those [value-added statements] available seem to be designed to show,
often by a "sale-cake" diagram, how much of the value-added goes to the employees
themselves, how much the government absorbs and how little the shareholder receives.[49]

A survey of firms with three years of experience with the published statements of value added showed a variety of treatments used, including those that follow.[50]

1. The location of the statement was mainly in the main accounts, although some firms included it in the employee report and supplementary report addressed to several groups.

2. The title of the statement included such orthodox titles as The Statement of Value Added, The Added-Value Statement, The Group Value Added, and Statement of Value Added and Its Distribution. Unorthodox titles included such examples as Where the Money Goes, How the Group Spends the Money It Receives, Who Benefits from Our Increase in Sales, Statement of Use of Total Income, Share of the Operating-Profit Cake, How We Created Wealth and Share It Out, Our Year's Work in Money Terms—The "Value Added" Way of Looking at Our Profit-and-Loss Account, and How Sales Were Built Up.[51]

3. The format included both subtractive and additive methods, as well as various mixes of tables, graphics, proportions, and narrative presentations.

4. Deferred taxes were handled in several ways: inclusion with taxation payable by companies describing taxation as applied to government; shown separately but described as applied to government; included with taxation and described neutrally; shown separately and described neutrally; and included with retentions.

5. The treatment of minority interest included such forms as the total amount shown as a separate application; the minority-interest dividends and retentions included with group allocation; the total included with dividends; the total included with retentions; and minority interests included in input costs.

6. The treatment of nontrading credits, such as associated companies' results, interest receivable, and other investment income, included an understatement of input costs; presentation as a separately disclosed addition to value added calculated by the subtractive method; netting against an application of value added; presentation as a separately disclosed deduction from value added calculated by the additive method; and elimination from the statement entirely.[52]

7. Methods of treating extraordinary items included inclusion in input costs, exclusion from statement, inclusion in nontrading credits (NTCs) added to value added, and separate application of value added.


## CONCLUSIONS

Value-added reporting is becoming more and more popular in Europe. Its adoption seems to reflect a greater European concern for the public interest and for what may be perceived as socioeconomic accounting. The greater concern for the rights and opportunities of individuals in the United States and Canada, for example, has not yet created a favorable climate for the introduction of value-added reporting. As accounting becomes more and more actively and explicitly recognized as an instrument of social management and change, value-added reporting will constitute a definite example of the intertwining of the accounting and the social worlds, because value-added reporting reveals something about the social character of production, something that is obscured by conventional reporting. With value-added reporting, the clear message would be that the wealth created in production is the result of the combined effort of a team of cooperating members.

## NOTES

1. B. Cox, *Value Added: An Application for the Accountant Concerned with Industry* (London: Heinemann and the Institute of Cost and Management Accountants, 1978), 15.

2. W. W. Suojanen, "Accounting Theory and the Large Corporation," *Accounting Review* (July 1954): 391–398.

3. Accounting Standards Steering Committee, *The Corporate Report* (London: Accounting Standards Steering Committee, 1975): 48.

4. Ibid.

5. Ibid.

6. Department of Trade, *The Future of Company Reports* (London: Her Majesty's Stationery Office, 1977): 7–8.

7. S. J. Gray and K. T. Maunders, *Value Added Reporting: Uses and Measurement* (London: Association of Certified Accountants, 1980), 10.

8. Engineering Employers Federation, *Business Performance and Industrial Relations* (London: Kogan Page, 1977), 50.

9. M. Woodmansay, *Added Value: An Introduction to Productivity Schemes* (London: British Institute of Management, 1978), 16.

10. S. Burchell, C. Clubb, and A. G. Hopwood, "Accounting and Its Social Context: Towards a History of Value Added in the United Kingdom," *Accounting, Organizations and Society* 10, no. 4 (1985): 387.

11. F. C. Jones, *The Economic Ingredients of Industrial Success* (London: James Clayton Lecture, Institute of Mechanical Engineers, 1976); F. C. Jones, "Our Manufacturing Industry: The Missing $100,000 Million," *National Westminster Bank Quarterly Review* (May 1978): 8–17; C. New, "Factors in Productivity that Should Not Be Overlooked," *The Times,* February 1, 1978.

12. S. Cameron, "Added Value Plan for Distributing ICI's wealth," *Financial Times,* January 7, 1977.

13. V. da Costa, *Testing for Success* (London: Mimeo, 1979).

14. M. Renshall, R. Allan, and K. Nicholson, *Added Value in External Financial Reporting* (London: Institute of Chartered Accountants in England and Wales, 1979).

15. M. F. Morley, *The Value Added Statement* (London: Gee & Co. for the Institute of Chartered Accountants of Scotland, 1978).

16. Cox, *Value Added,* 15.

17. Gray and Maunders, *Value Added Reporting,* 15.

18. R. Ruggles and N. D. Ruggles, *National Income Accounts and Income Analysis,* 2d ed. (New York: McGraw-Hill, 1965): 50.

19. Morley, *The Value Added Statement,* 3.

20. Ibid., 19.

21. Accounting Standards Steering Committee, *The Corporate Report,* 96.

22. M. F. Morley, "The Value Added Statement in Britain," *Accounting Review* (July 1979): 626.

23. Ibid., 628.

24. M. F. Morley, "The Value Added Statement: A British Innovation," *Chartered Accountant Magazine* (May 1978): 33.

25. B. A. Rutherford, "Published Statements of Value Added: A Survey of Three Years' Experience," *Accounting and Business Research* (Winter 1980): 23.

26. Morley, *The Value Added Statement*, 87.

27. Accounting Standards Steering Committee, *The Corporate Report*, 50.

28. Rutherford, "Published Statements of Value Added," 28.

29. Morley, "The Value Added Statement: A British Innovation," 32.

30. Morley, "The Value Added Statement in Britain," 621.

31. Ibid.

32. Ibid., 622.

33. Cox, *Value Added*, 67–82.

34. G. Sinha, *Value Added Income* (Calcutta: Book World, 1983), 130–137.

35. K. T. Maunders, "The Decision Relevance of Value Added Reports," in *Frontiers of International Accounting: An Anthology*, ed. F. D. Choi and G. G. Mueller (Ann Arbor, MI: UMI Research Press, 1985), 241.

36. Morley, "The Value Added Statement in Britain," 623.

37. M. F. Morley, "Value Added Reporting," in *Developments in Financial Reporting*, ed. T. A. Lee (London: Philip Allan, 1981), 259.

38. Maunders, "The Decision Relevance of Value Added Reports," 225–245.

39. Ibid., 229.

40. Ibid., 228.

41. B. Lev and J. A. Ohlson, "Market Band Empirical Research: A Review, Interpretation and Extension," *Journal of Accounting Research* (Supplement, 1982): 239–322.

42. P. Karpik and A. Belkaoui, "The Relative Relationship between Systematic Risk and Value Added Variables," *Journal of International Financial Management and Accounting* (Fall 1989): 259–276.

43. Ibid., 273.

44. Morley, "The Value Added Statement in Britain," 624.

45. R. R. Gilchrist, *Managing for Profit: The Value Added Concept* (London: Allen and Unwin, 1971).

46. Morley, "The Value Added Statement: A British Innovation," 30.

47. Rutherford, "Published Statements of Value Added," 52.

48. Morley, *The Value Added Statement*, 141.

49. da Costa, *Testing for Success.*

50. Rutherford, "Published Statements of Value Added," 17.

51. Ibid.

52. Ibid., 23.

## BIBLIOGRAPHY

Accounting Standards Steering Committee. *The Corporate Report*. London: Accounting Standards Steering Committee, 1975.

Ball, R. J. "The Use of Value Added in Measuring Managerial Efficiency." *Business Ratios* (Summer 1968): 5–11.

Beattie, D. M. "Value Added and Return on Capital as Measures of Managerial Efficiency" *Journal of Business Finance* (Summer 1970): 22–28.

Bentley, T. "Value Added and Contribution." *Management Accounting* (March 1981): 17–21.

Burchell, S., C. Clubb, and A. G. Hopwood. "Accounting and Its Social Context: Towards a History of Value Added in the United Kingdom." *Accounting, Organizations and Society* 10, no. 4 (1985): 381–413.

Chua, K. C. "The Use of Value Added in Productivity Measurement." In *Productivity-Measurement and Achievement, Proceedings of Accountancy.* Victoria, NZ: University of Wellington, 1977.

Cox, B. *Value Added: An Application for the Accountant Concerned with Industry.* London: Heinemann and the Institute of Cost and Management Accountants, 1978.

Cruns, R. P. "Added-Value: The Roots Run Deep into Colonial and Early America" *Accounting Historian Journal* (Fall 1982): 25–42.

Dewhurst, J. "Assessing Business Performance." *Accountant* 188 (March 3, 1983): 17–18.

Egginton, D. A. "In Defense of Profit Measurement: Some Limitations of Cash Flow and Value Added as Performance Measures for External Reporting." *Accounting and Business Research* (Spring 1984): 99–110.

Foley, B. J., and K. T. Maunders. *Accounting Information Disclosure and Collective Bargaining.* London: Macmillan, 1977.

Gilchrist, R. R. *Managing for Profit: The Value Added Concept.* London: Allen and Unwin, 1971.

Gray, S. J., and K. T. Maunders. "Recent Developments in Value Added Disclosures" *Certified Accountant* (August 1979): 255–236.

_____. "Recent Developments in Value Added Reporting." *Certified Accountant* (August 1979): 229–236.

_____. *Value Added Reporting: Uses and Measurement.* London: Association of Certified Accountants, 1980.

Karpik, P., and A. Belkaoui. "The Relative Relationship between Systematic Risk and Value Added Variables." *Journal of International Financial Management and Accounting* (Fall 1989): 259–276.

Lev, B., and J. A. Ohlson. "Market Band Empirical Research: A Review, Interpretation and Extension." *Journal of Accounting Research* (Supplement, 1982): 239–322.

McLead, C. C. "Use of Value Added." *Bests Review* (January 1984): 80–84.

McLeay, S. "Value Added: A Comparative Study." *Accounting, Organizations and Society* 8, no. 1 (1983): 31–56.

McSweeney, B. "Irish Answer to Value Added Reports." In *Frontiers of International Accounting: An Anthology,* edited by F. K. Choi and G. G. Mueller, 225–245. Ann Arbor, MI: UMI Research Press, 1985.

Morley, M. F. "Value Added Reporting." In *Developments in Financial Reporting,* edited by T. A. Lee, 251–269. London: Philip Allan, 1981.

_____. *The Value Added Statement.* London: Gee & Co. for the Institute of Chartered Accountants of Scotland, 1978.

_____. "The Value Added Statement in Britain." *Accounting Review* (July 1979): 618–689.

————. "The Value Added Statement: A British Innovation." *Chartered Accountant Magazine* (May 1978): 31–34.

Pendrill, D. "Introducing a Newcomer: The Value Added Statement." *Accountancy* (December 1977): 92–94.

Purdy, D. E. "Value Added Statement: The Case Is Not Yet Proven," *Accountancy* (September 1981): 121–122.

Renshall, M., R. Allan, and K. Nicholson. *Added Value in External Financial Reporting*. London: Institute of Chartered Accountants in England and Wales, 1979.

Rutherford, B. A. "Easing the CCA Transition in Value Added Statements." *Accountancy* 93 (May 1983): 121–122.

————. "Five Fallacies about Value Added." *Management Accounting* (September 1981): 31–33.

————. "Published Statements of Value Added : A Survey of Three Years' Experience." *Accounting and Business Review* (Winter 1980): 15–28.

————. "Value Added as a Focus of Attention for Financial Reporting: Some Conceptual Problems." *Accounting and Business Research* (Summer 1972): 215–220.

Sinha, G. *Value Added Income*. Calcutta: Book World, 1983.

Woolf, E. "Case of Added Value." *Accountants* (March 3, 1983): 13–16.

————. "Time to Scrap the P&L Account?" *Accountancy* (August 1981): 93–95.

# INDEX

**About the Author**

**AHMED BELKAOUI** is Professor of Accounting at the University of Illinois at Chicago. He has written some twenty previous books on accounting subjects including *Multinational Management Accounting* (Quorum, 1991), *Cost Accounting: Theory and Practice* (Quorum, 1991), *Judgment in International Accounting* (Quorum, 1990), and *Human Information Processing in Accounting* (Quorum, 1989).